IMAGES
of America

ONTARIO COUNTY

THE GOLDEN AGE OF RAILROADS AND BASEBALL

IMAGES
of America

ONTARIO COUNTY

THE GOLDEN AGE OF RAILROADS AND BASEBALL

Tim Munn and Matt Vitticore

ARCADIA
PUBLISHING

ISBN 978-0-7385-6407-4

Published by Arcadia Publishing
Charleston, South Carolina

Printed in the United States of America

Library of Congress Catalog Card Number: 2009921959

For all general information contact Arcadia Publishing at:
Telephone 843-853-2070
Fax 843-853-0044
E-mail sales@arcadiapublishing.com
For customer service and orders:
Toll-Free 1-888-313-2665

Visit us on the Internet at www.arcadiapublishing.com

Cover Image: In 1917, this photograph was taken at King's Diamond during the third and final series game between the Sayre Colemans of Pennsylvania and Manchester. Sayre was defeated in 14 innings by a score of 5-4. Pictured, from left to right, are Bill Segbers, Johnny Kerins, Tommy Kerins, Neal O'Harrigan, and Francis Clary. The scorekeeper (furthest to the right) remains unidentified.

Contents

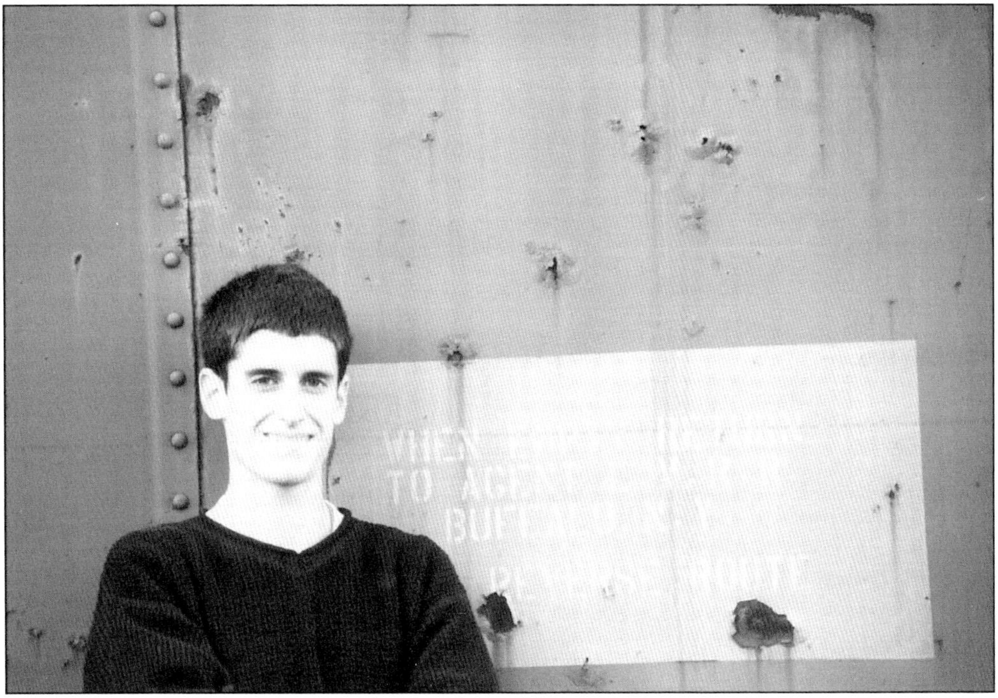

Author Matt Vitticore.

With the roar of a locomotive
and the crack of a bat
may we never forget those
who laid the first track.

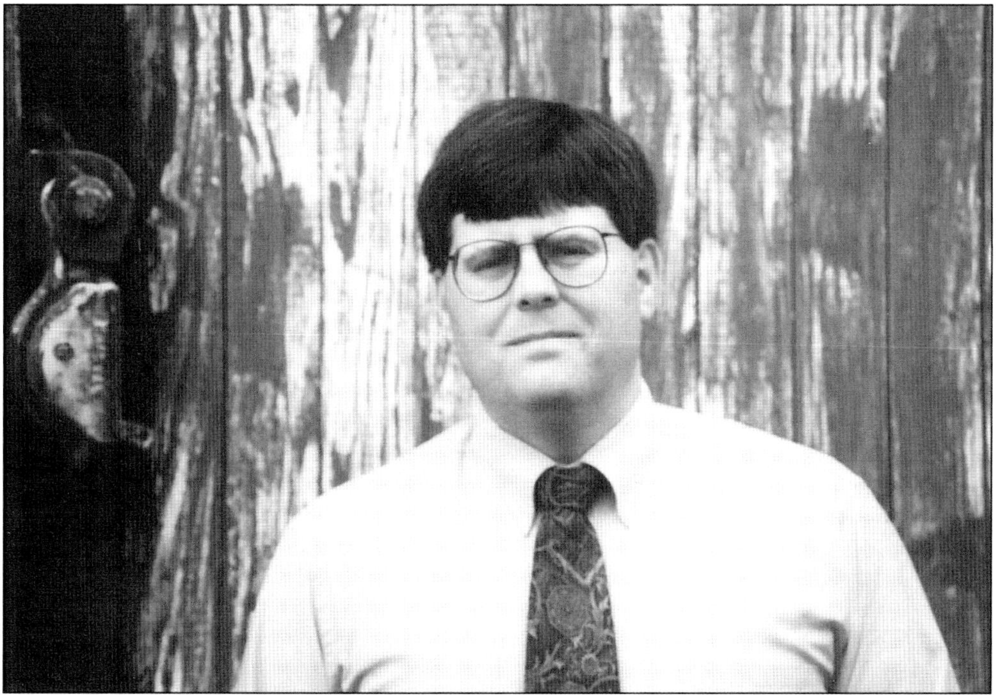

Author Tim Munn.

INTRODUCTION

As an amateur historian and longtime coach, I am privileged to have had the opportunity to preserve one of the great periods in Ontario County. Without the writing talents of co-author Matt Vitticore, a former player of mine, this book would not have been possible. Matt and I wish to extend our sincere thanks to Ed Varno and the Ontario County Historical Society, the Segbers family, Carrie Adams, Jo Lane, Margaret Vienna, Joe Boardman, Richard Boardman, James Romeiser, Craig Mott, the Angeline family, Linda Van Caeseele, Olivia Stambach, Marlene DeGloma, Rand Darrow, Mayor Phil D'Arduini, Angela D'Arduini, Rita Gurewich, Dorothy Ann Liberati, Richard Simonds, the Victor Historical Society, the Prouty Chew Museum, Charles Bauder, Steve O'Malley, Dan O'Donnell, Rick Barnard, Roger Halderman, Helene Downey, the Gwilt family, Rachel Vaughn, the Moore family, Ann Walker, George Childs, C.J. Cooley, George Grube, and William Eddinger III. We would also like to extend our gratitude to the Vitticore family, Jillian Eddinger, Daniel Munn, and Nancy Munn for their patience and support throughout this endeavor.

To all the dye in the wool fans,

Sincerely,
Tim Munn

One

THE RAILROAD

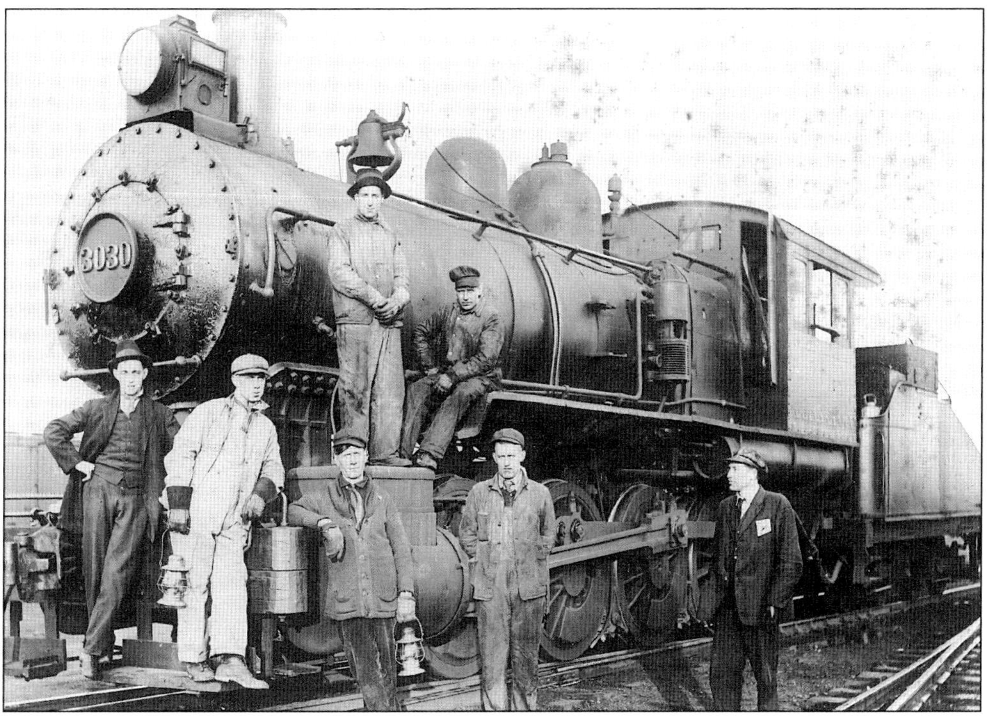

This six-wheeled steam locomotive acted as a switcher and frequently utilized Manchester's freight transfer yard in the early part of the 20th century. William Eddinger II is shown here under the bell on a 3030 engine model along with Ed Shepard (seated), Asa Baker (furthest right), Harry Van Orman, John Sloppy, Milt Parmele, and an unidentified operator. In 1936, Manchester's freight transfer was the second largest in the United States. The transfer had 72 electric trucks, 415 employees, sorted 3 million packages per year, and had an annual payroll of $600,000.

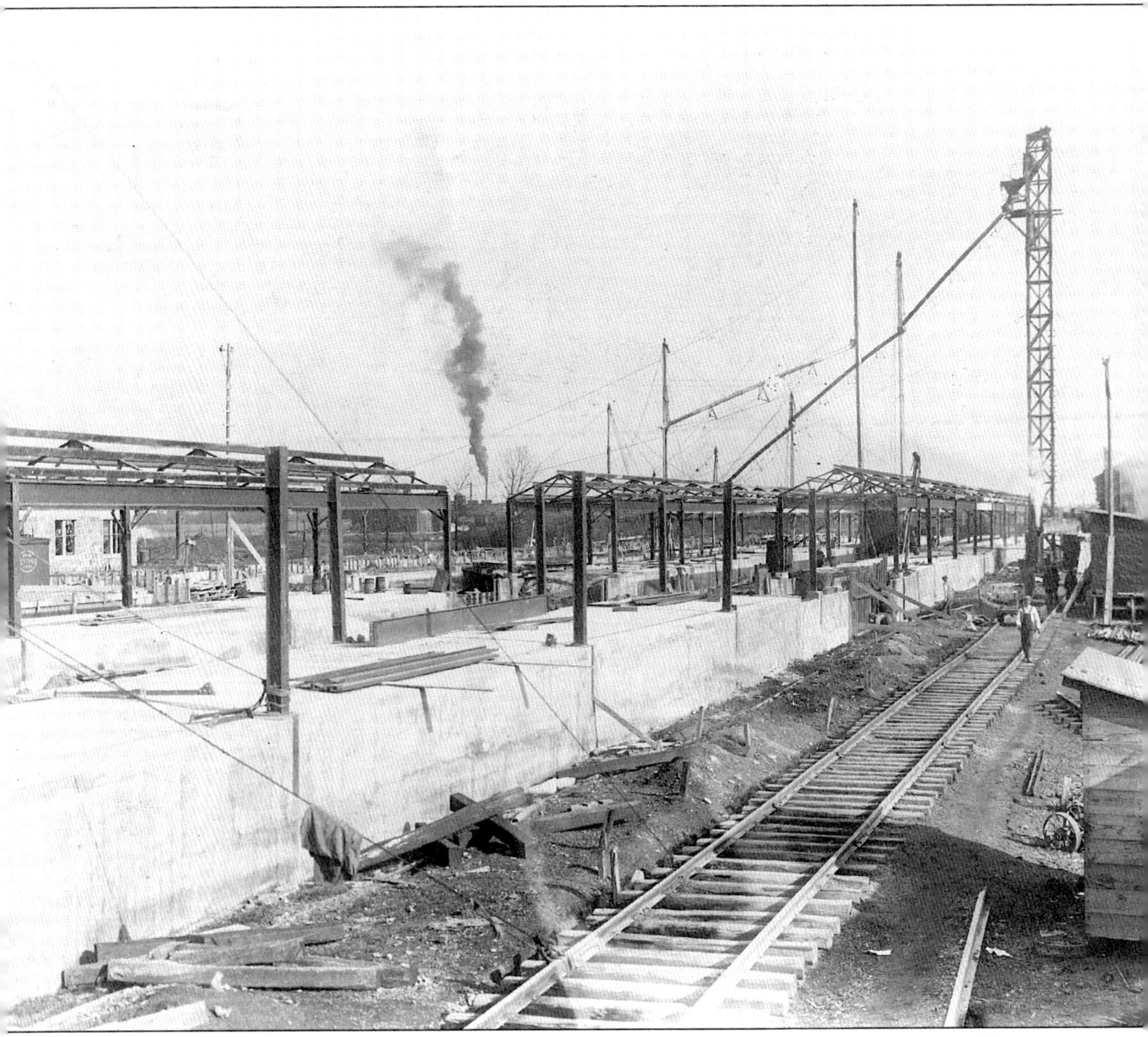

Upon the arrival of the Lehigh Valley Railroad (LVRR) in 1892, Manchester's semblance was forever changed. However, it wasn't until 1914 that the expansion of the freight transfer yard began. The expansion signified a migration of immigrants, turning Manchester into a distinct cross-section of multicultural men and women.

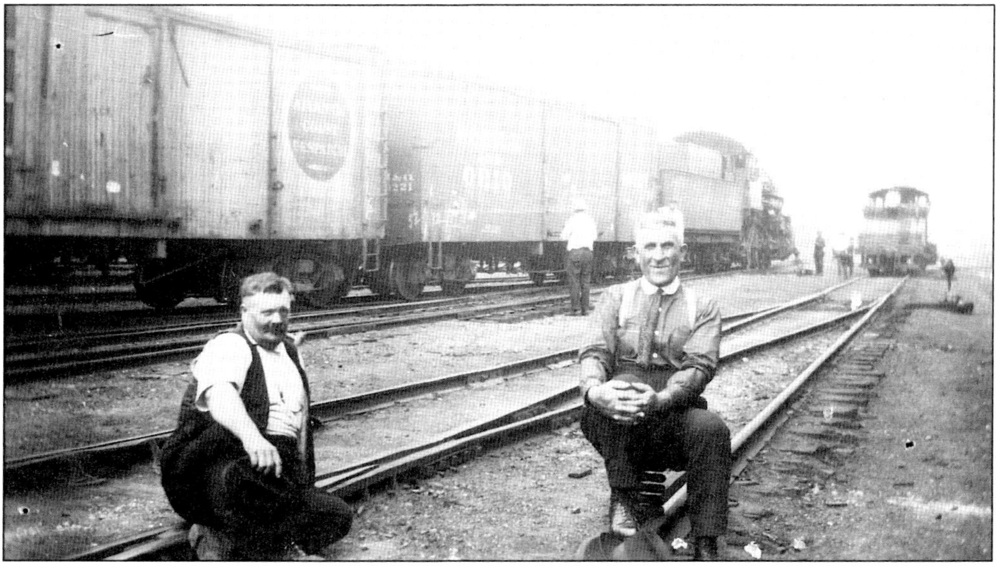

By 1914, freight cars from all over the United States began to roll into the Lehigh Valley Freight transfer yards in Manchester, New York. Pictured here are two wooden boxcars known as the Mobile and Ohio boxcars.

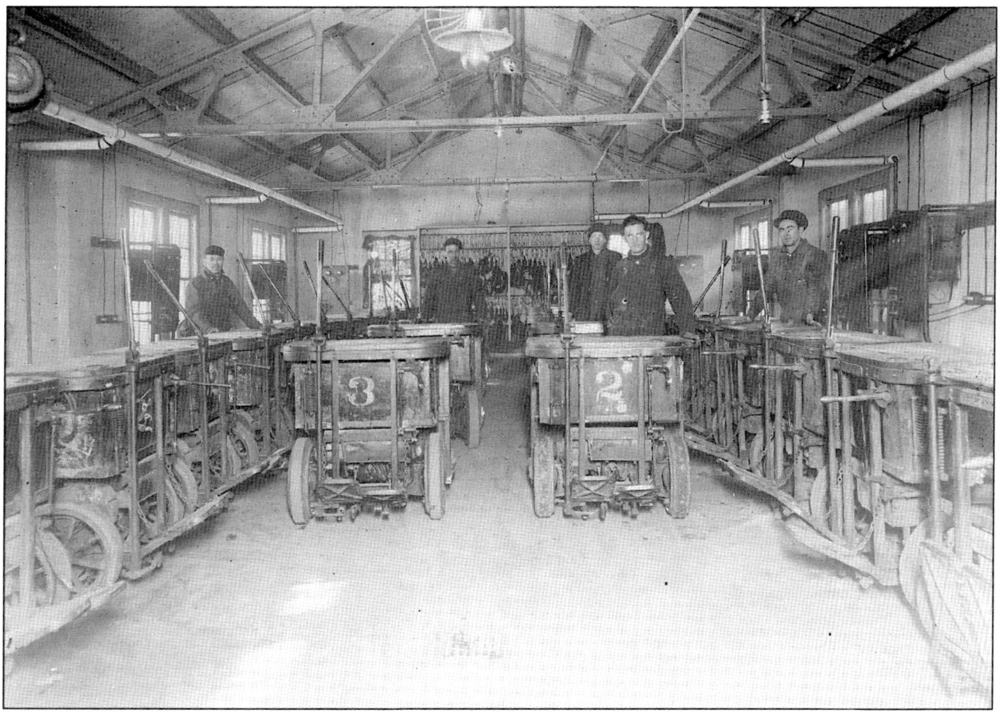

This photograph offers a rare glimpse of battery-operated transfer carts in 1914 at the Lehigh Valley transfer yard in Manchester. The carts hauled cargo from one boxcar to another traveling to several different locations in the United States.

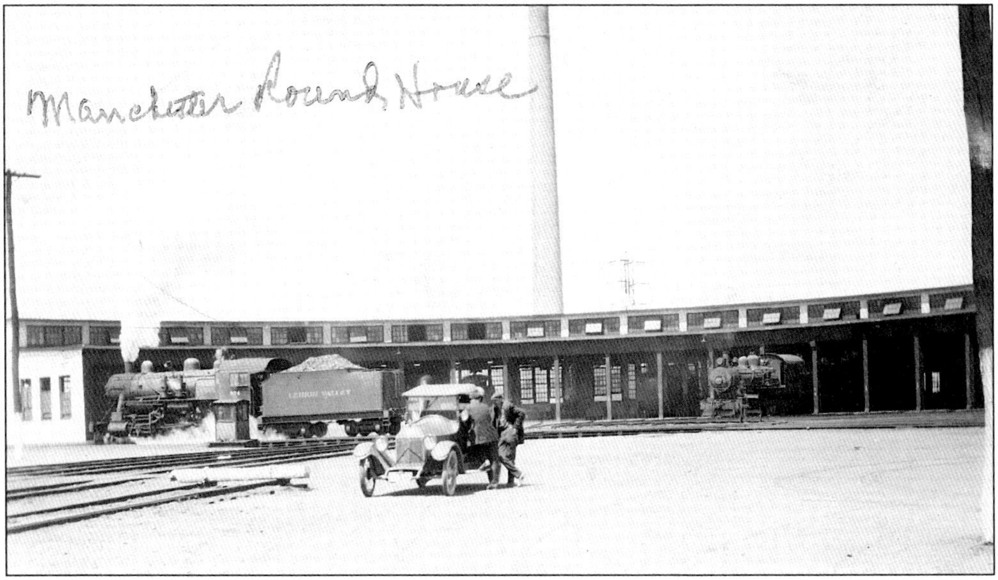

The Lehigh Valley roundhouse, shown here in 1928, guides a 904 out off the turntable in Manchester. The turntable, which was 100 feet in diameter, helped guide the steam engines into any one of 35 bays. This roundhouse was constructed in 1916 and was the last of three that were built in Manchester. In 1918, a turntable mishap claimed the life of a man when the boiler of the locomotive exploded, scalding the victim to death in Manchester's roundhouse.

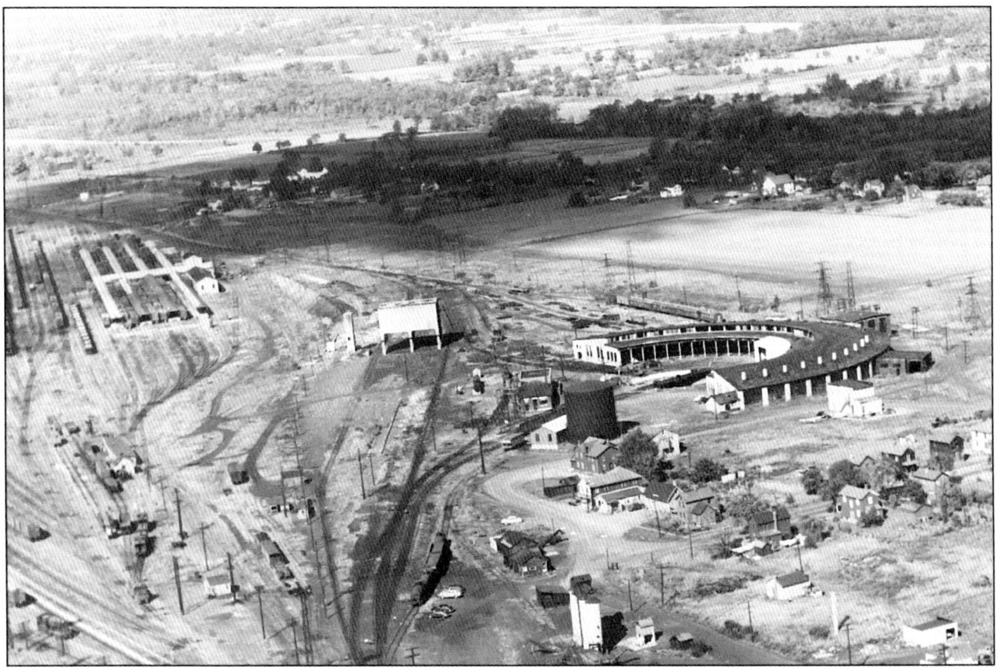

This aerial survey by Henry DeWolf portrays Manchester's freight yards in the early part of the 20th century. Note the turntable within the roundhouse. During World War II, Manchester acted as a major player among the big East Coast cities. Manchester's transfer station was essential in the shipping of military hardware to the New York harbor. At the time, Manchester had the second largest freight transfer yard in the world.

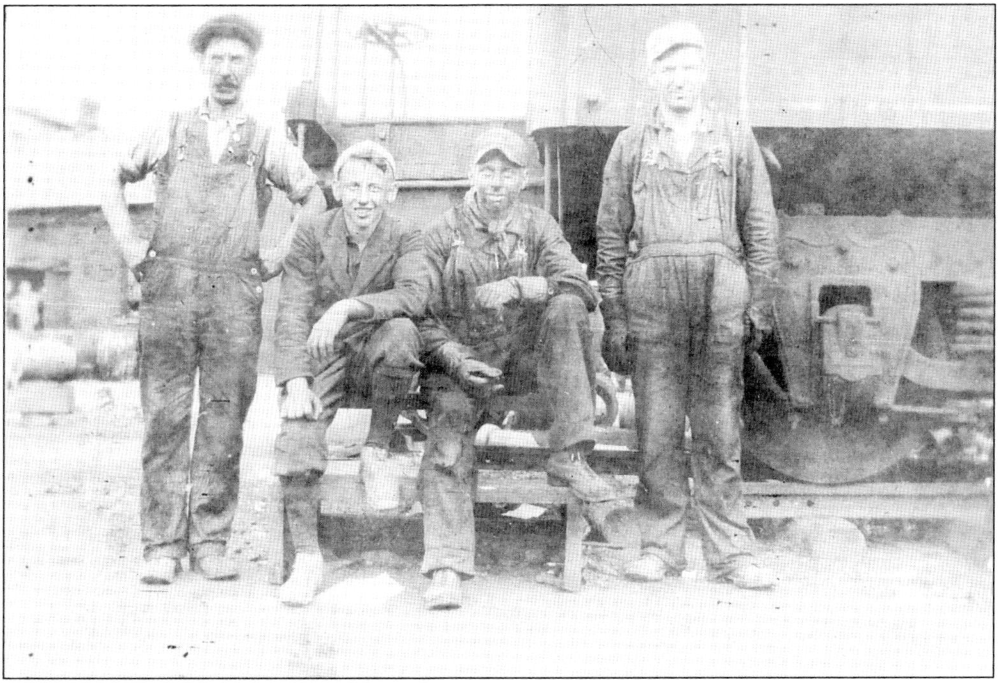

These fellows, known as the pit crew, worked 12 to 14 hours a day as they maintained the locomotives in the pits of the roundhouse.

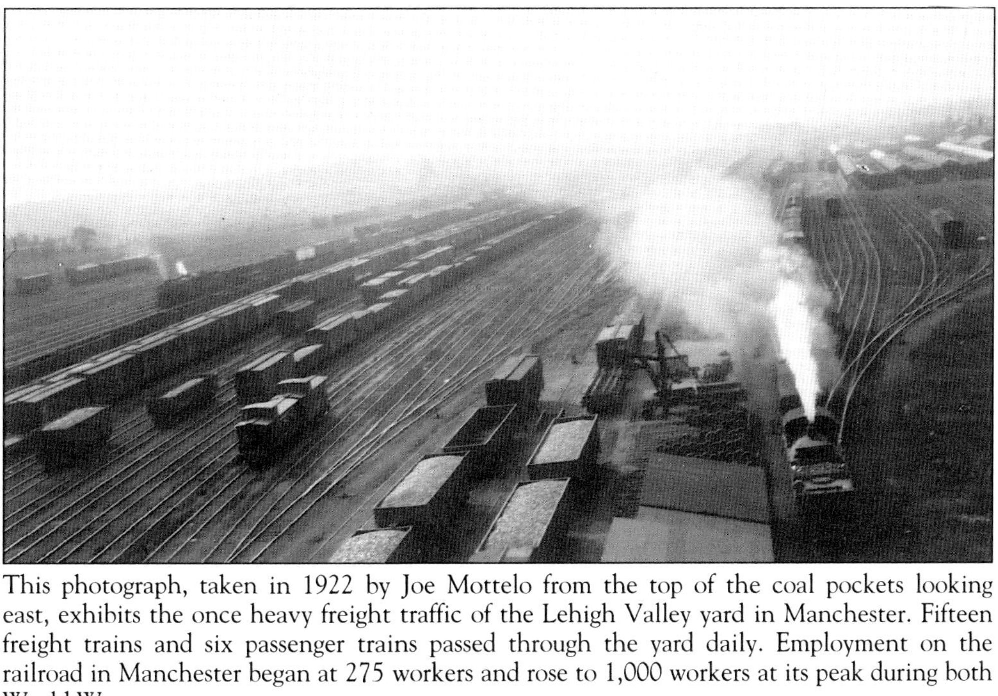

This photograph, taken in 1922 by Joe Mottelo from the top of the coal pockets looking east, exhibits the once heavy freight traffic of the Lehigh Valley yard in Manchester. Fifteen freight trains and six passenger trains passed through the yard daily. Employment on the railroad in Manchester began at 275 workers and rose to 1,000 workers at its peak during both World Wars.

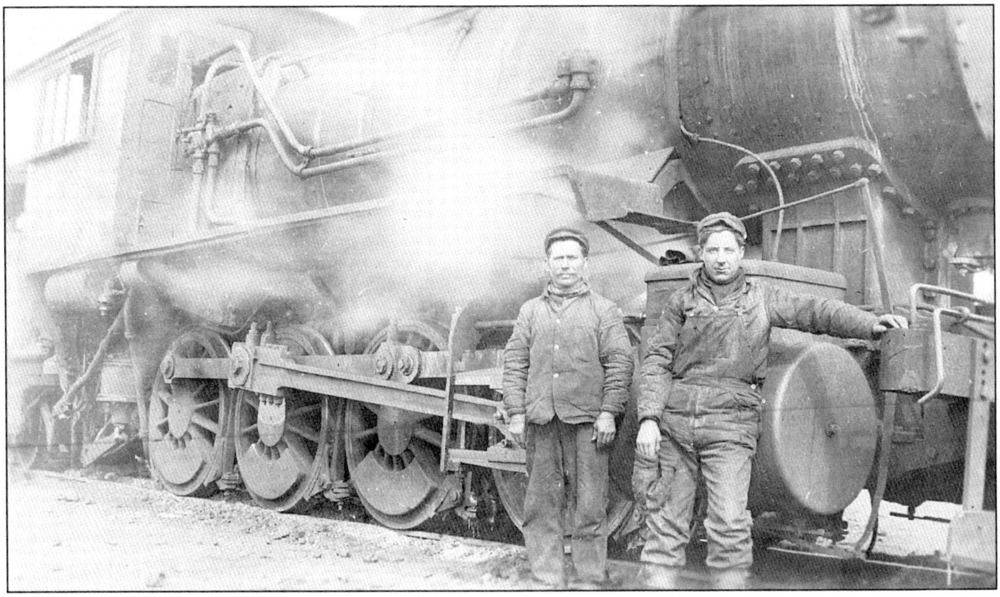

The Baldwin 0-8-0 Switcher stayed mainly in the Manchester yard due to the instability of the tracks. The engine, seen here in 1916, was chiefly used as a transfer engine that brought boxcars to the transfer warehouses.

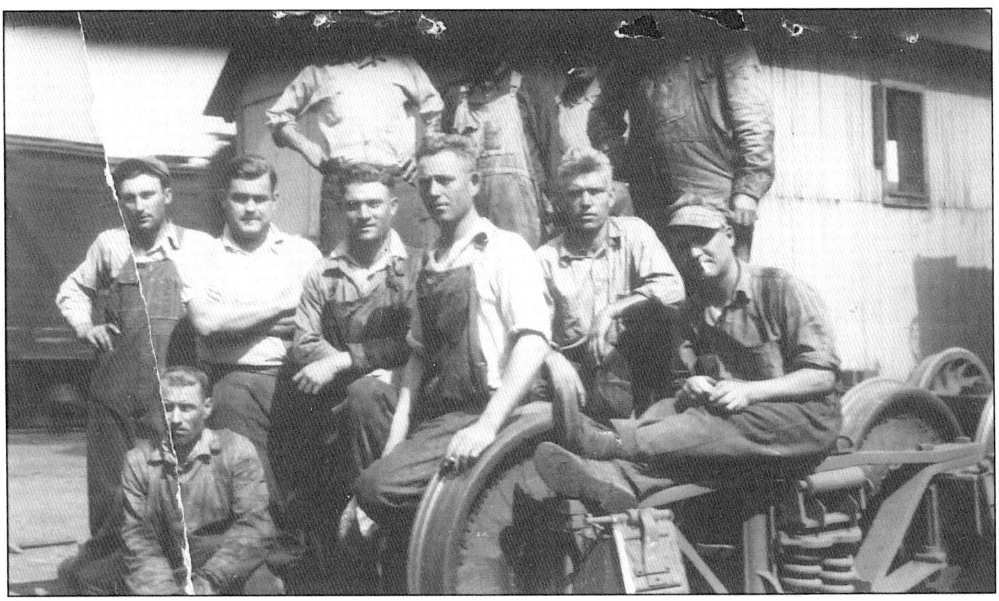

The men of the cripple track in Manchester, otherwise known as the "car-knockers," were often immigrants. These men were mainly Syrians, Poles, Ukranians, and Italians who had relocated from the mines of Pennsylvania. The work involved was physically grueling and considered undesirable.

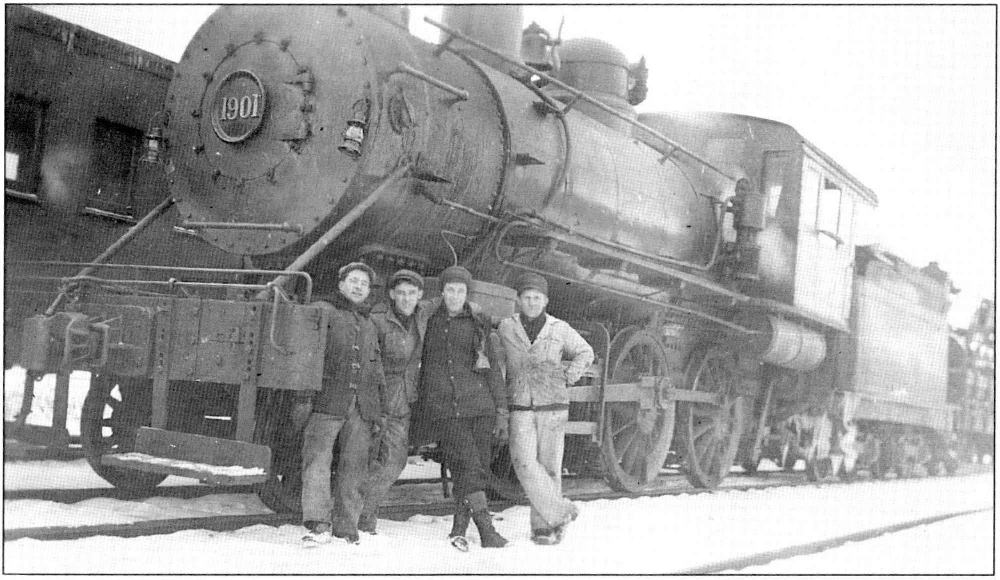

This winter 1916 photograph depicts engine 1901, which was a 2-6-0 Alco model of the American Locomotive Company. It is identified as a switcher due to the footsteps at the front of the engine. Because it could not generate huge speeds, it was considered a work train, and it pulled boxcars along the system with a massive tractive power of 29,000 pounds.

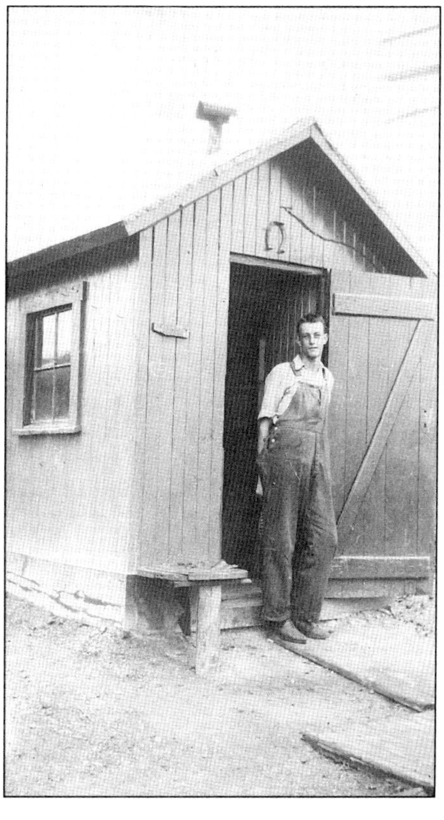

This photograph of Fred Ellis, a blacksmith for the railroad who began working at the Manchester yard at 17 years of age, was taken in 1919. Railroad work was difficult and dangerous, and the sacrifice involved was both feared and respected. On a sunny day in July of 1920, Fred's wife, Edna, commented on the conditions of the day: "What a beautiful day it is, Fred," she said. Fred responded by noting the ambient factors in the rail yards. "Maybe for you, but for me, every day is a cloudy day on the railroad."

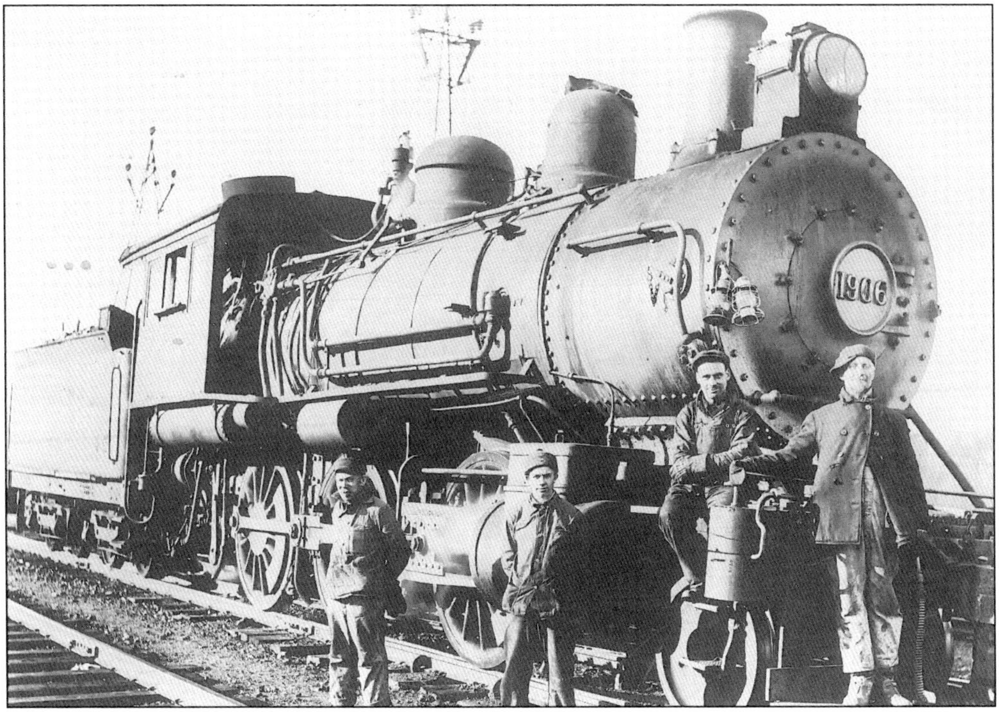

Standing before a 1906 model engine, conductor William Eddinger I and his crew pause near the coal pockets on January 24, 1916. The towering coal pockets covered nearly an acre of land and served as a refueling station for the steam locomotives. Engineers maneuvered a train underneath the pockets so the workers could guide the shoot to fill the tender of the locomotive. The coal pockets of Manchester serviced east- and westbound engines simultaneously.

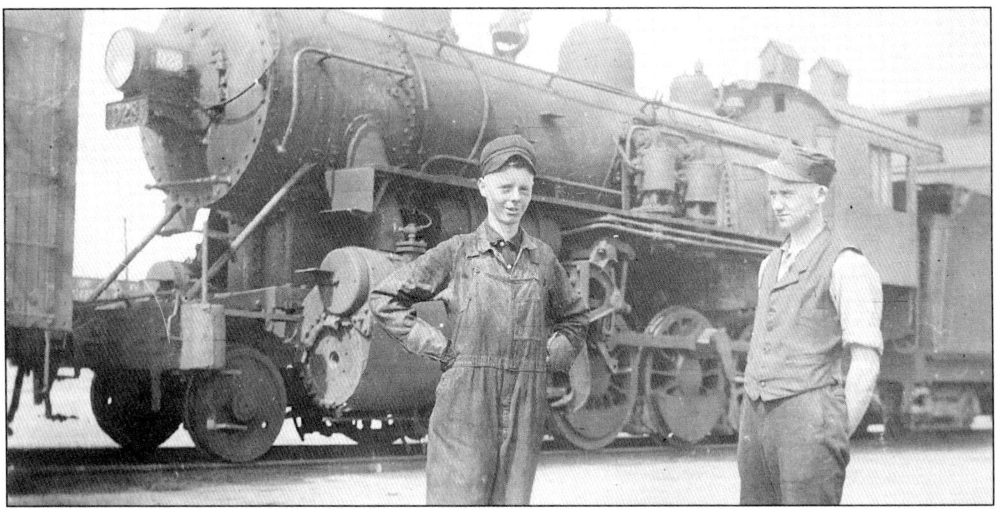

This photograph depicts Engine 928, a 2-6-0 Switcher, parked in front of the roundhouse. Two of the railroad's youngsters (Charlie Snyder and Johnny Boardman) pose for the camera in 1921. Young men of the railroad often worked as brakemen, and although the job paid well, the risks were acknowledged as some of the worst and most terrifying on the railroad. Brakemen worked on moving boxcars in order to separate and reroute incoming freight.

In this photograph, Johnny Boardman is shown standing in the cripple track storeroom in 1921. The building supplied parts for the maintenance of damaged trains. In 1921, cripple track workers made less than 40¢ an hour, a mere fraction of the brakemen's hourly wage.

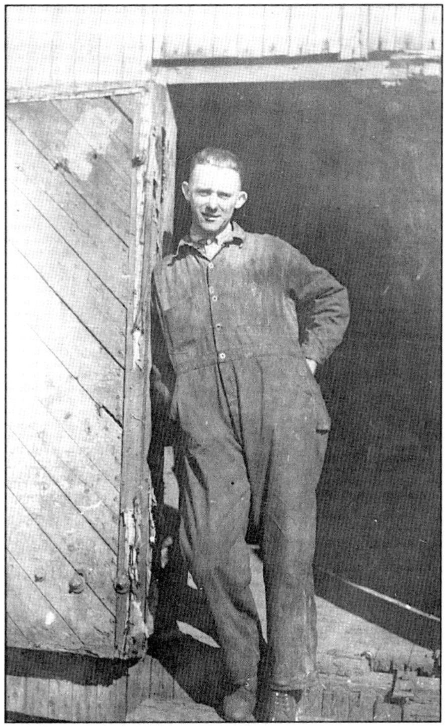

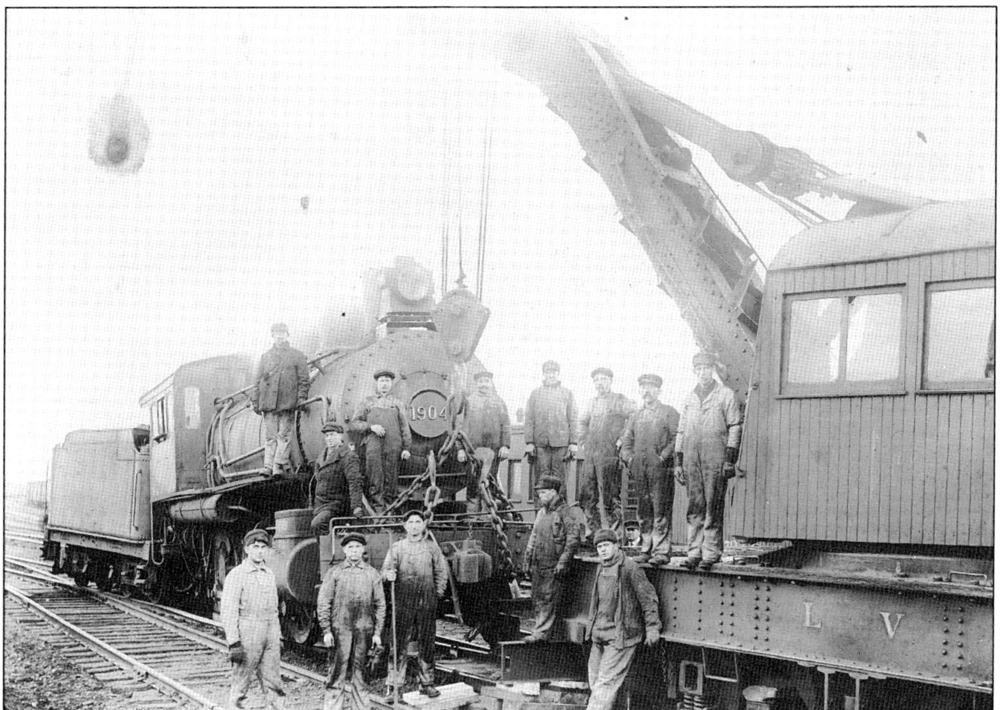

The Lehigh Valley "wreck train crane" (shown here in 1916) was utilized to remove damaged boxcars and crippled engines from the tracks in Manchester. Repairs were then made, allowing the ever-busy freight traffic to continue.

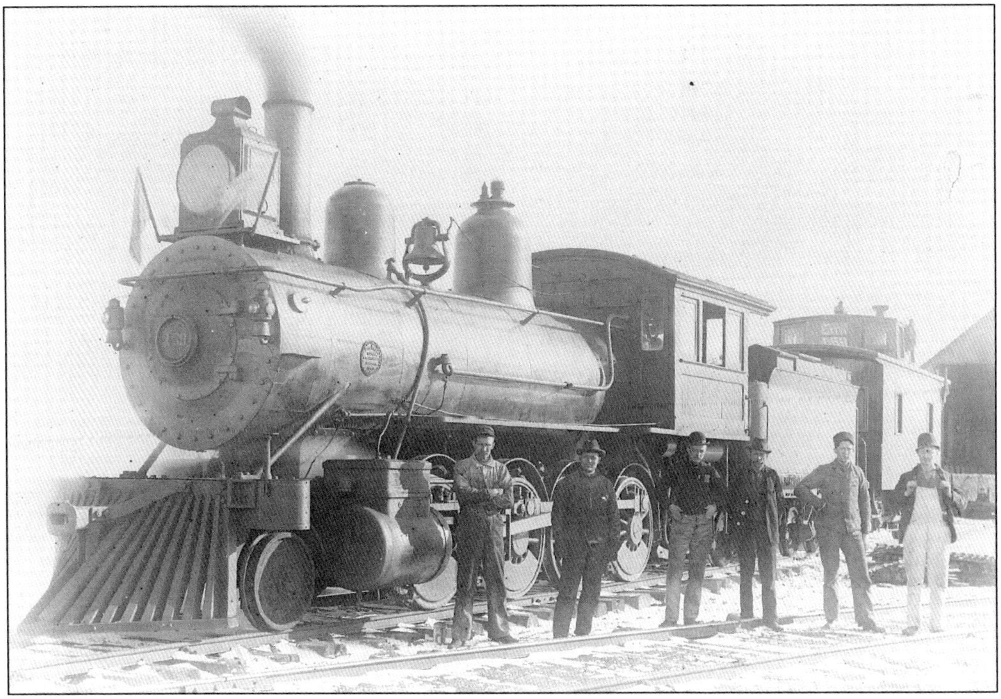

This is perhaps one of Manchester's earliest railroad photographs. The 159 steamer transported freight crews from Buffalo and Sayre, Pennsylvania.

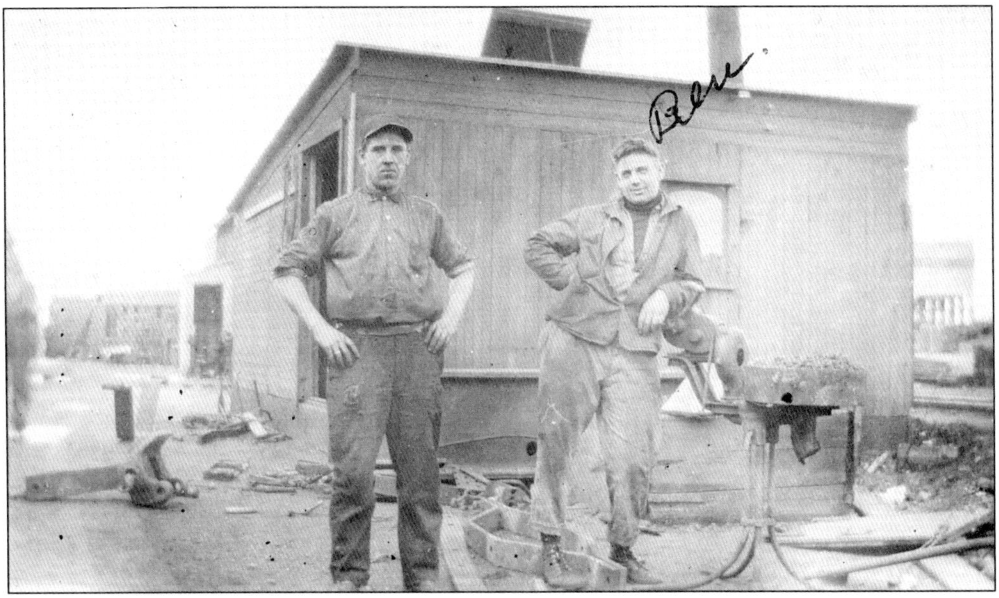

Once a paperboy for the *Saturday Evening Post*, Ben Knauss and an unidentified co-worker pause from train repairs in the cripple track section. The photograph was taken in 1917.

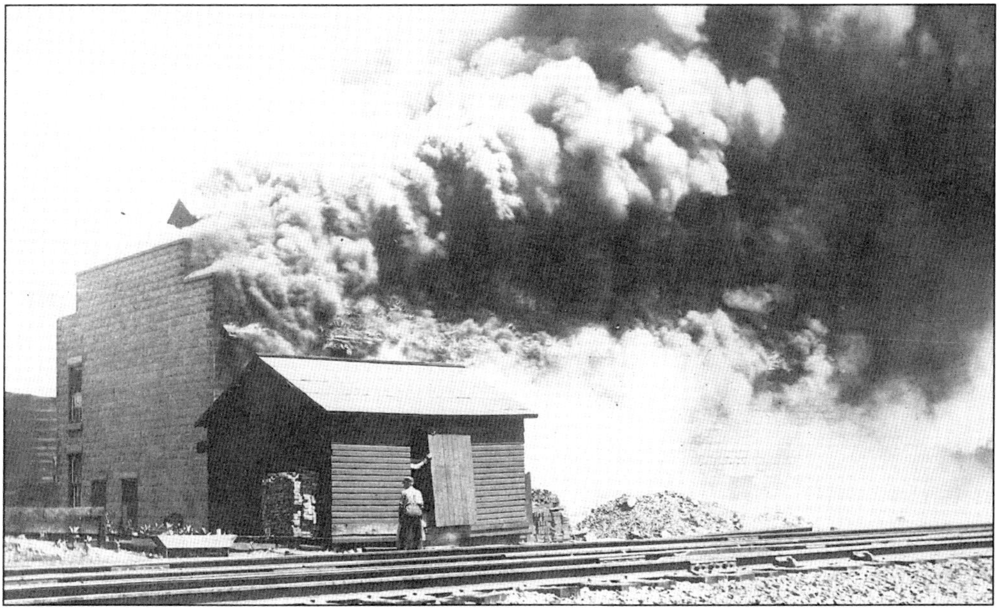

Manchester's early series of postcards consisted of many different pictures from freight transfer yards. This postcard is of the 1913 dry house and canning factory fire in the rail yards of Manchester. The fire was controlled by a new water system built in Manchester earlier that year; however, Manchester did not purchase a fire truck until 1915, so the fire had to be fought by the volunteer bucket brigade.

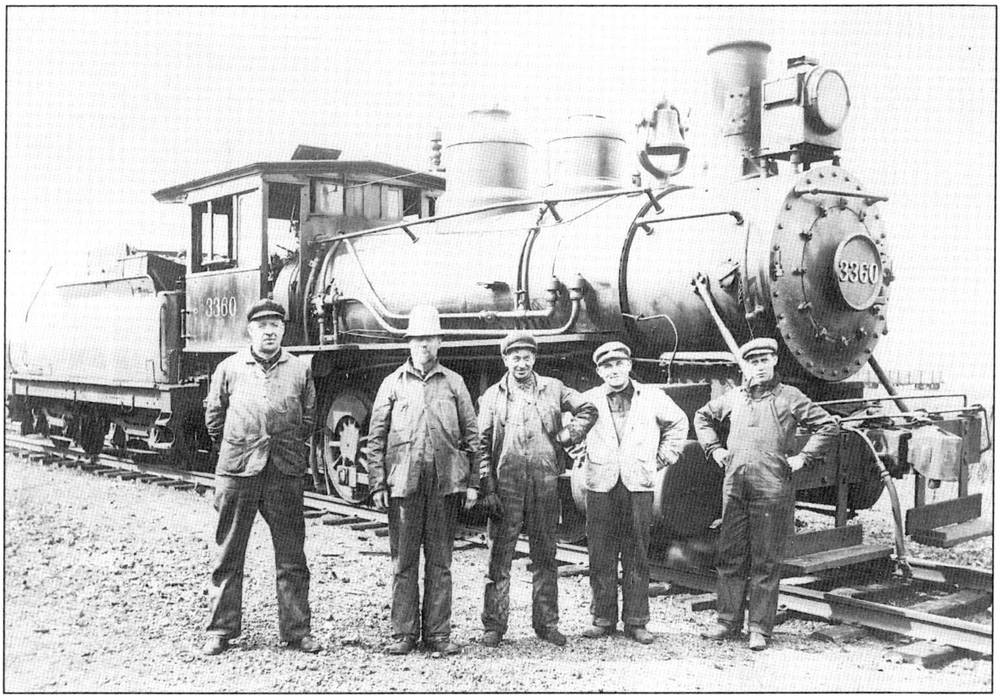

On a sunny day in 1915, Mike Langdon, William Eddinger I (conductor), Harry Maynard, Harry Herman, and Lee Smith stand before steamer 3360. Irishmen secured the highest paying positions of the LVRR in Manchester.

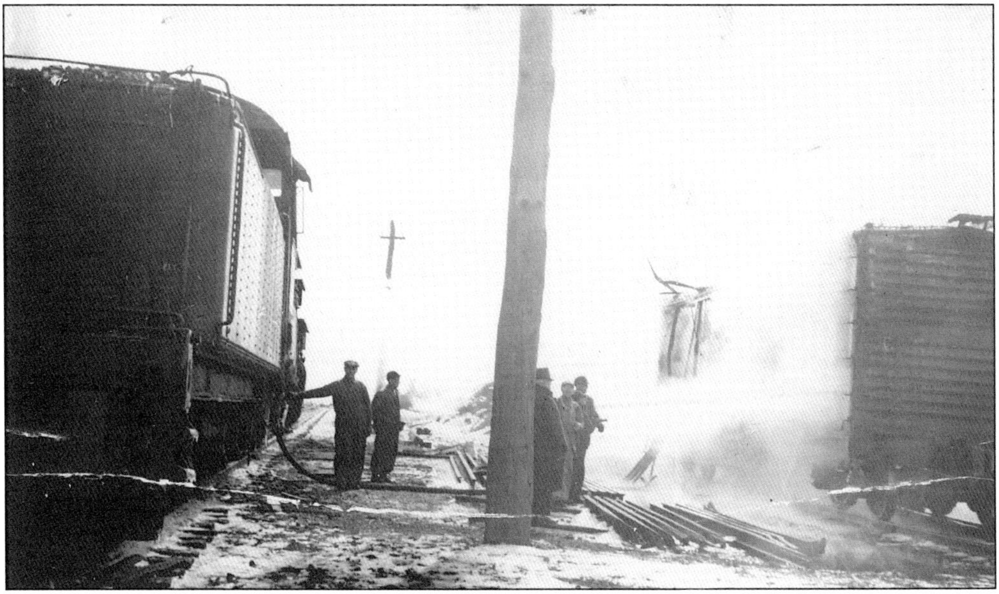

On March 28, 1937, a chemical explosion resulted from one of many perilous hazards that existed in the freight yards of Manchester. No one was hurt by the blowout, but the damage was considerable as several boxcars burned and a substantial amount of freight was destroyed.

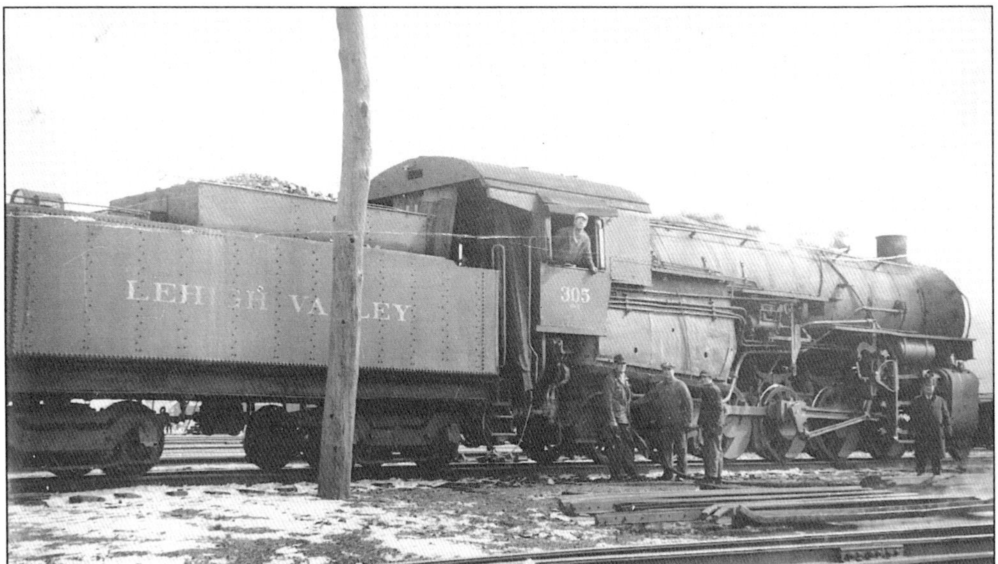

Following the March 28th disaster, engine 305 received special attention from C.A. Quinter, foreman; C. Colvin, fireman; Francis McShea; P.O. O'Brian, general yard master; and the train's engineer, W. Grassly. Francis McShea, a lifelong LVRR worker, was once a star shortstop for the Manchester Railroaders.

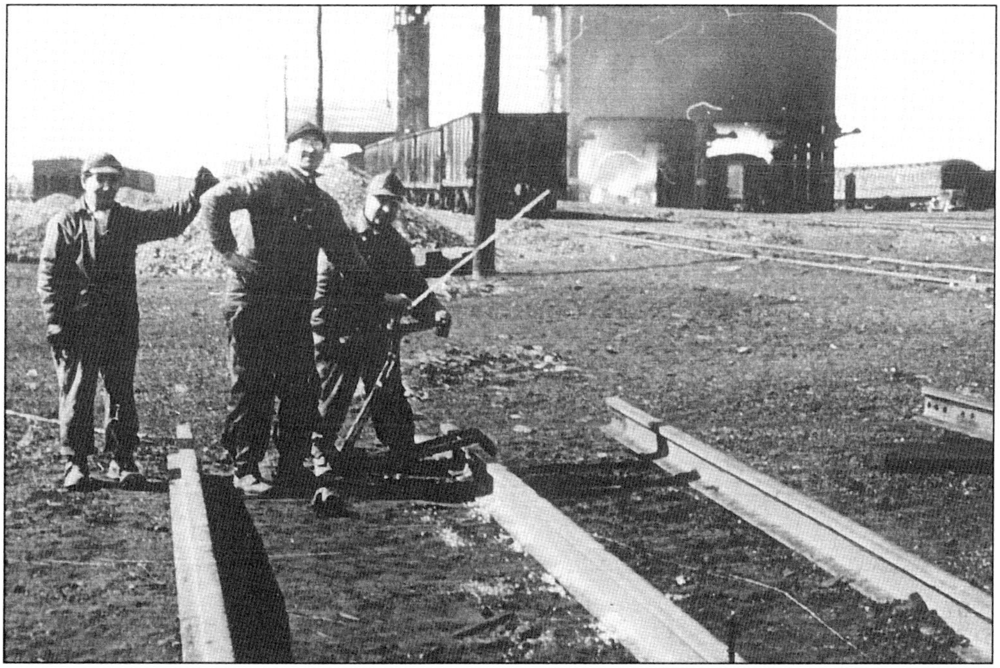

A trio of gandy dancers, Louis Pasquale, Joe Weaver, and Joe Minute, pause before the coal pockets in Manchester during the Depression era. The term "gandy dancer" is derived from the railroad tools manufactured in Chicago. The dancers were renowned for their strategic work rhythm and playful railroad songs. Often the dancers covered several miles in a day's work. Harlan Munn, the father of co-author Tim Munn, worked as a gandy dancer for the Dansville Mount Morris Railroad. Note the tenders being filled beneath the coal pockets.

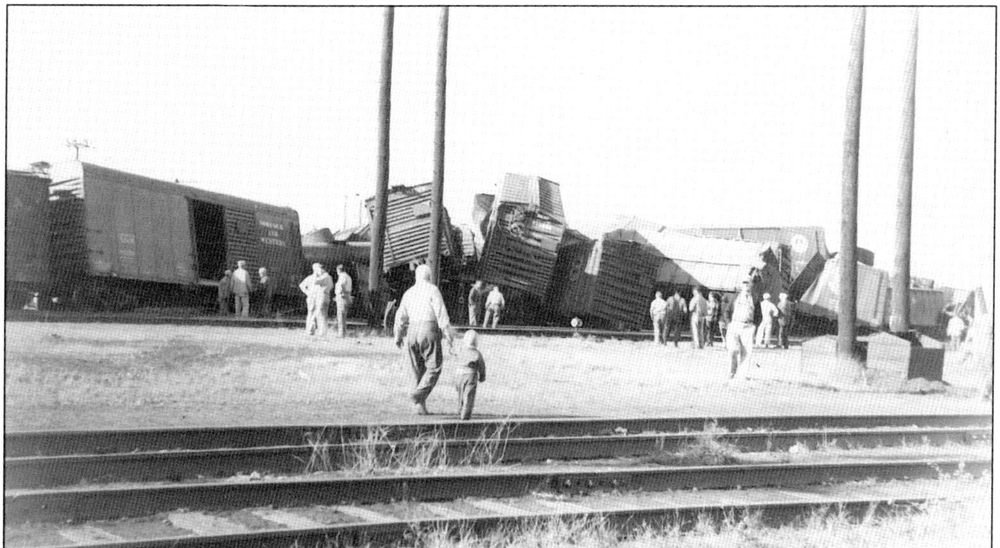

Frank Angeline and his grandson investigate the 1953 Lehigh Valley derailment in the Manchester yard. The air brakes on the locomotive failed, causing the train to slam into a line of LVRR boxcars. The noise from the crash was reported more than 5 miles away in Clifton Springs.

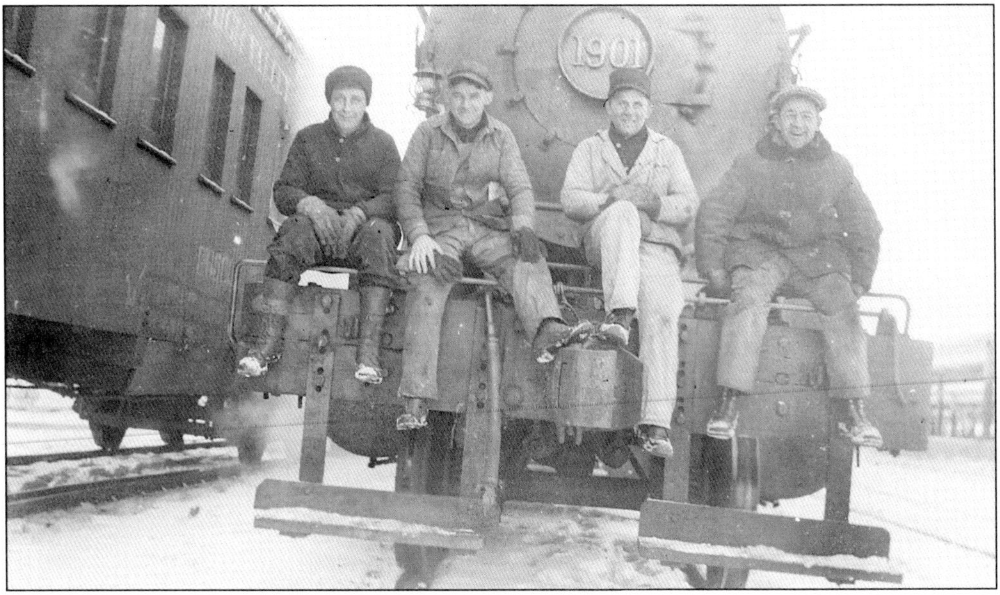

Not even the frigid winters of upstate New York could damper the spirits of this hearty crew of engine 1901. The weather was troublesome and often dangerous in addition to the already hazardous conditions of the railroad. To the left is a classic wooden Pullman of the LVRR.

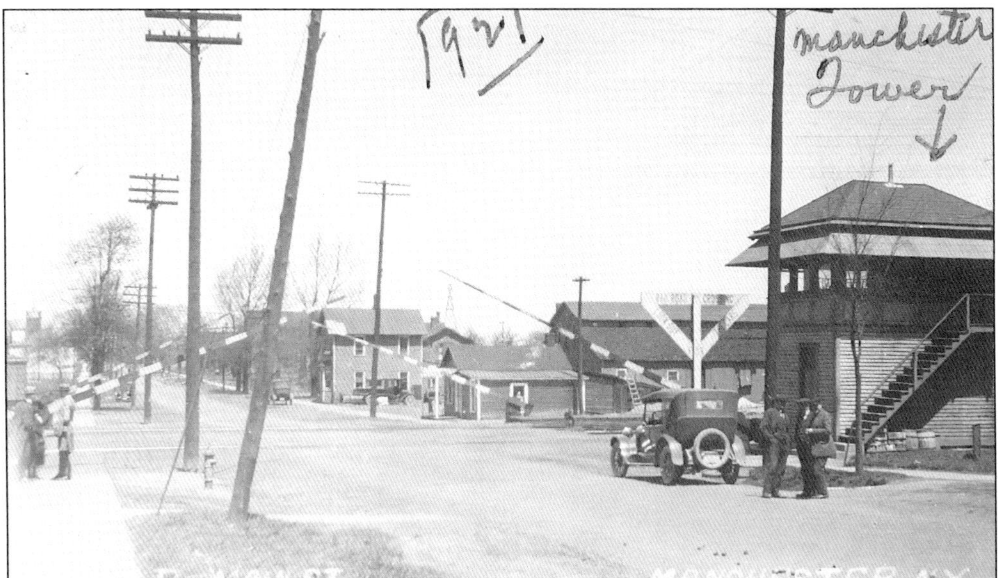

For more than 60 years, Manchester's control tower operated for the LVRR. In 1934, an underpass system was sculpted to accommodate street traffic on what is currently Route 21. The control tower was demolished in 1968. Occasionally, small trains can be seen crossing the bridge at a snail's pace, giving today's populace a symbol of what once ruled the town.

One of Manchester's nicknames in its early history was "Tank Town." John McNally is shown here in 1920 standing in front of the water supply tanks, which filled the steam locomotives of the LVRR.

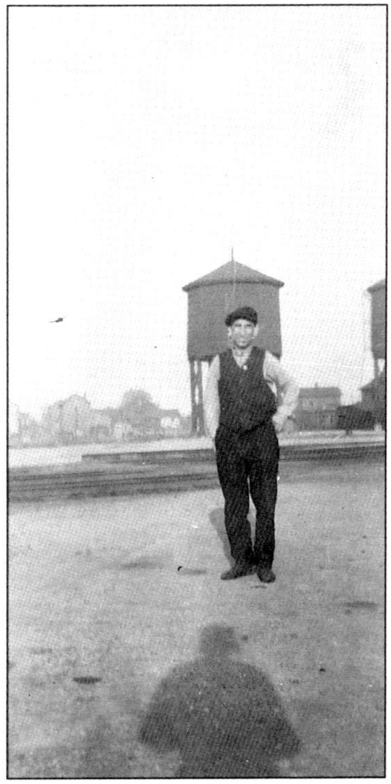

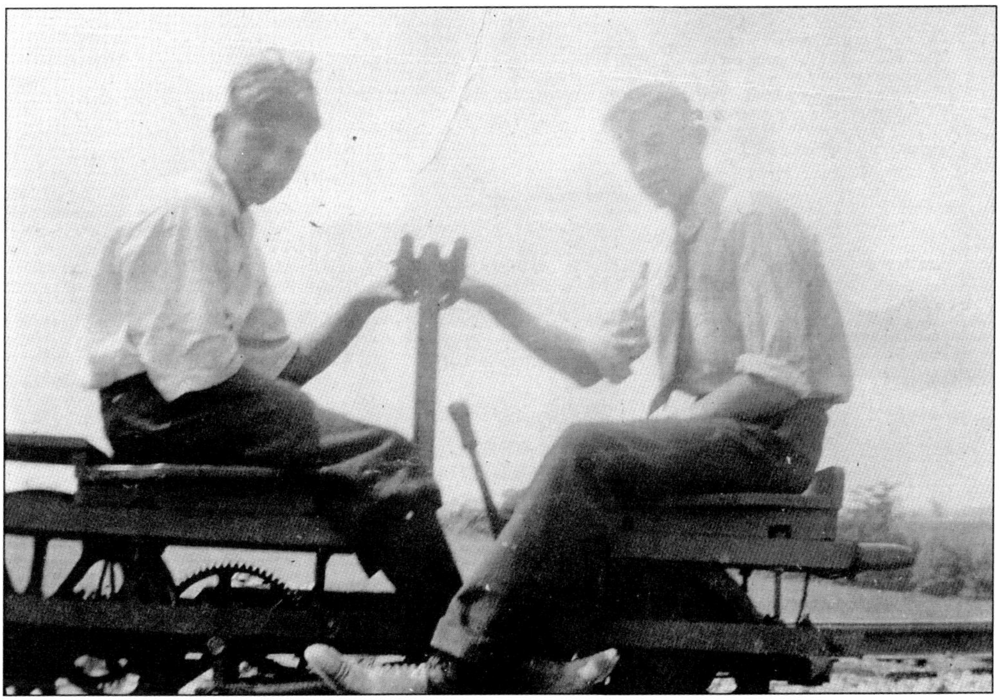

Two young lads operate an early railroad invention called the handcar. Handcars were used for running supplies to a section gang, also known as gandy dancers. The section gang required adequate assistance as the handcars carried the spikes, hammers, and water buckets—the essential equipment needed for a hard day's work.

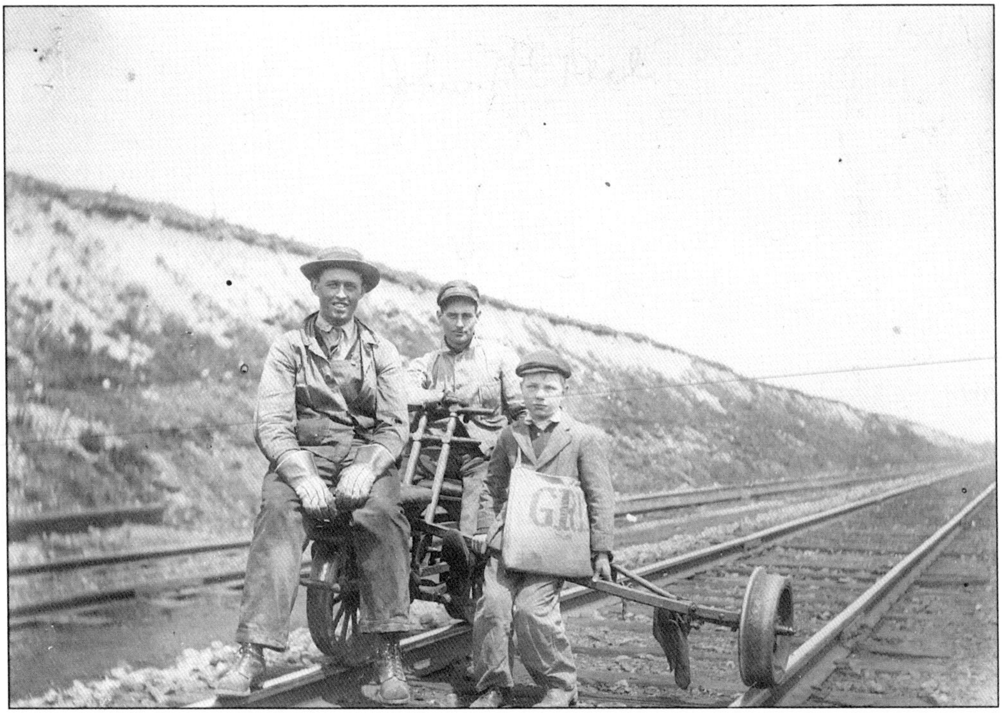

Jim McNeal operates his rail motorcycle near the West End of the yard in Manchester. "Grit," seen on the side of the bag, was a national newspaper in the early part of the century. Children gladly worked the paper routes of the ever-growing town.

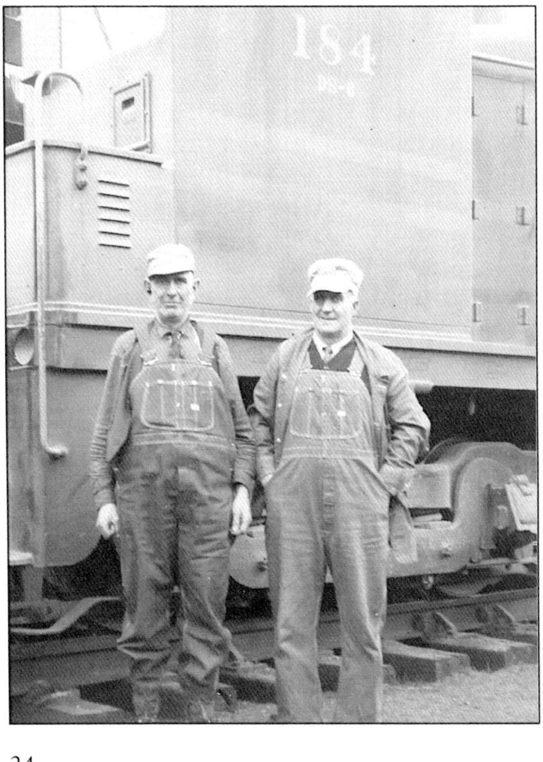

Venerable Lehigh Valley men, Joe Pulling and William Eddinger II, stand proudly before diesel locomotive 184 in the early 1960s. These two men began as fireman on the LVRR during the steam locomotive era and concluded as engineers of the diesel era.

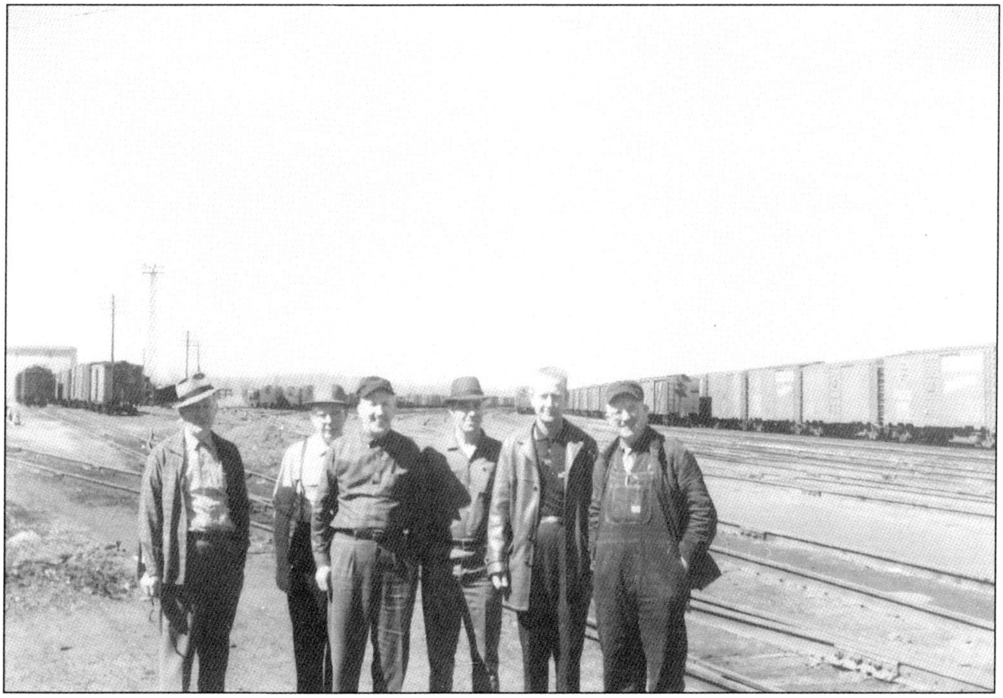

Veteran railroaders, from left to right, Mullen, Hartnett, Boardman, Vienna, Conlon, and Johnny Boardman return to the rail yard in May of 1963. Manchester's rail yard officially closed in 1970.

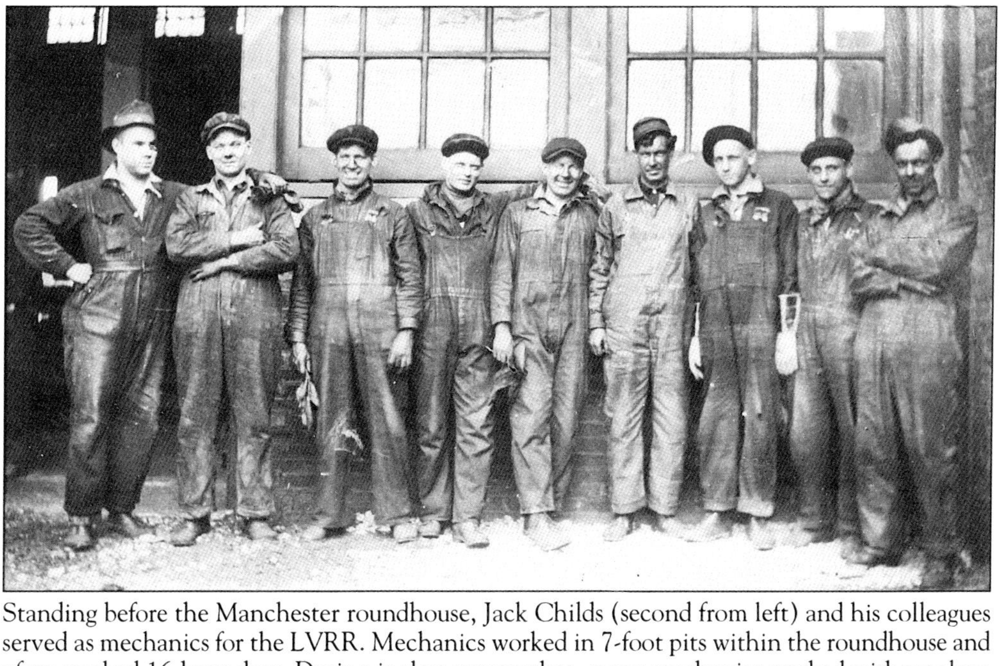

Standing before the Manchester roundhouse, Jack Childs (second from left) and his colleagues served as mechanics for the LVRR. Mechanics worked in 7-foot pits within the roundhouse and often worked 16-hour days. During inclement weather, many mechanics worked without sleep for 24 hours.

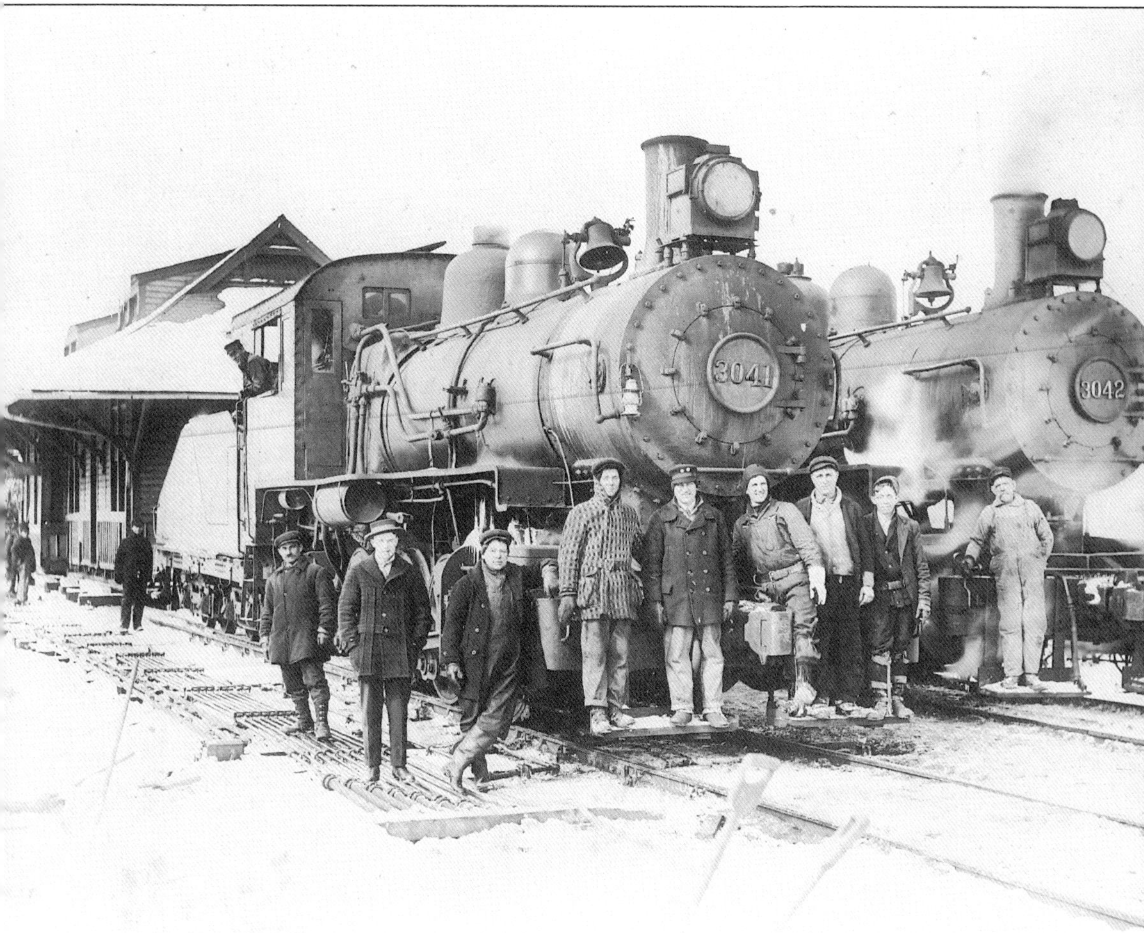

Two steam engines and their crews pose in front of the newly built bunkhouse in the early 1900s. The bunkhouse provided warm meals and adequate sleeping quarters for the various workers on the LVRR, most notably the engineers, firemen, brakemen, and conductors.

Two

THE TOWN

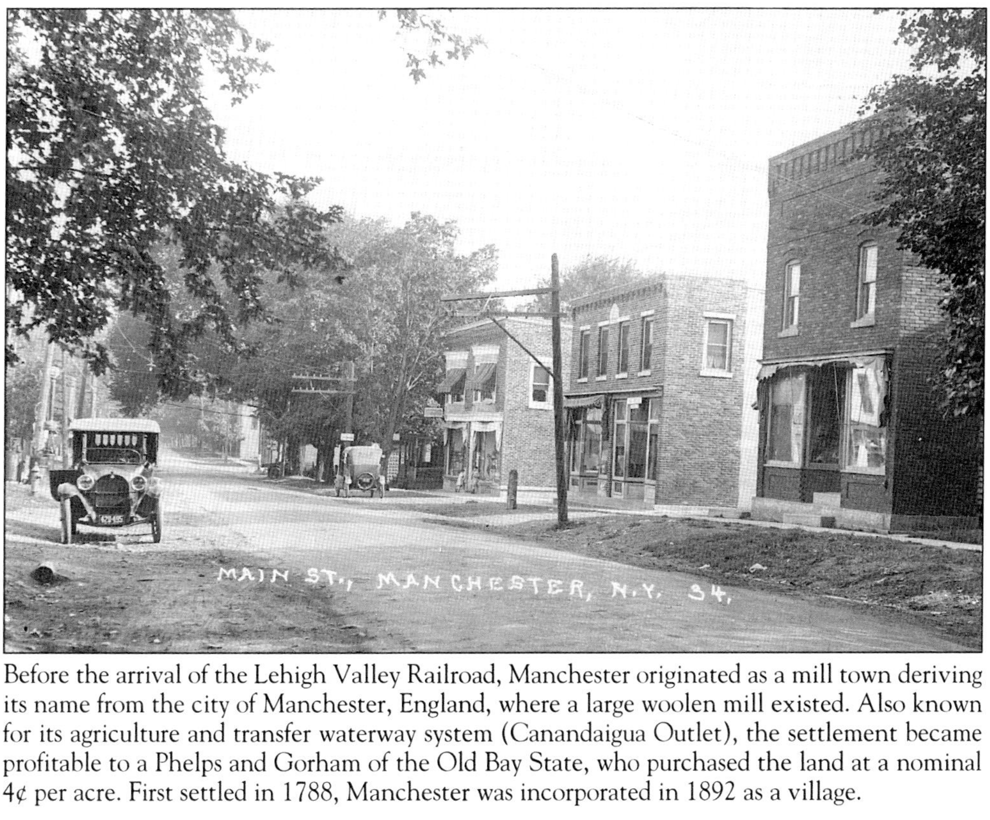

Before the arrival of the Lehigh Valley Railroad, Manchester originated as a mill town deriving its name from the city of Manchester, England, where a large woolen mill existed. Also known for its agriculture and transfer waterway system (Canandaigua Outlet), the settlement became profitable to a Phelps and Gorham of the Old Bay State, who purchased the land at a nominal 4¢ per acre. First settled in 1788, Manchester was incorporated in 1892 as a village.

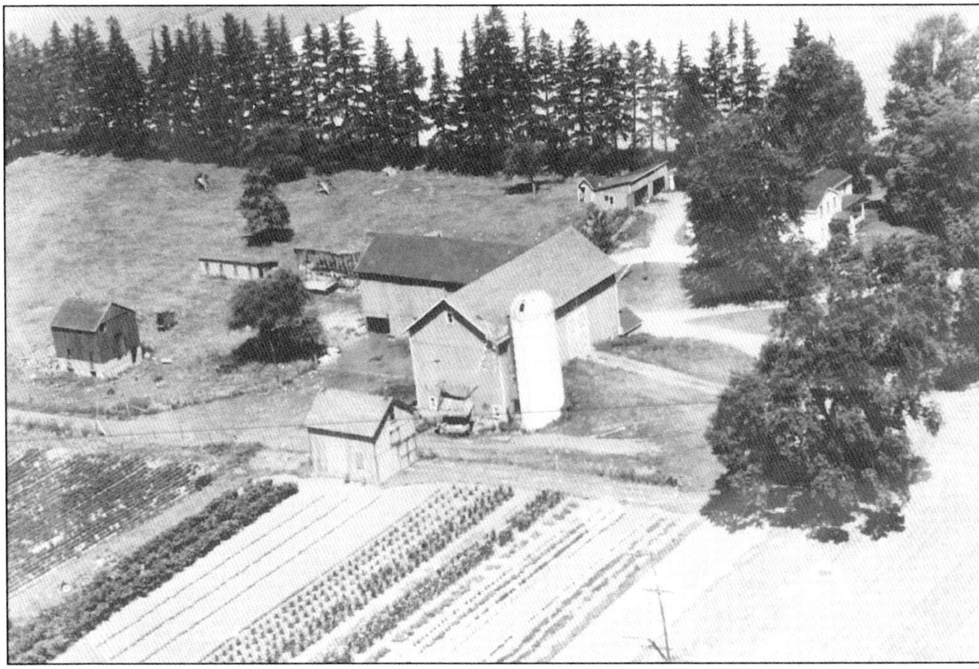

Before the construction of the New York State Thruway, many farms in Manchester flourished. The Stafford farm, which was over a century old, was the oldest of many farms in Manchester. The framework of the farmhouse consisted of portions of the home belonging to Joseph Smith, founder of the Mormon religion. The Lupolds owned the farm at the time this aerial photograph was taken in 1950; the farm was cut in half by the thruway construction in the early 1950s. The historic farm still stands on Stafford Road and now belongs to the VanCaeseele family.

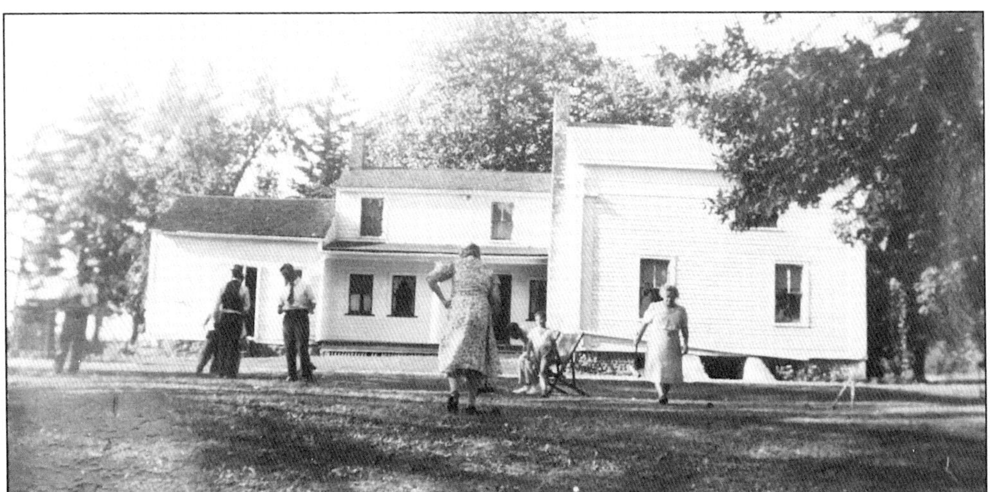

This photograph depicts a classic scene of the Lupold family during a warm, tranquil summer day in 1944. In the early years, Sunday was the only day for rest for farming families. After church, men would customarily pitch horseshoes and talk about politics, while women would prepare the traditional Sunday dinner. It was also popular for families to play croquet on Sundays.

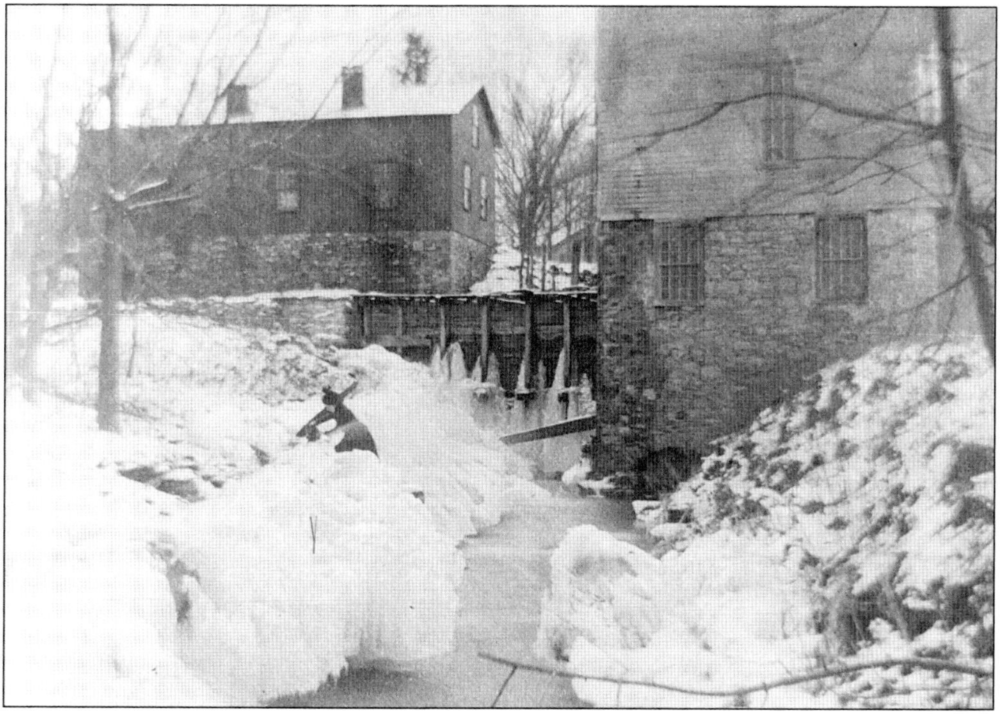

A courageous woman rescues her cat from the icy banks of the outlet. In the background stands Mason's gristmill, a woolen mill of the late 19th century. Children were paid 15¢ to 25¢ a day to work at the old woolen mill. Mason's was eventually converted to a wheat and flower mill and was finally torn down in 1919.

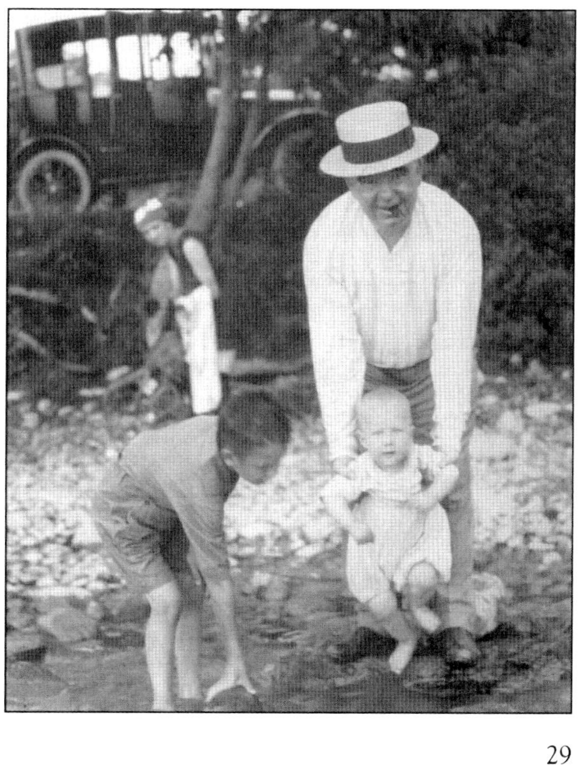

This time-honored portrayal of a grandfather and his grandchildren was taken at the Canandaigua outlet in 1919. Many locals like Grandpa Segbers (shown here) used the outlet for recreation during time off from work.

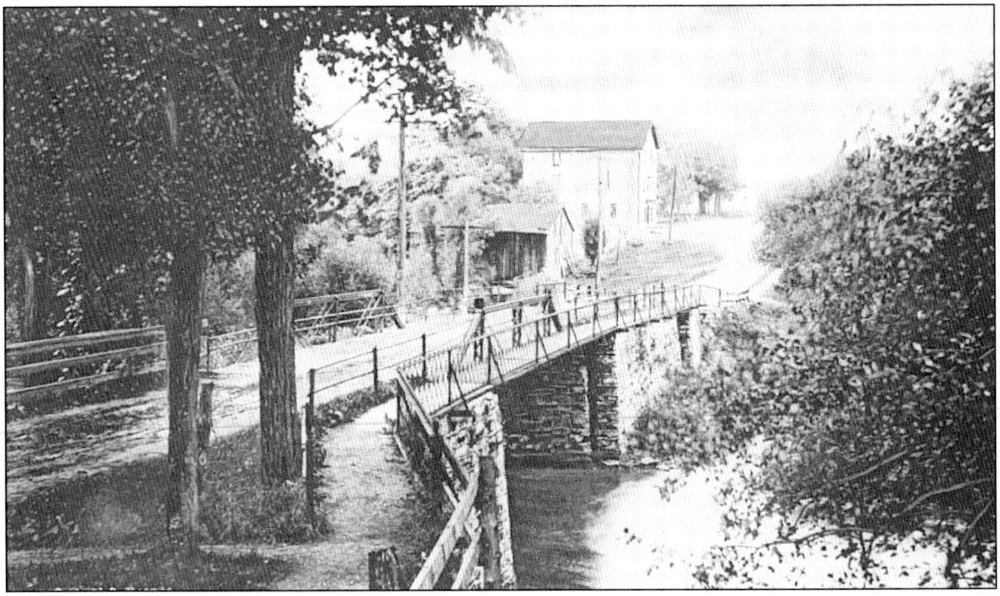

This is a 1908 photograph of the Outlet Bridge leading to "old mill hill," where Mason's gristmill and Russell's sawmill operated by waterpower until 1919. Early settlers used flat-bottom boats known as bateau or Durham boats to carry supplies, trade goods, and transport other useful commodities on the outlet. The site of Manchester's Boy Scout camp, off the picture to the left of the bridge, was used as a landing by settlers as early as 1788.

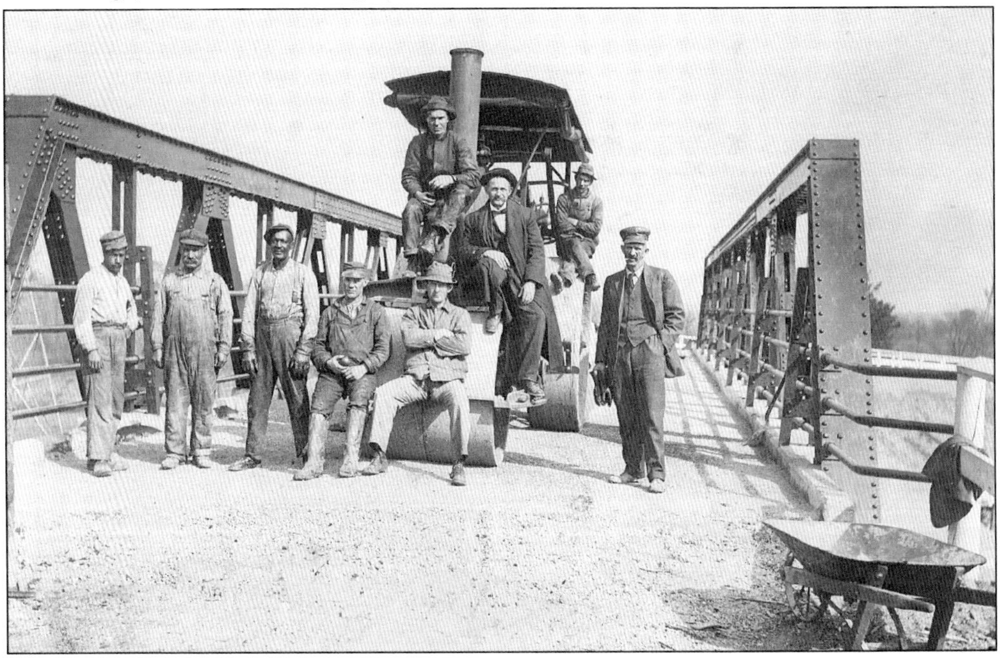

Shown here are men contending with the railroad. Posing in front of a coal-fed steamroller in 1914, N. Brophy and his co-workers pause for recognition during the construction of the State Street bridge. The bridge was used temporarily as a safer transportation route but was demolished in the mid-1960s because of cost and disuse. A section of the bridge remains and is located near Payne Cemetery, Manchester. State Street is the old Route 96.

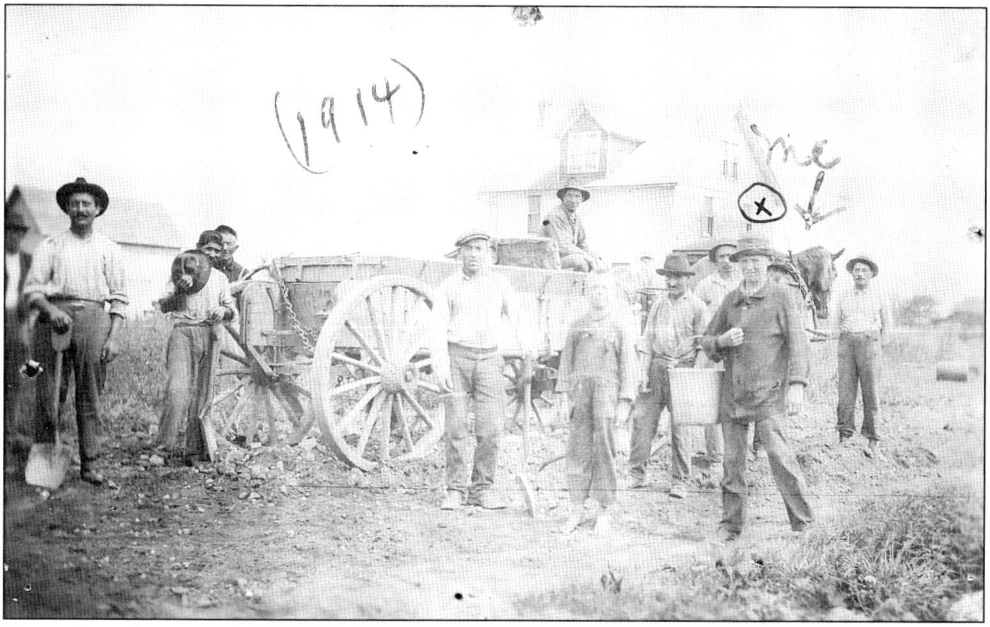

Soon after the reconstruction of State Street in 1914, a large number of rail workers claimed plots and purchased land. Pick axes and shovels were the common tools workers used to clear the roads. Johnny Boardman is shown here carrying water to the workers.

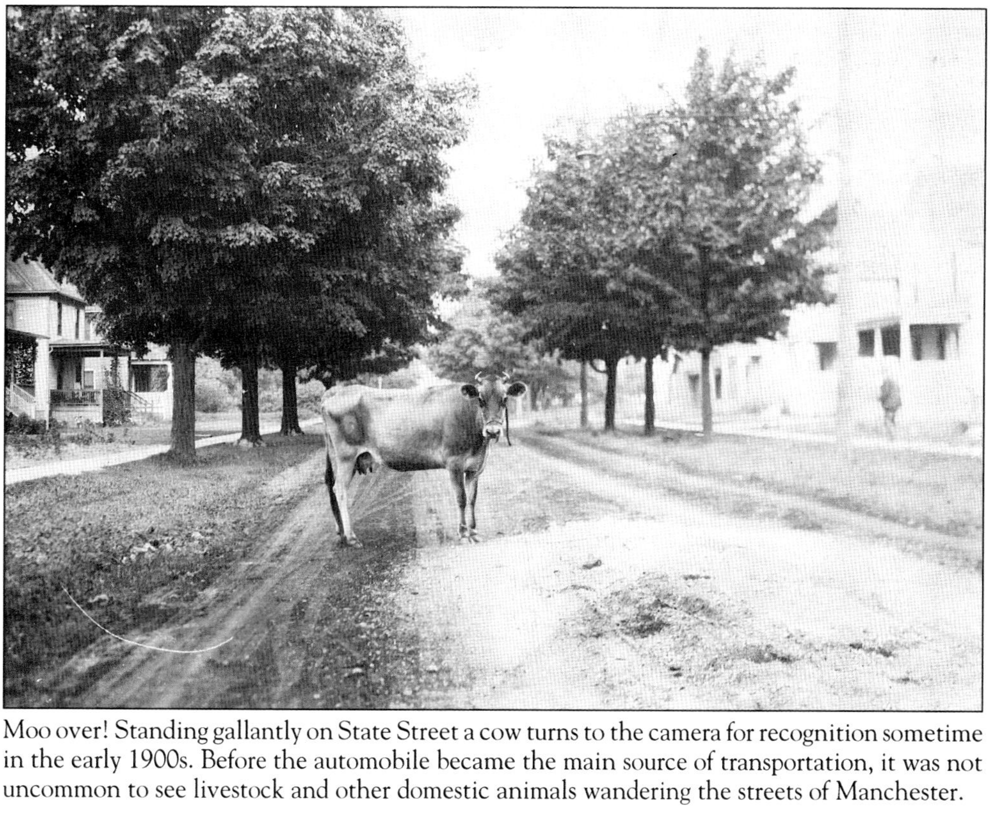

Moo over! Standing gallantly on State Street a cow turns to the camera for recognition sometime in the early 1900s. Before the automobile became the main source of transportation, it was not uncommon to see livestock and other domestic animals wandering the streets of Manchester.

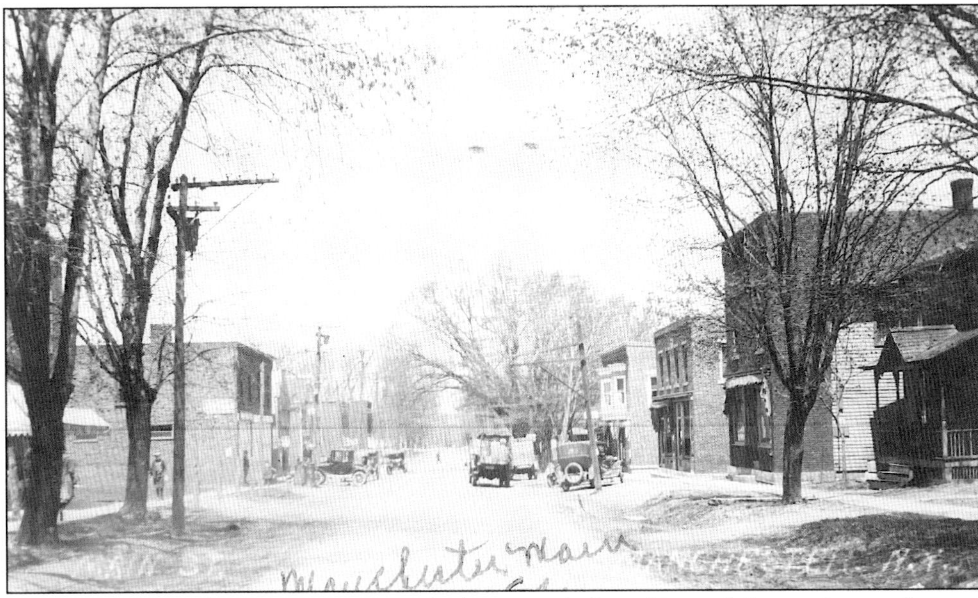

This 1921 view of South Main Street looking north from Howard Street shows what was considered the main business district in Manchester. Note the delivery truck parked in front of Knapp's drug store.

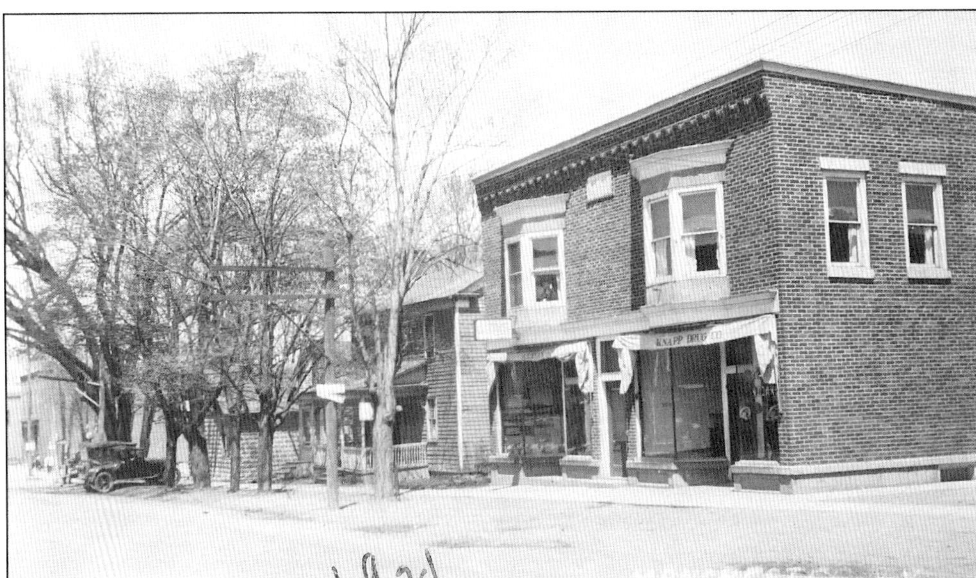

A secret room lies hidden within the walls of Knapp's drug store. The town speakeasy was separated by a sliding wall that still exists within Twin Cities restaurant in Manchester.

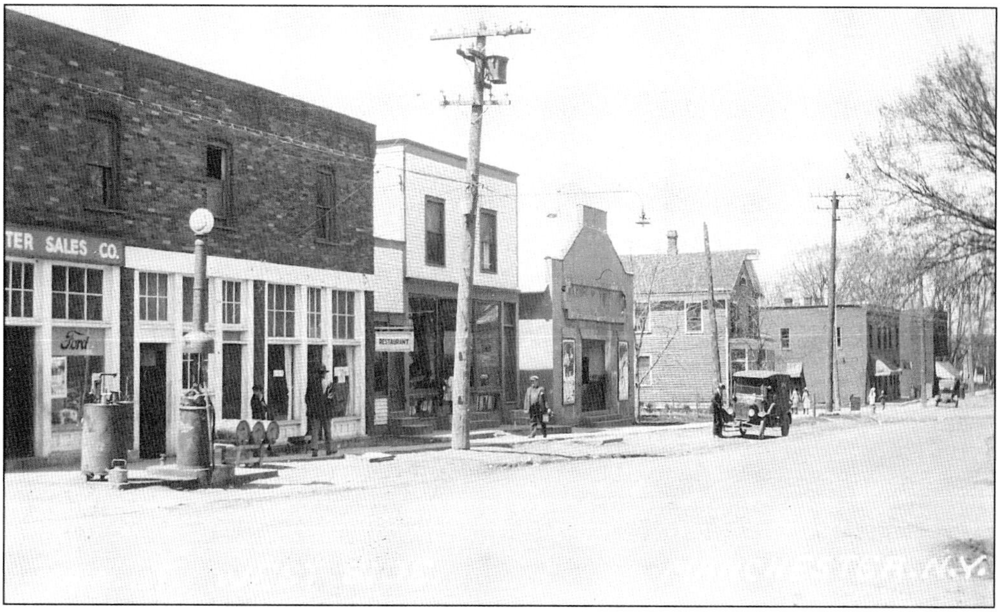

George McGurk's garage, now the site of Gravino's barbershop, is shown here on the west side of Main Street in 1921. Looking further, one can see, from left to right, Manchester's car company, a restaurant, a picture show theater, and Hawkes bakery.

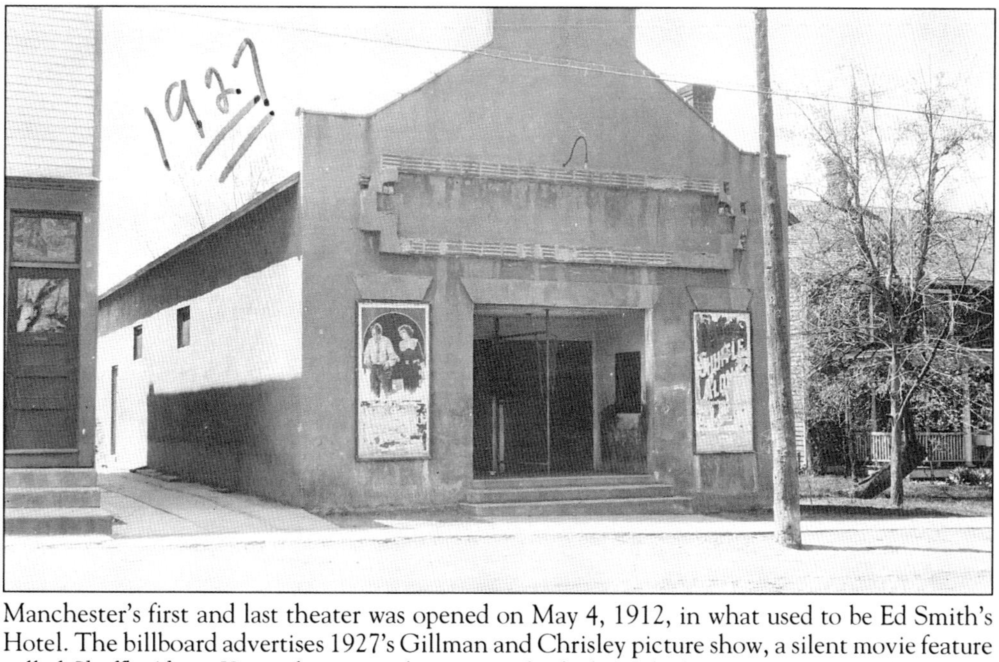

Manchester's first and last theater was opened on May 4, 1912, in what used to be Ed Smith's Hotel. The billboard advertises 1927's Gillman and Chrisley picture show, a silent movie feature called *Shuffle Alone*. Young boys were known to climb through the men's room window to get a free peak at the popular movies. In 1947, the theater closed due to increasing film costs and low attendance.

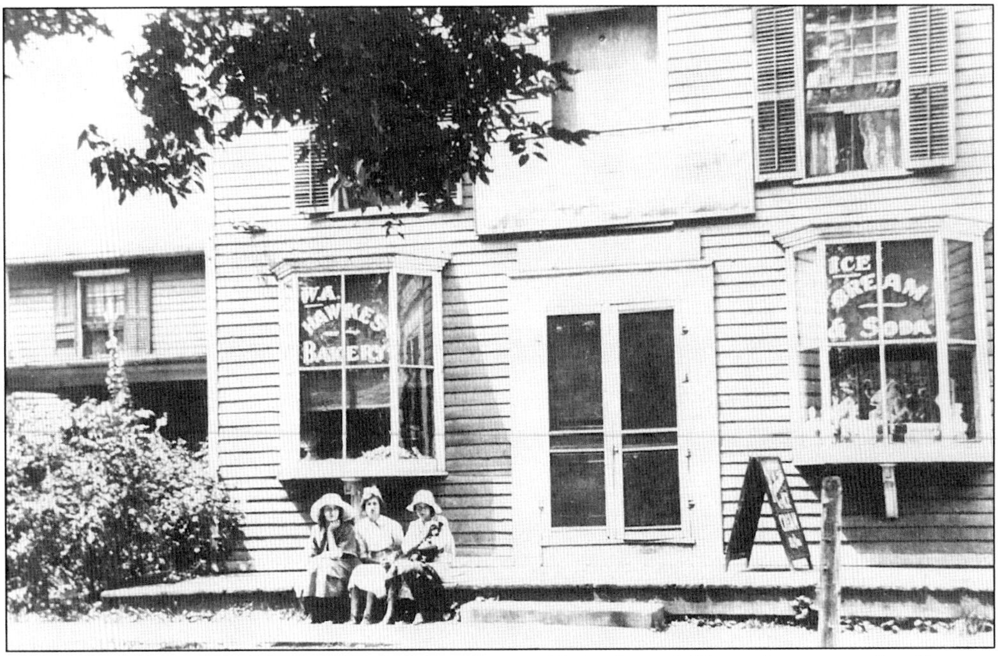

Hawkes bakery, a Manchester landmark, was established in 1892 and was run by Stewart and Genevieve Hawkes. It moved in 1904 to the corner of State and Main Streets, where it flourished for over 70 years. In 1963, the bakery was demolished and replaced with the Atlantic Service station. Today, the site is owned by Express Mart Mobile.

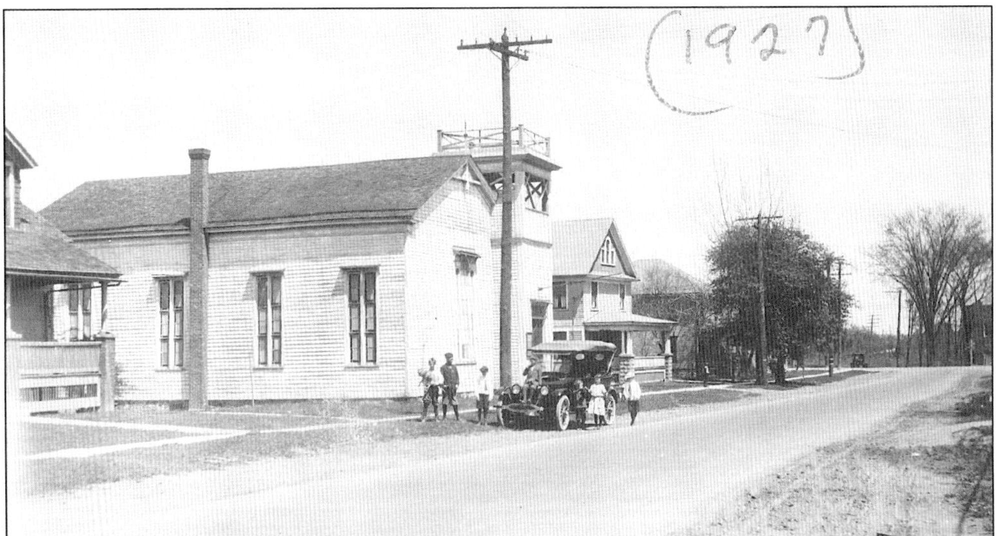

Built to seat 200 people in 1840, Manchester's Methodist Church, pictured here in 1927, played an important part in the town's history. Perhaps the most noteworthy of the building's components was its extraordinary church bell. To alert Manchester's bucket brigade, the mighty bell would sound during all village fires. After the news of the Armistice signing, the bell rang triumphant and melodious as Manchester celebrated the end of World War I. It also sounded on the New Year but was most recognized for its commemoration of the deceased through the years.

Manchester's Baptist Church, with its place of worship built in 1849, consisted of a congregation of farmers. Many families, like the Dewey family, traveled to church by driving an ox team. Ed Watkins, an African-American farmhand for Deacon Howland, had an exclusive pew at the stairs in the gallery for many years. Watkins served in the Civil War.

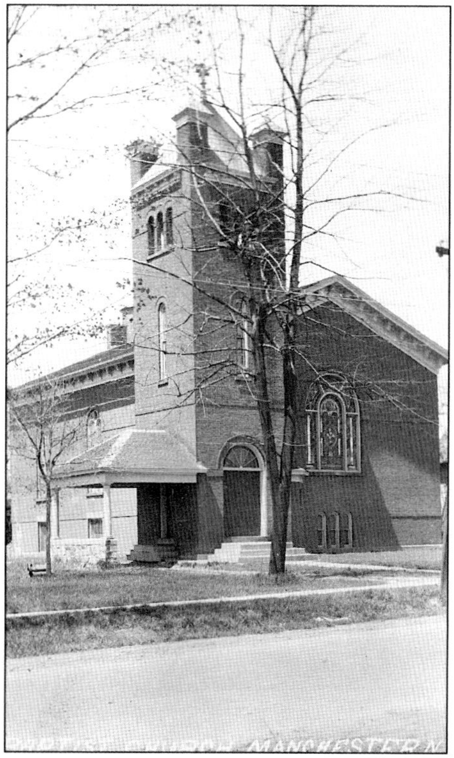

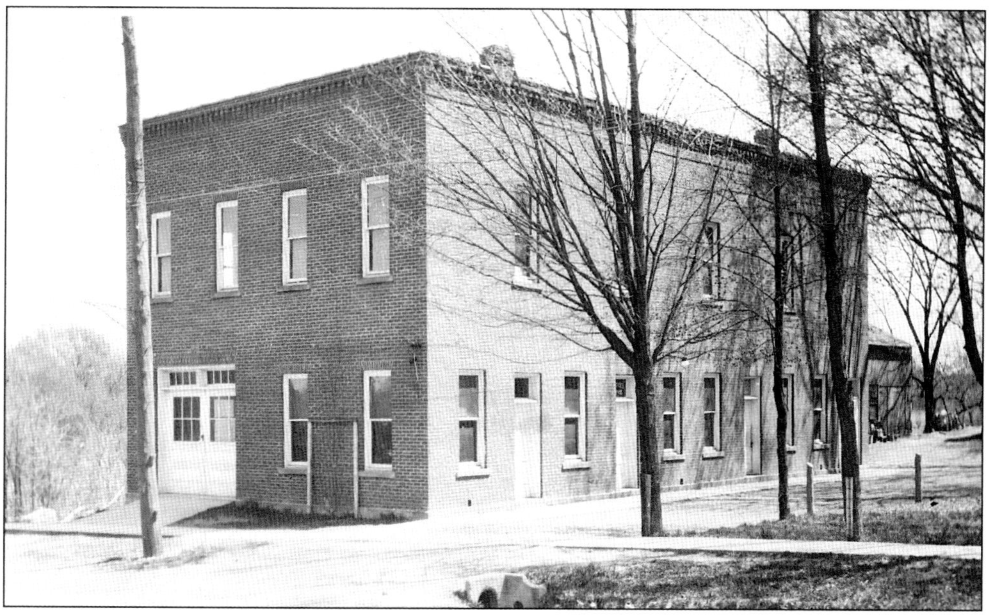

Manchester's old village hall and fire company is shown here in 1921 near the old blacksmith shop and town bandstand. The upstairs of the fire hall held many smokers (meetings, dances, and banquets) as well as many Manchester Arrows and Rochester Centrals semi-pro basketball battles. Although the baskets were 10 feet high, the ceiling was only 5 feet higher. Maintenance men had to attend games with ladders and extra light bulbs to replace many broken lights through the years.

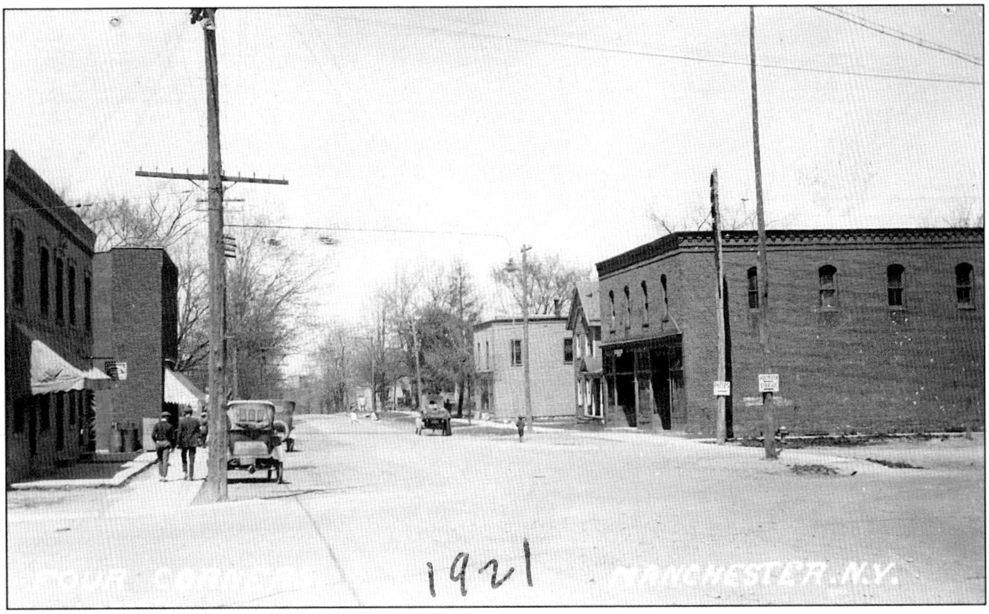

This 1921 view of the North Main Street intersection of State Street and Clifton Street captures the area once used as the finish and starting lines for early century bicycle and horse races in Manchester. The building to the left was known as the Johnson General and Bennett store. During the early 1900s, it operated as the temporary site of the Catholic Church, which was attended by many railroad families.

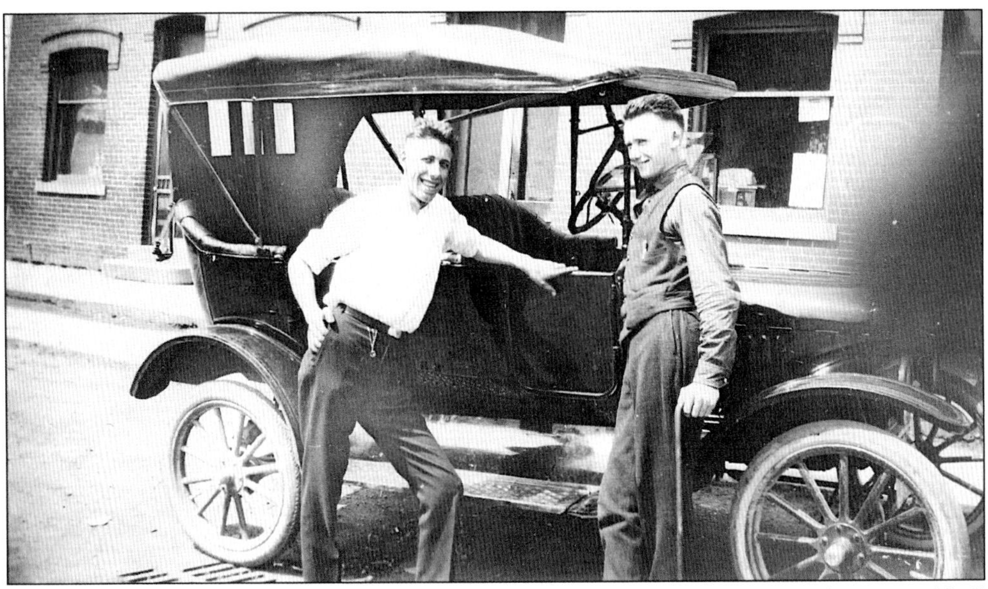

Elmer Vienna and Johnny Boardman lean against a Model T in front of Manchester pool hall and meat market trading stores on the corner of Route 21 and State Street. This photograph was taken in 1919.

Manchester's bandstand, built in the public square on Mill Hill Park in 1886, was financed by donations from the following: Luther Walters of Manchester, J.R. Pratt, M.D., the Wilson & Allen Co., L.H. Aldrich, Al Knapp, Orin Vine, William M. Wells, N.C. Herendeen, H.S. Lyke, J.F. Aldrich, N.K. Cole, J. Lyke, Newton Smith, R.C. Herendeen, Mark Pomeroy, C.H. Herendeen, Mrs. H.A. Brewster, Charles Bumpus, Allen Power, Mrs. H. Hart, Jim Gavin, A.M. Snadeker, J. Rushmore, A.W. Hawkes, J. Hakes, H.E. Hawkes, N.V. Wilson, W.H. Post, J.W. Ovaracre, J.F. Clarck, E.P. Herendeen, William McComb, A.H. Dewey, L.S. Newton, Thomas Lathbury, Charles McLouth, and J. Tate.

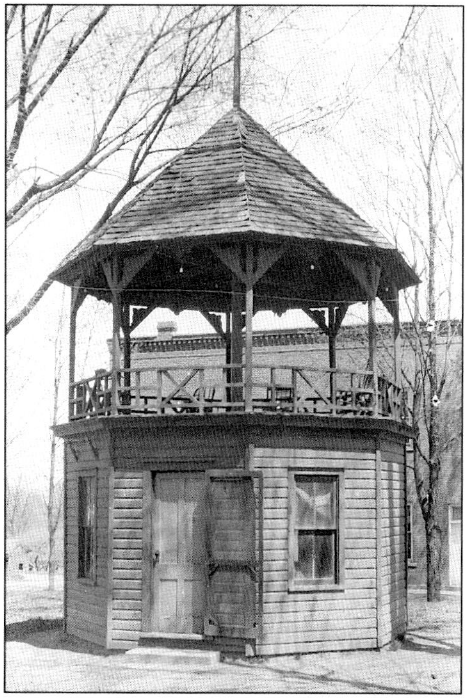

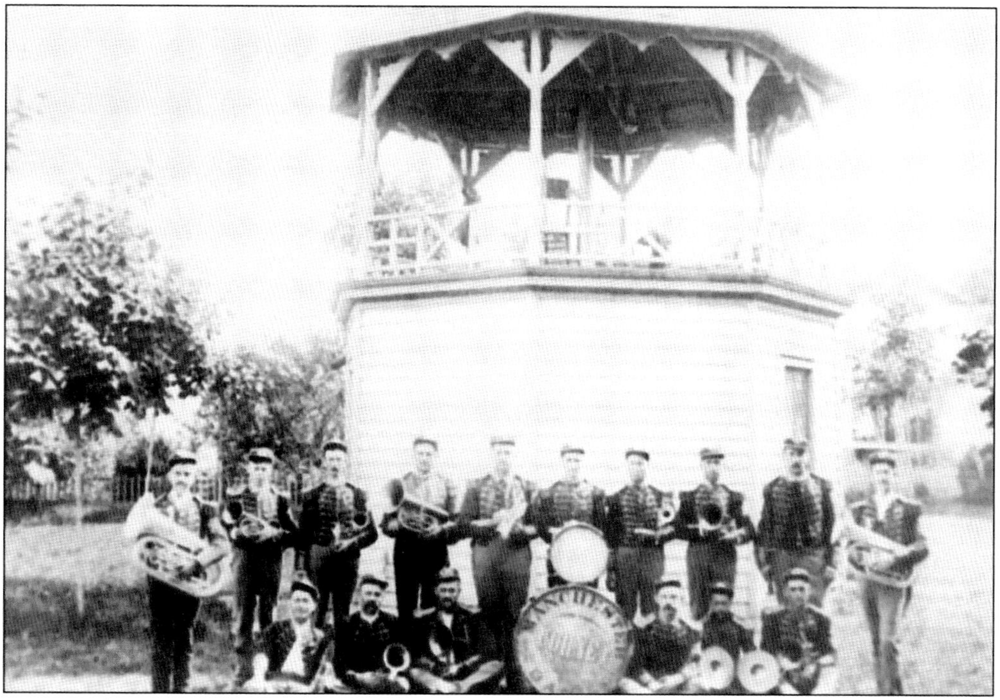

In 1899, the Smith Cornet Band became Manchester's official military band under the direction of Mr. Edward Lyman, a graduate of the Boston Conservatory of Music. The band became popular throughout western New York and gave several moonlit concerts on Canandaigua Lake aboard the *Onalinda*, the *Orgarita*, and the *Orianna*. The songs of John P. Sousa were featured during these performances.

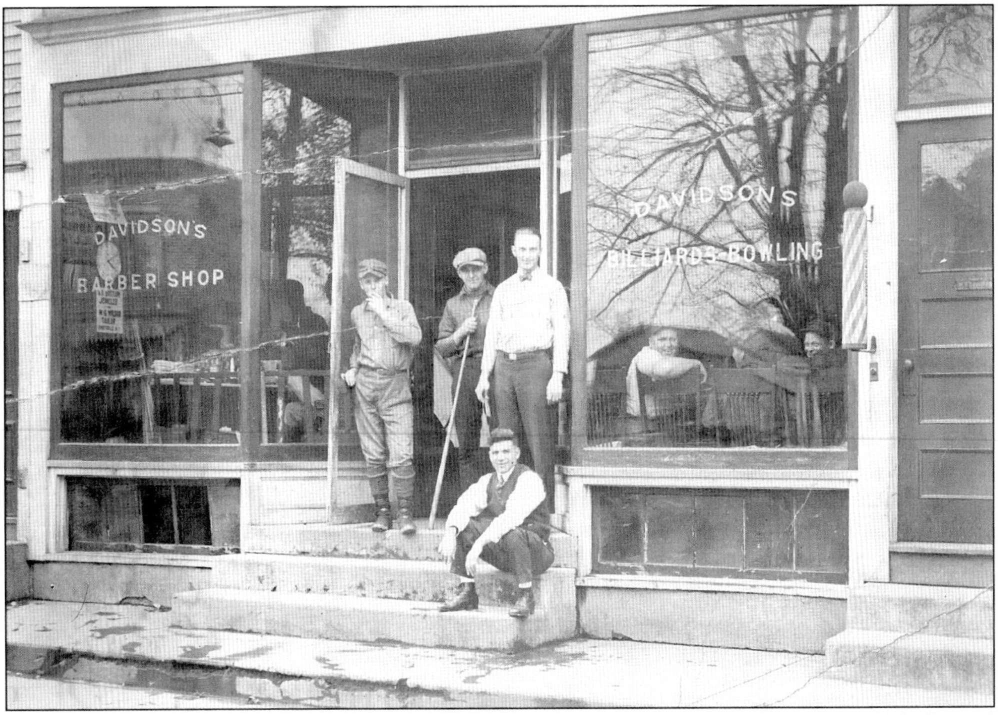

A known betting parlor and afternoon speakeasy, Davidson's barber shop, billiard hall, and bowling company (pictured here in 1910) entertained the people of Manchester for many years.

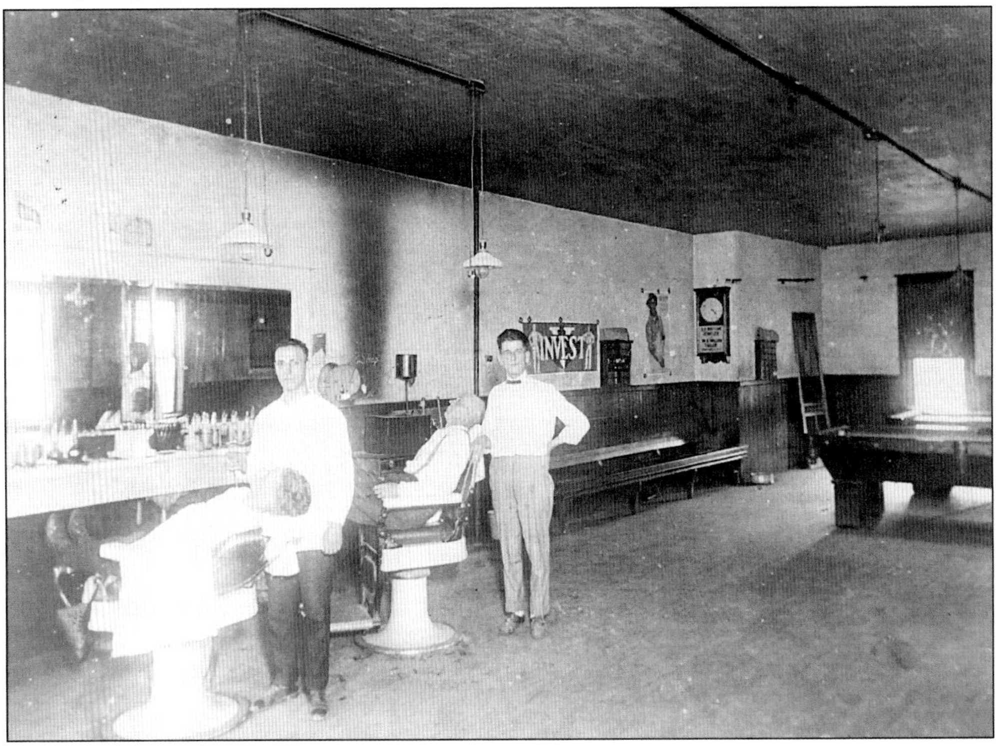

At work in 1911, the Davidsons charged a bargain price of 20¢ for a shave and 25¢ for a haircut.

The Vecchi Brothers bakery of Canandaigua, pictured here in 1911, delivered baked goods to Grandma Mottelo's grocery store, located by the roundhouse on Merrick Circle in Manchester.

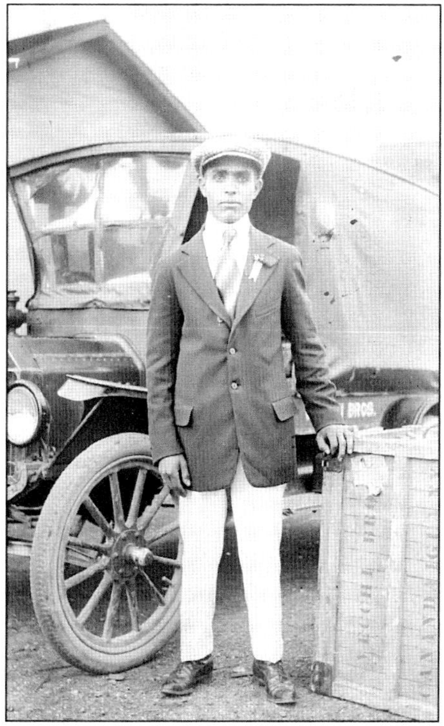

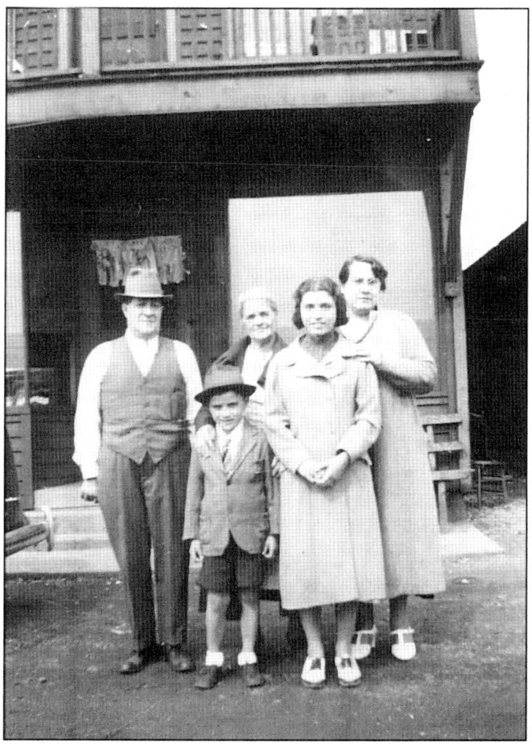

Grandma Mottelo (second from left), acclaimed for her unconditional generosity, served free meals to hobos and transient railroaders in Manchester for many years at the Mottelo store. Seen here, from left to right, are Mr. Cilento, Fred Angeline (the little boy), Grandma Mottelo, Mary Angeline, and Preasa Mottelo.

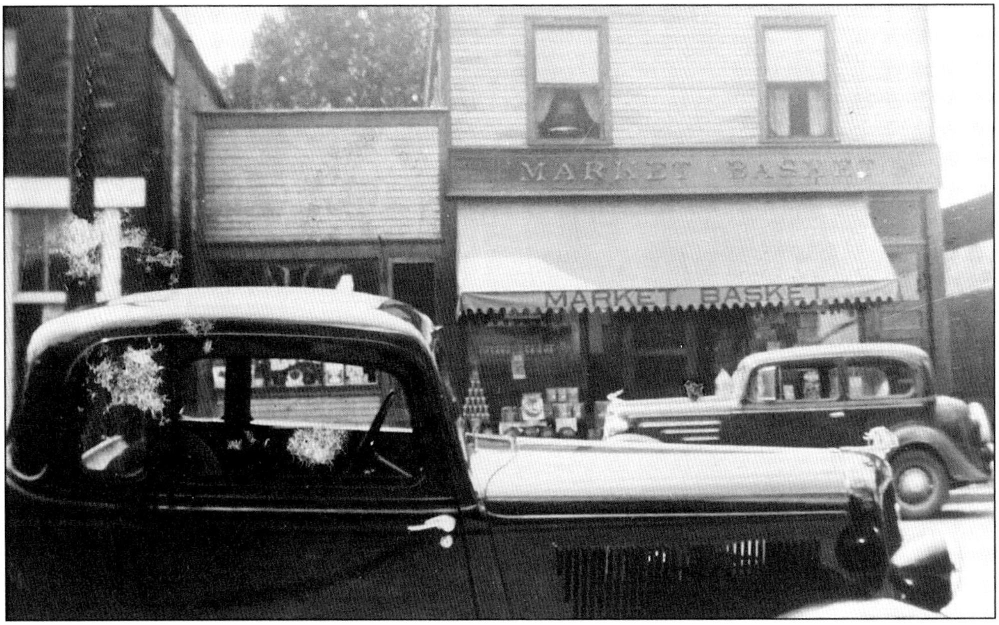

This photograph offers a view of Manchester's Market Basket grocery store (owned by the Geise family), which was later taken over by P&B market (owned by Phil and Ben D'Arduini). Gordon Hover opened the Market Basket grocery store in the former site of the theater in 1947. Manchester, like many villages during the post-World War II era, contained several neighborhood grocery stores that could not compete with national wholesale chains like Market Basket. Eventually, neighborhood stores in Manchester disappeared.

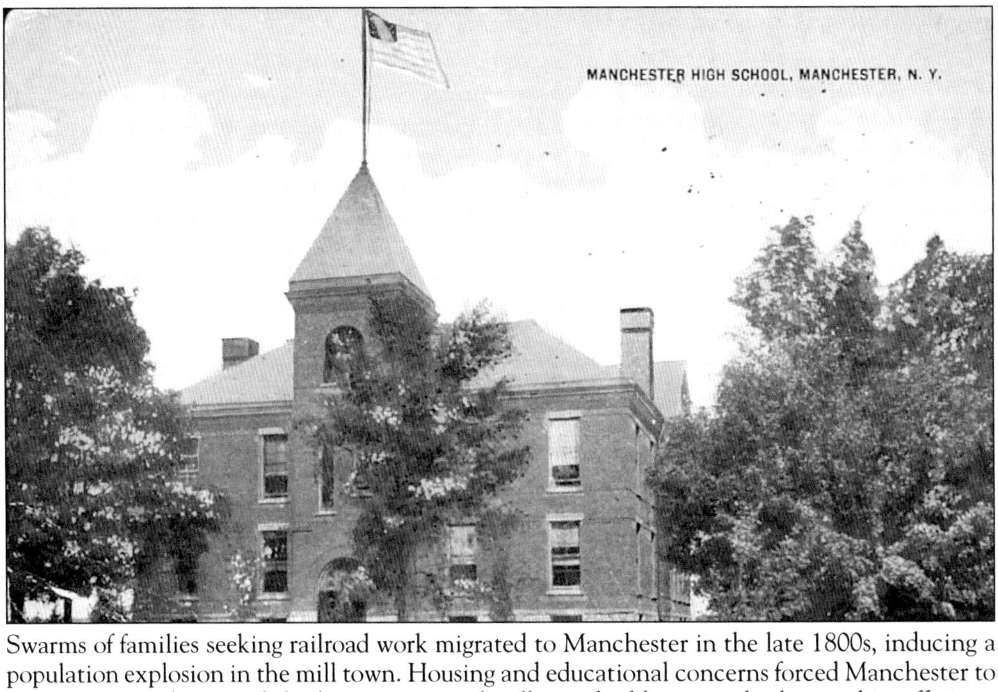

Swarms of families seeking railroad work migrated to Manchester in the late 1800s, inducing a population explosion in the mill town. Housing and educational concerns forced Manchester to construct more homes while the two-room schoolhouse had become obsolete and insufficient. A new Union School, built for $10,000 on North Main Street, opened on February 19, 1896.

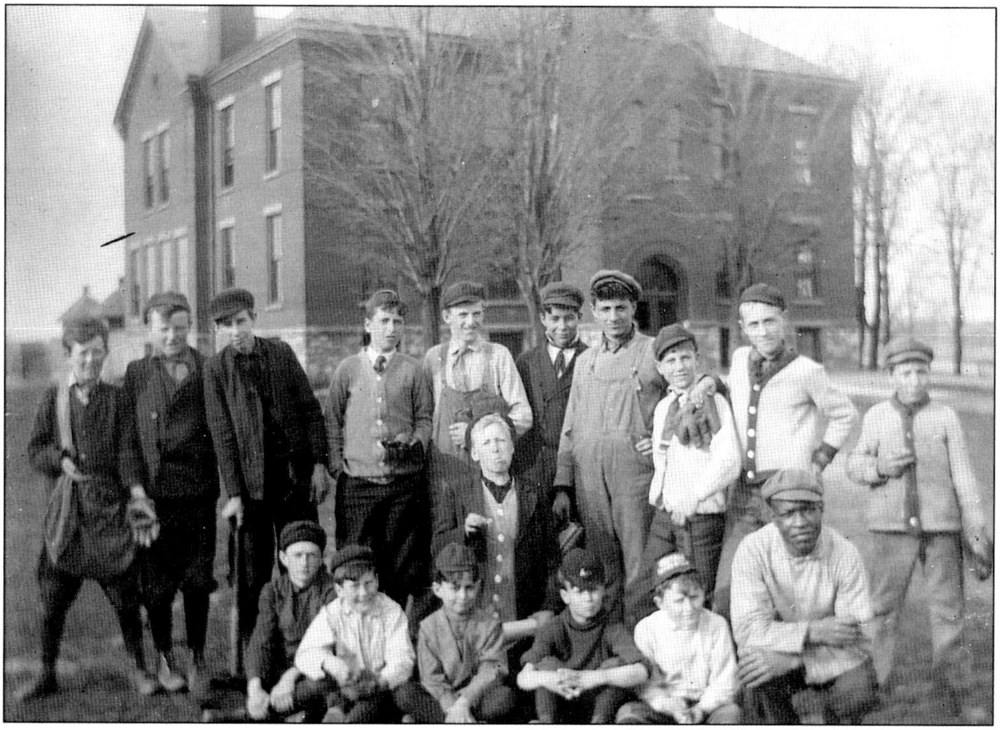

Manchester boys pose in front of the three-story Union School No. 8 as they prepare to play baseball during recess. For many years, baseball dominated Manchester as the main source of recreation in the town. Although Manchester was diverse in culture, baseball offered a common form of entertainment accepted by native and immigrant families.

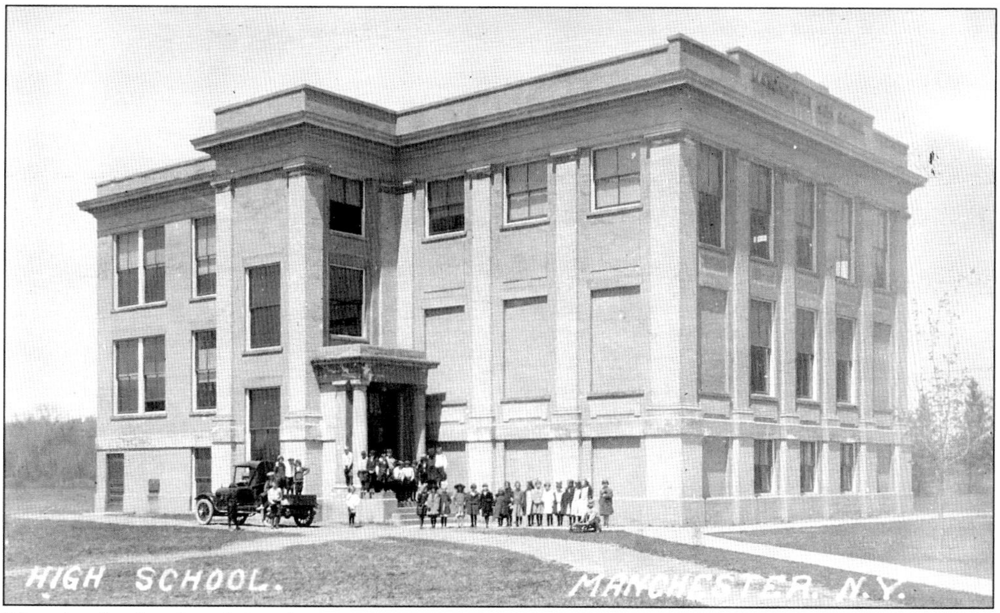

The third school in Manchester was erected on North Main Street in 1915 and included a modern auditorium and a grand balcony. The land of the school's property extended to the Black Brook in Manchester.

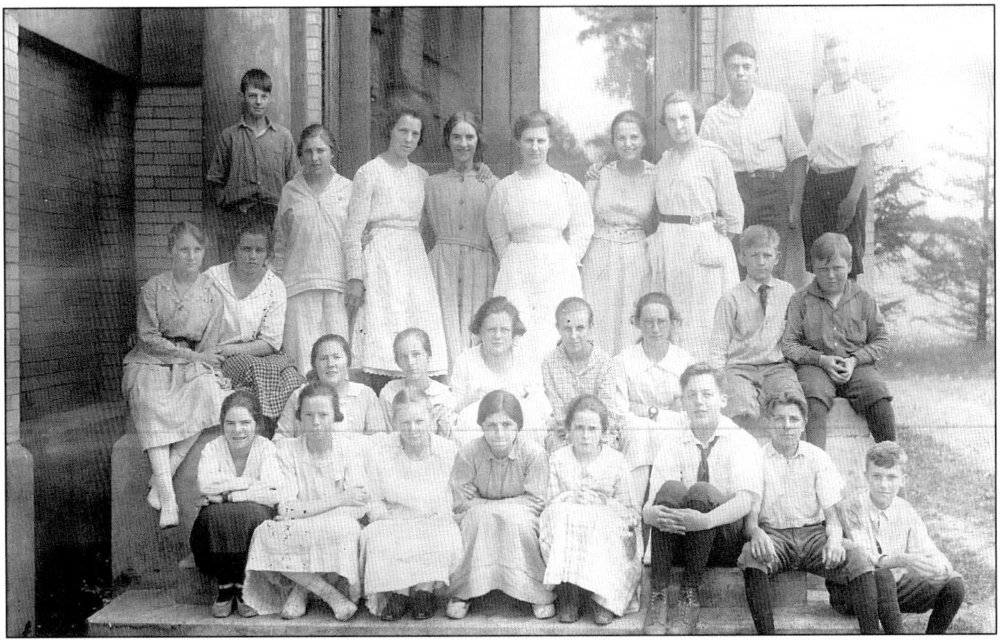

Shown here is the 1918 Manchester school photograph. From left to right are as follows: (bottom row) Mary Manion, Mildred Devitt, Pearl White, Sarah Hesseny, Marion Bard, Fred Hudson, Pete Demott, and Claire Barrows; (middle row) Helene Downey, Elsie Craig, Josephine McLouth, Margaret Gillis, and Sybil Randall; (on posts) Ruth Pratt, Delma Bunnell, Kenneth Herman, and Ernest Pilcher; (top row) Russell Werner, Ida Stroud, Doris Bennett, Pauline Macumber, Miss De May, Mabel Pratt, Margaret Murray, Joseph Mottelo, and Stewart Macumber.

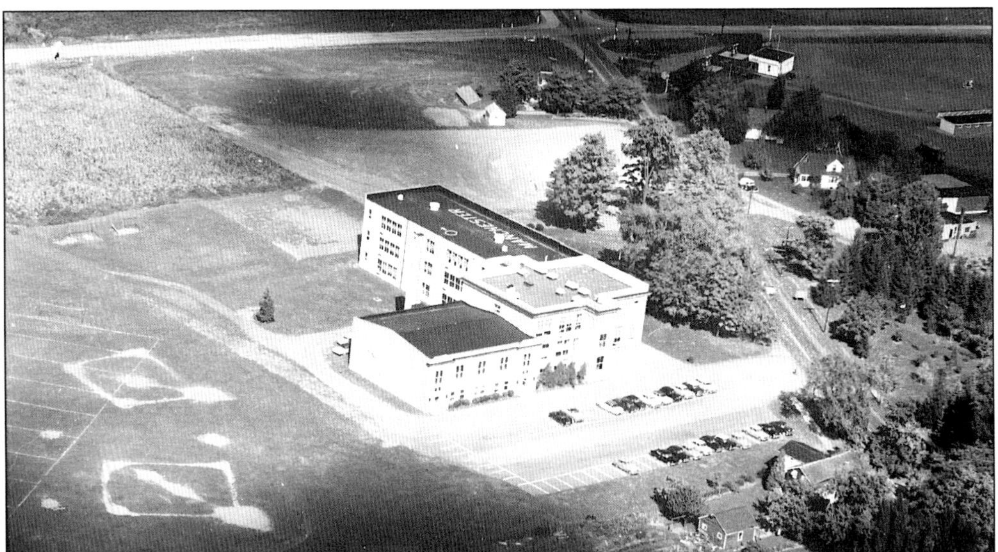

This is a 1956 aerial photograph of Manchester's fourth school, which was built in 1931 at a cost of $180,000. Home economics, industrial arts, and science departments were added to the system. Also, a nurse's office and a large gymnasium were added along with locker and shower facilities.

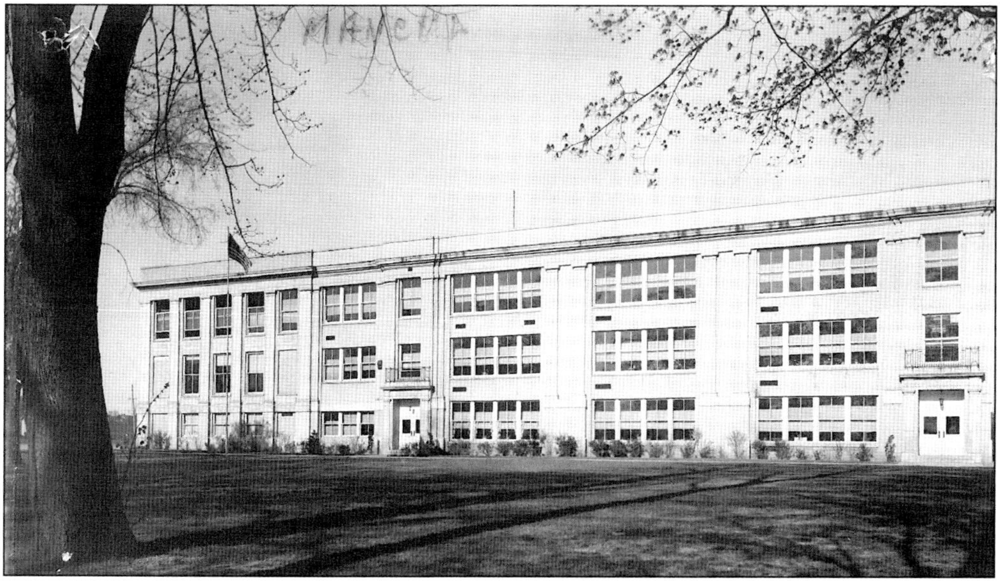

In 1950, ten years after this photograph was taken, Manchester merged with Shortsville to form a centralized school of adjacent districts. After many debates, both sides voted and agreed to name the new school Red Jacket. Red Jacket, an Iroquois chief and orator of the Seneca nation, had appeared in Canandaigua and Ontario County in the fall of 1794, where the Pickering Treaty was signed with the Senecas of the Iroquois Federation. Manchester's team colors had been green and white and Shortsville's had been purple and white. The two sides agreed that red and white would suffice for the team colors.

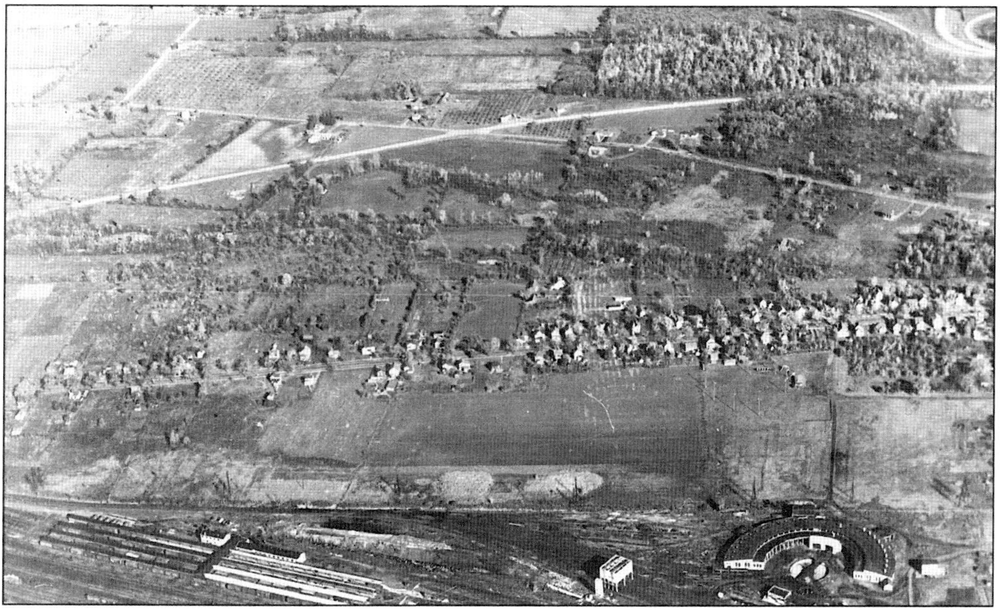

This epic aerial photograph of Manchester in 1963 shows, to the upper right, exit 43 of the New York State Thruway, completed on December 31, 1953. The Lane Construction Company built a section of about 10 miles, and this construction changed the landscape drastically as roads were cut off and farms were cut in half. The addition would eventually cause Manchester's famous Black Brook to dry out.

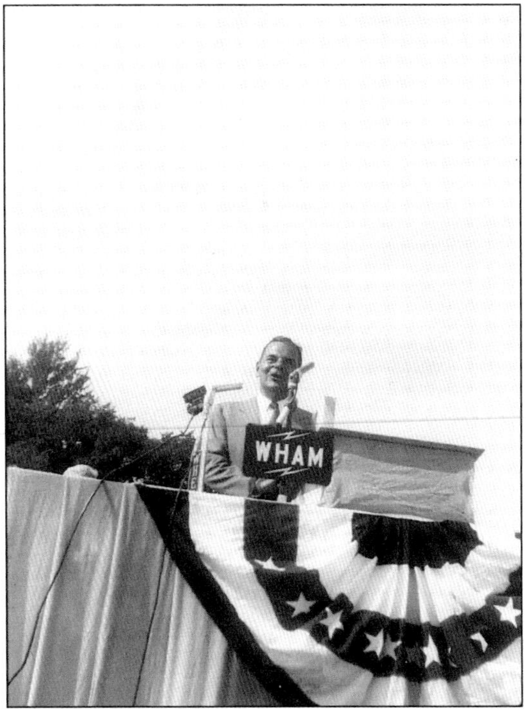

Before a large crowd in 1954, former New York State governor Thomas Dewey dedicated exit 43 to Manchester at Red Jacket High School. The WHAM microphone belonged to Rochester's oldest radio station, which produced 50,000 watts of clear channel power that could be heard as far west as Indianapolis, Indiana.

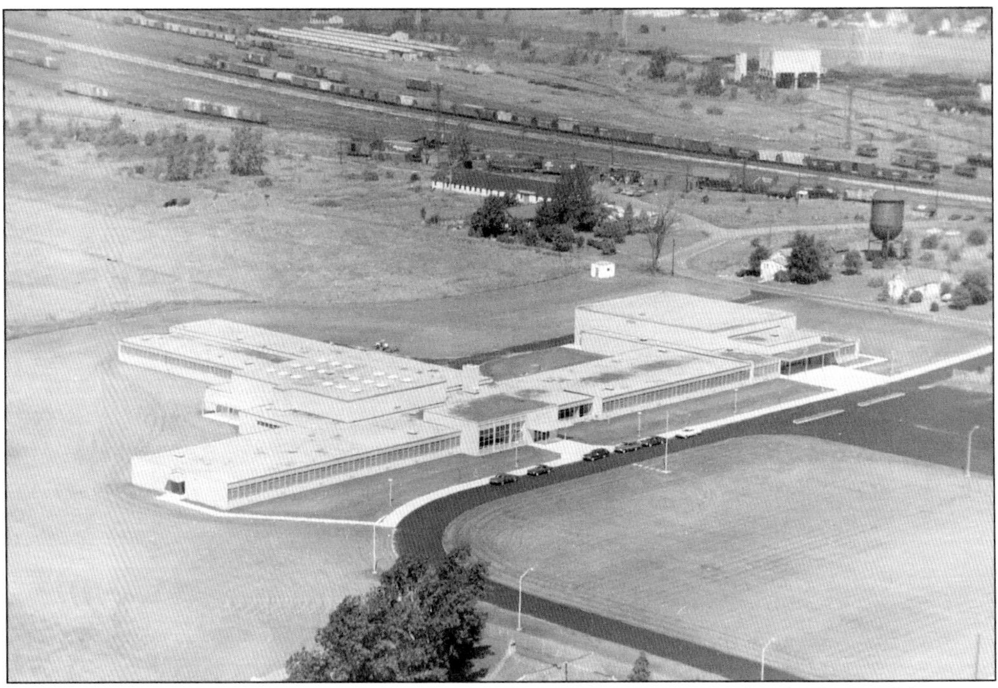

This is a 1967 aerial photograph of what was known as "no man's land" (located between Manchester and Shortsville), the present-day location of Manchester-Shortsville Central, formerly known as Red Jacket. The school became the pride and joy of the late Neil Harkenreider, the former principal of Red Jacket. The Manchester freight yards can be seen at the top right, below the old Ellis farm of Shortsville.

Three

AMERICA'S PASTIME

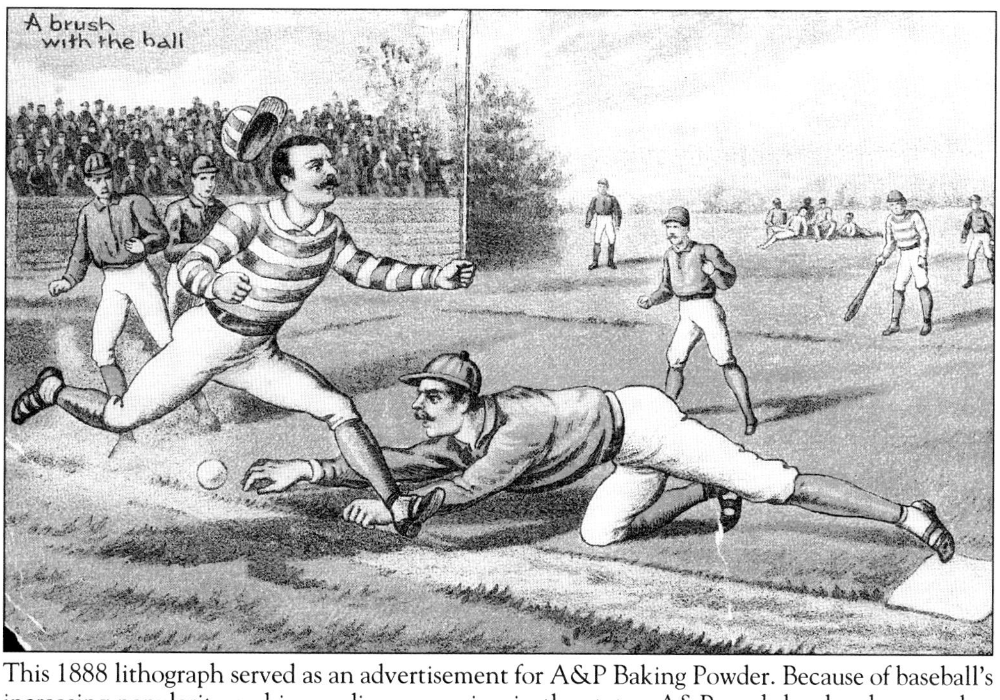

This 1888 lithograph served as an advertisement for A&P Baking Powder. Because of baseball's increasing popularity and impending expansion in the states, A&P used the sketch to market America's future pastime.

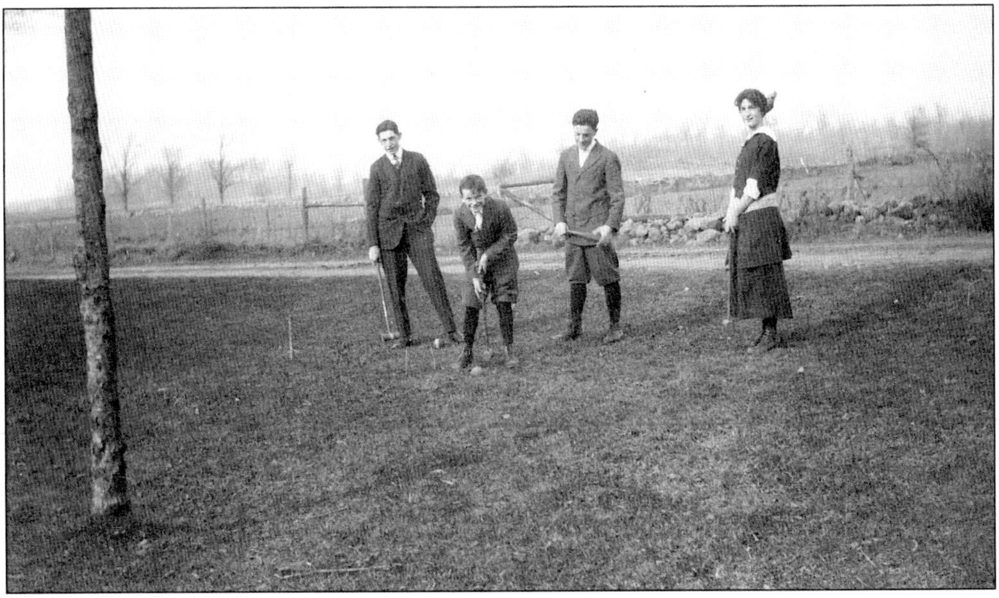

A local family pauses for a picture during "Sunday on the lawn." Because the playing of baseball had been forbidden on Sundays, croquet became the traditional entertainment instead.

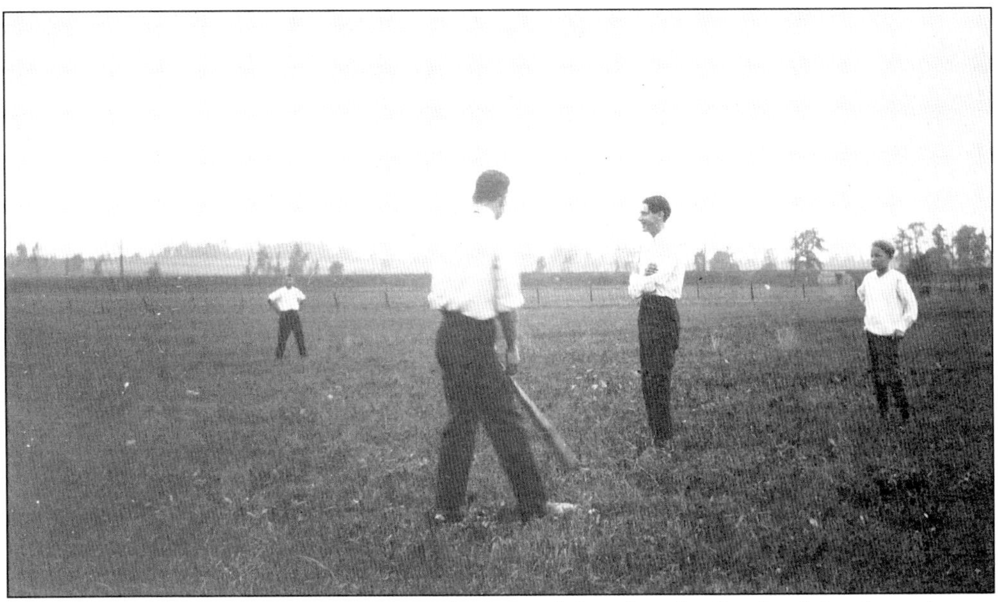

These amateur athletes are swinging in style. Dressed their best for Sunday, Manchester's men and boys abandon high-class croquet for baseball on a sunny afternoon in 1919. The famed Charles Ebbetts, the former owner of the Dodgers, scheduled and played the first big league game on a Sunday in New York in 1918.

Baseball in its early form required no gloves and suited players in pointed leather boots as shown in this 1880 lithograph. Underwood & Wagner (a boot, shoes, and leather store) of Penn Yan, NY, produced this lithograph as an advertisement on the front side and as a scorecard on the back side.

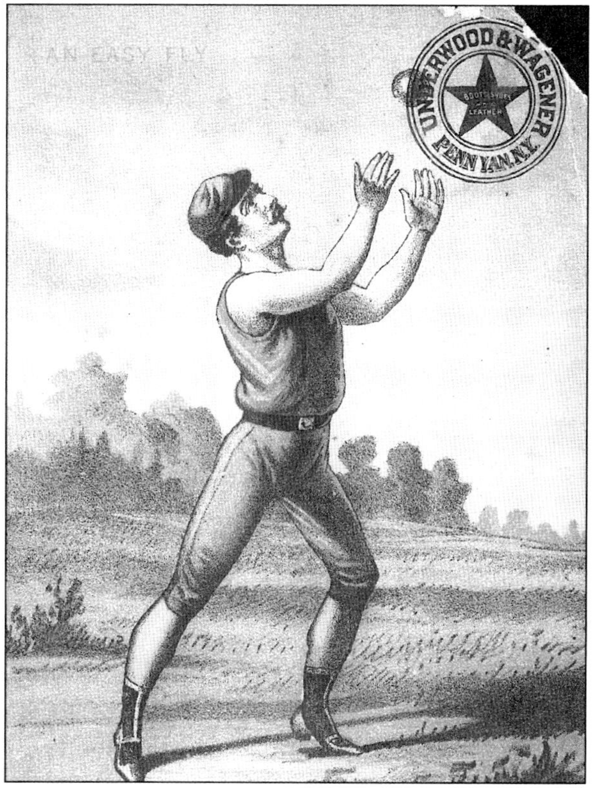

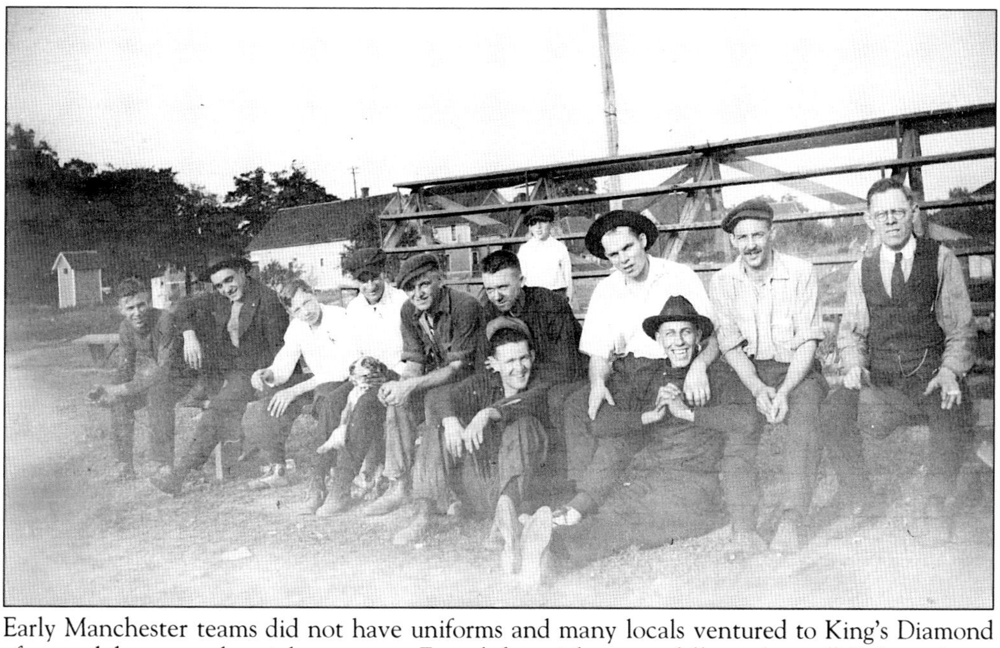

Early Manchester teams did not have uniforms and many locals ventured to King's Diamond after work hours to play pick-up games. From left to right are as follows: (seated) R. Lounsberry and E. Vienna; (on bench) E. Gailbreth, Jas. Bennett, S. Macumber, unidentified, G. Growney, J. Boardman, R. Durant, T. Edmunds, and R. O'Hearn.

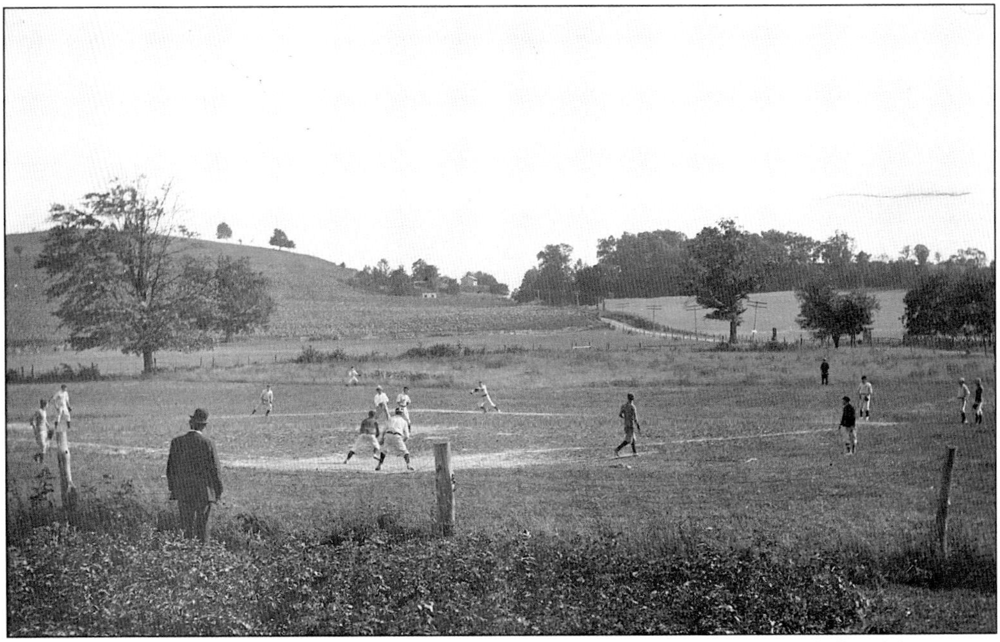

Considered to be one of the most beautiful regions in the country, the rolling hills of the Finger Lakes hosted countless ball games for barnstorming and professional teams during the industrial league era. Small towns throughout the Finger Lakes were exposed to several significant changes affecting the sport of baseball, such as the modified artistry of pitching. The curveball, once known as "slants," as well as other off-speed pitches, came into play at the turn of the century. Most small town pitchers relied on the fastball because the curveball was considered to be a method of deception and was determined to be unethical in its early form.

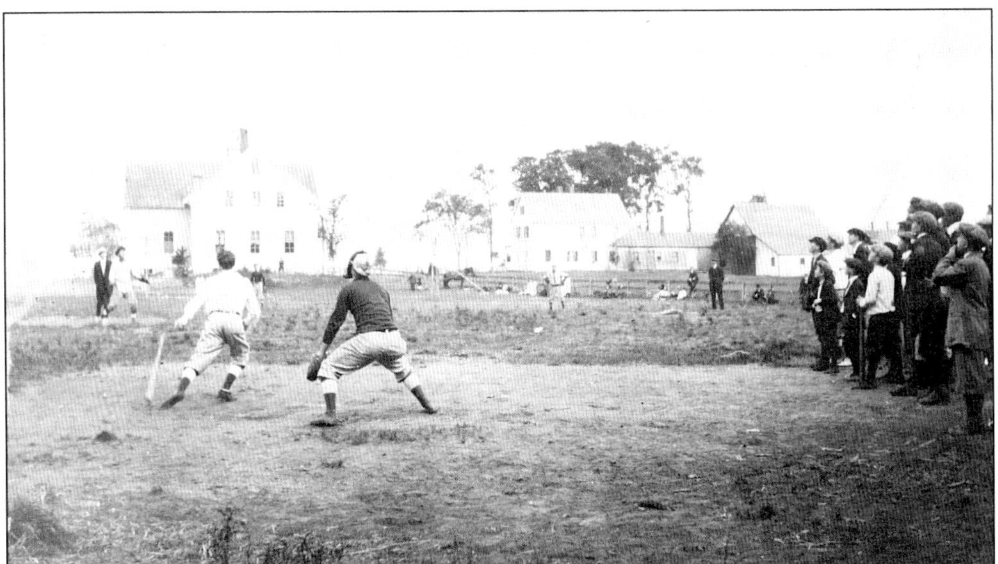

Traveling teams journeyed from town to town in what was known as barnstorming. Industrial baseball teams would often bunk in neutral haylofts until the next morning.

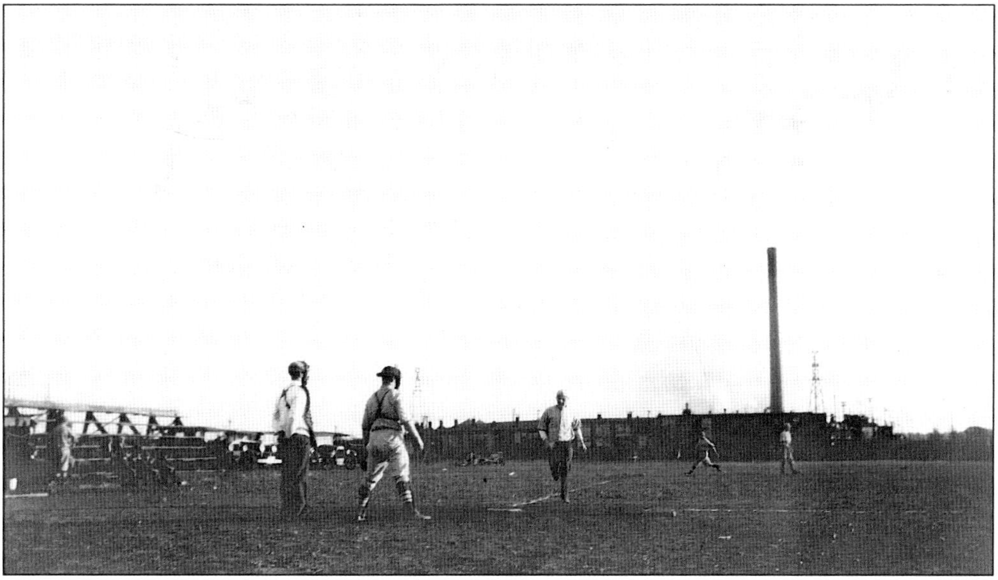

Known as "Roundhousers," the men pictured here in 1928 often played games in the early morning hours, before their initial work shift began. The roundhouse stands at the deepest part of left field.

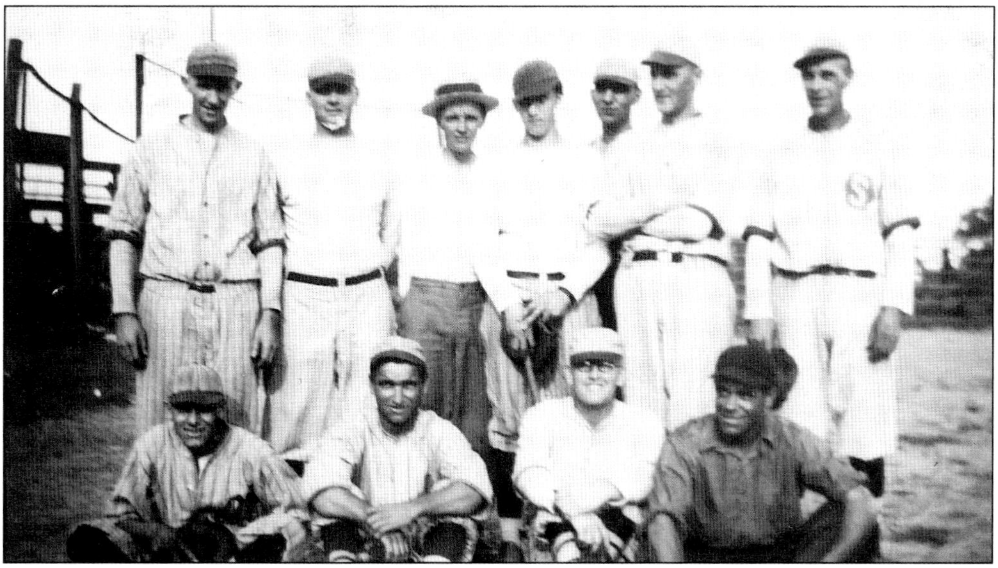

An August 1928 Manchester Railroaders team photograph shows players, from left to right, as follows: (front row) Delgatto, Dean, Sprague, and Mottelo; (back row) Boardman, Childs, Turner (umpire), Werner, Delgatto, Murray, and Craig.

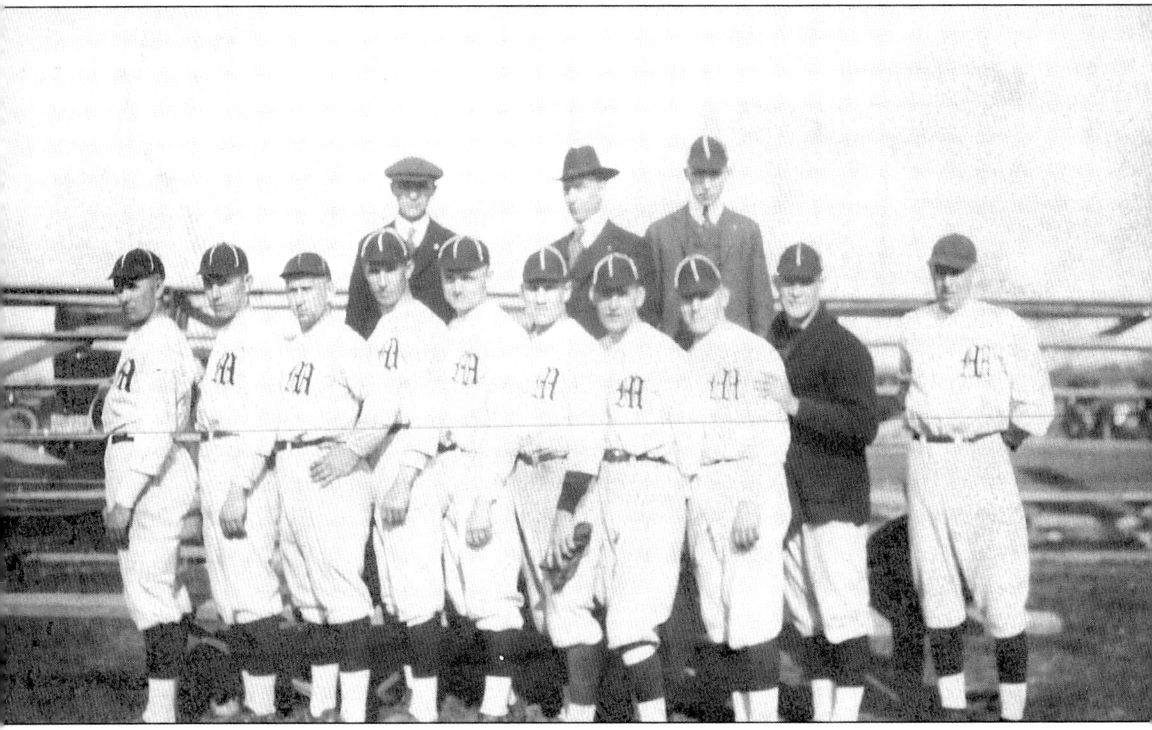

In 1914, the arrival of Charles McCormick (top center) signified the beginning of semi-professional baseball in Manchester. McCormick, a freight boss from Queens, New York, chose ten elite players to represent the boys from "Transfer Town."

Four

CHAMPEEN STRETCHERS AND GANDY DANCERS

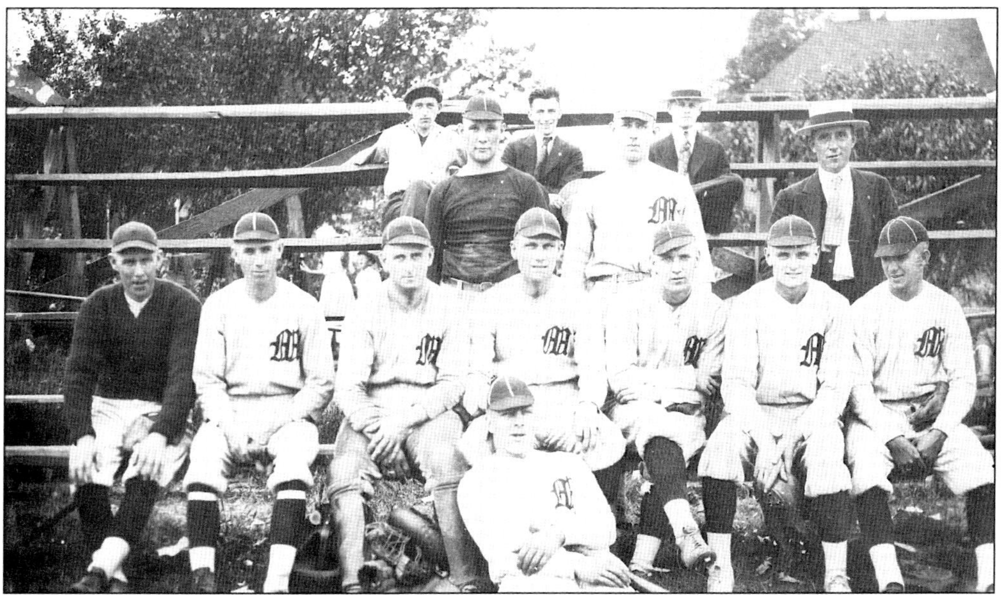

One of New York's most dominant industrial league teams, the Manchester Railroaders semi-professional baseball team boasted 13 championship seasons spanning 1914 to 1929. Here is a photograph of the 1919 Railroaders. From left to right are as follows: (seated) Joe McKenna (from Canandaigua); (second row) E. Potter, J. Kerins, F. Clary, Neal O'Harrigan, Ed Quigley, "Beans" Cooley, and Tommy Kerins; (third row) Bill Segbers, T. Cleary, and manager Charles McCormick; (fourth row) bat boys A. Doody, B. Dailey, and J. Rodney.

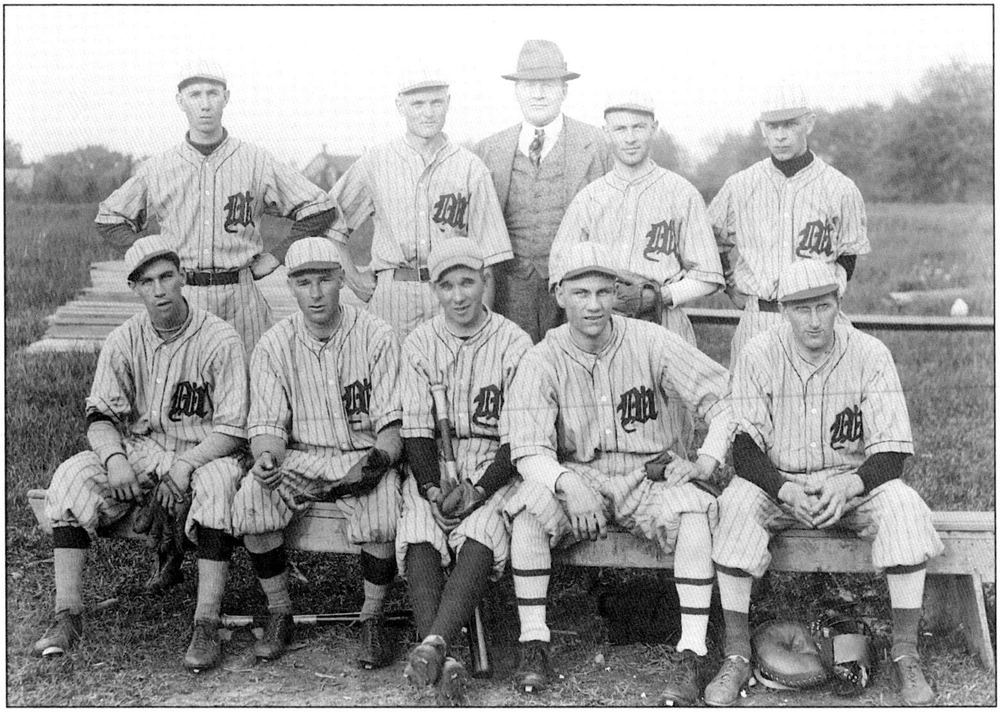

The Manchester Railroaders of 1916 were granted an industrial league franchise in what was known as the Tri-State (LVRR) Steel League from 1914 until 1919. This league consisted of teams from the Bronx, Brooklyn, and Elmira, New York; as well as Allentown, Coxton, and Pittston, Pennsylvania. The wool uniforms in this picture were provided by the LVRR.

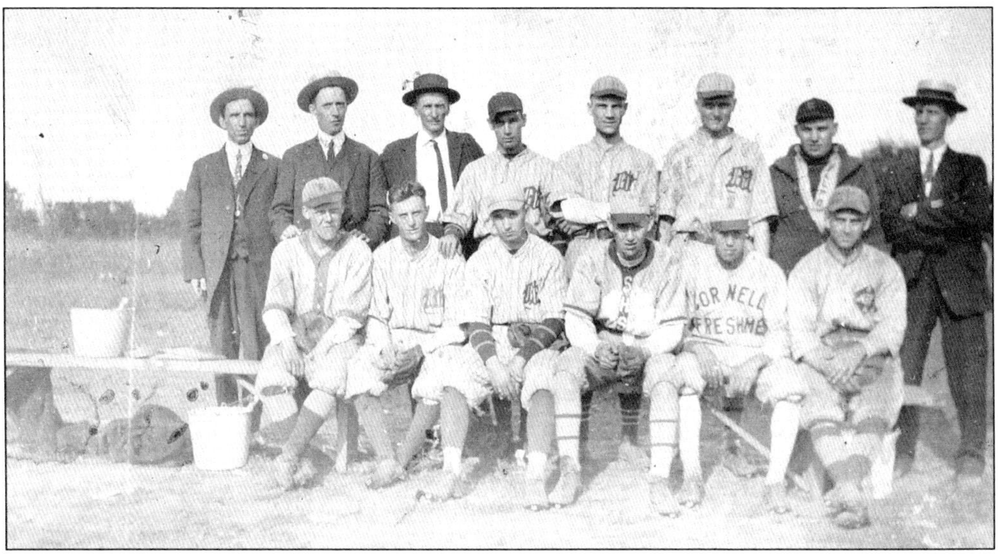

The Western New York Semi-Pro Circuit consisted of teams from Canandaigua, Fashion Park (Rochester garment district), Honeoye Falls, Webster, Newark, Fairport, and the Kodak Park Athletics. The 1918 team photograph shows the players, from left to right, as follows: (bottom) St. John, L. McNally, Curran, Potter, Brown, and Francis Clary; (top) Jim McNally, Charlie McCormick, George Stoddard, Sittler, Neal O'Harrigan, Beans Cooley, Stoddard, and Betz.

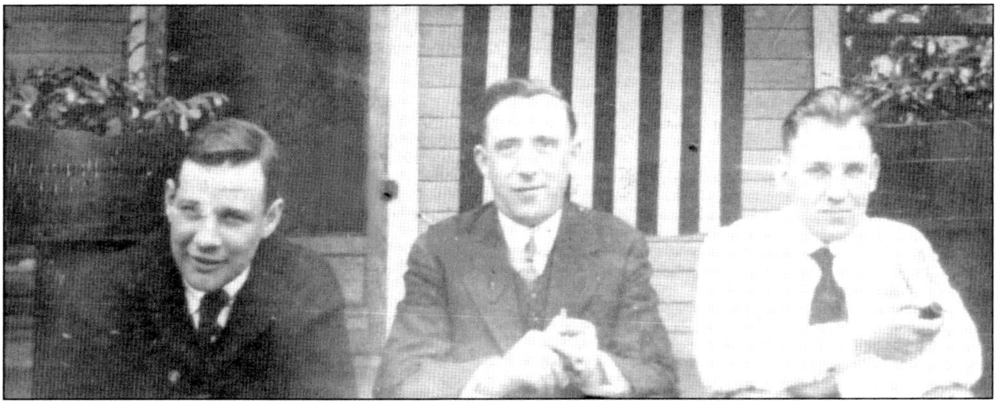

Bill Segbers, Charles McCormick, and his associate sit on the porch of Segbers's home on State Street on Independence Day, 1917. McCormick (an Irishman) and Segbers (a German) developed a mutual companionship through the years, beginning in Queens, New York, and continuing on the railroad in Manchester. During this time period, it was a national tradition to play baseball on Independence Day throughout the United States.

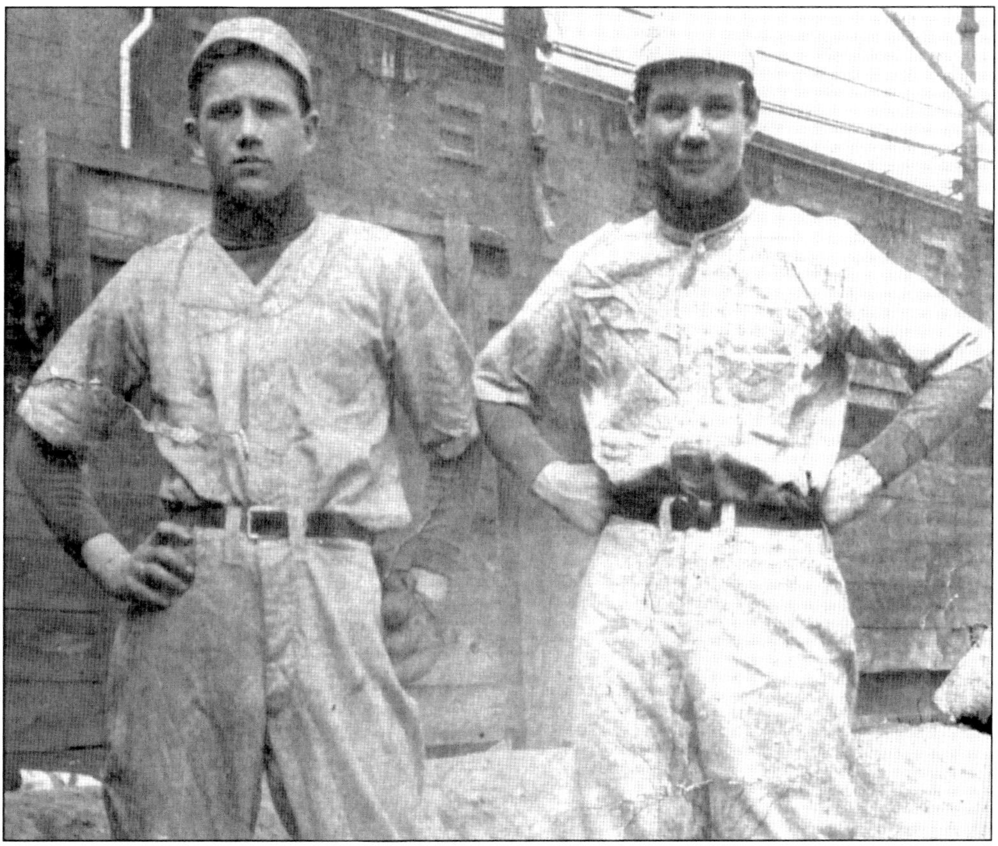

Ed "the Quigs" Quigley and "Big" Bill Segbers pose for this 1914 photograph in the Bushwick district of New York City. Both men had played for the Lourdes Athletic Club of Queens and for the Brooklyn Blue Sox of New York City before coming to play for Manchester. The presence of Quigley and Segbers marked a new era of international adeptness in the small railroad town.

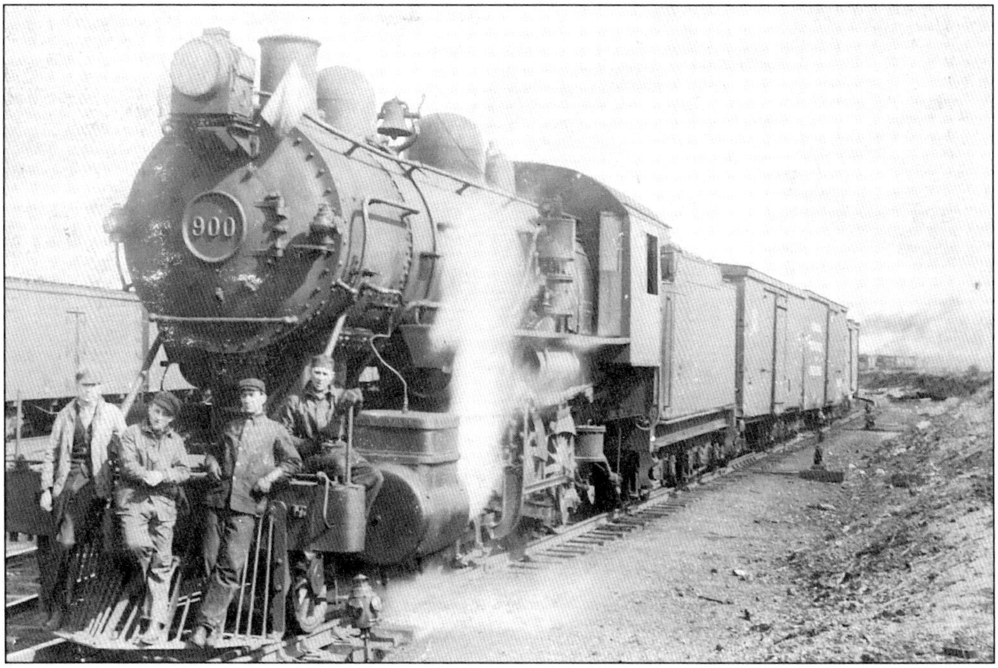

Four men rest on the front of a 1919 steamer locomotive 900. Boxcars carried the baseball team to Tri-State Steel League opponents in Allentown, Pittstown, Poston, and Elmira.

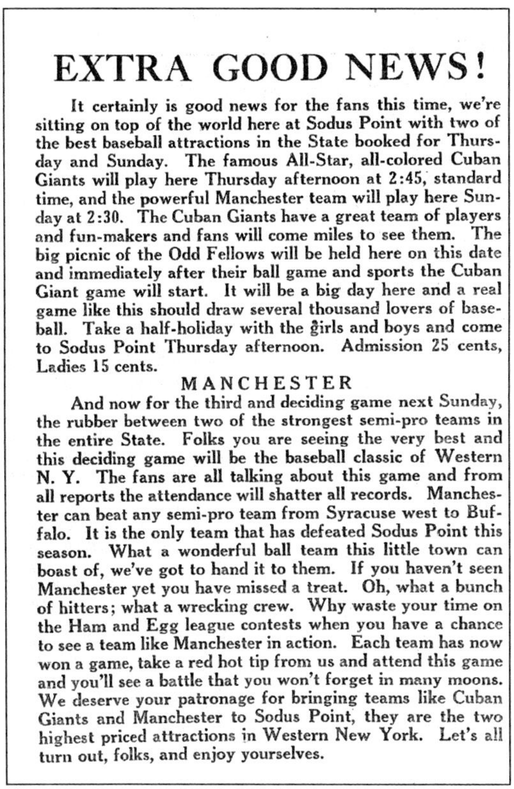

EXTRA GOOD NEWS!

It certainly is good news for the fans this time, we're sitting on top of the world here at Sodus Point with two of the best baseball attractions in the State booked for Thursday and Sunday. The famous All-Star, all-colored Cuban Giants will play here Thursday afternoon at 2:45, standard time, and the powerful Manchester team will play here Sunday at 2:30. The Cuban Giants have a great team of players and fun-makers and fans will come miles to see them. The big picnic of the Odd Fellows will be held here on this date and immediately after their ball game and sports the Cuban Giant game will start. It will be a big day here and a real game like this should draw several thousand lovers of baseball. Take a half-holiday with the girls and boys and come to Sodus Point Thursday afternoon. Admission 25 cents, Ladies 15 cents.

MANCHESTER

And now for the third and deciding game next Sunday, the rubber between two of the strongest semi-pro teams in the entire State. Folks you are seeing the very best and this deciding game will be the baseball classic of Western N. Y. The fans are all talking about this game and from all reports the attendance will shatter all records. Manchester can beat any semi-pro team from Syracuse west to Buffalo. It is the only team that has defeated Sodus Point this season. What a wonderful ball team this little town can boast of, we've got to hand it to them. If you haven't seen Manchester yet you have missed a treat. Oh, what a bunch of hitters; what a wrecking crew. Why waste your time on the Ham and Egg league contests when you have a chance to see a team like Manchester in action. Each team has now won a game, take a red hot tip from us and attend this game and you'll see a battle that you won't forget in many moons. We deserve your patronage for bringing teams like Cuban Giants and Manchester to Sodus Point, they are the two highest priced attractions in Western New York. Let's all turn out, folks, and enjoy yourselves.

"What a wonderful ball team this little town can boast of," a remark made in a Sodus Point newspaper referring to the Manchester Railroaders. The author validates that, in the 1920 game between the Railroaders and Cuban Giants, these teams were "the two highest priced attractions in Western New York." Manchester finished the season with 27 wins and 8 losses.

This team represented Manchester at the games played in Brooklyn. Manager Charles McCormick took Manchester, considered one of New York's finest semi-professional baseball teams, to New York City to play baseball's most celebrated semi-pro team—the Brooklyn Blue Sox. In the article to the right, McCormick displays his confidence that Manchester has the advantage as two former Blue Sox, Ed Quigley and Bill Segbers, suit up to play against their old team.

MANCHESTER'S TEAM FOR BROOKLYN GAME

CHARLEY MC-CORMACK COLLECTS BUNCH OF HEFTY PLAYERS FOR OPENING BATTLE ON APRIL 22

Manager Charley McCormack of the Manchester club has snared a likely bunch of diamond dwellers for his opening game against the Bushwicks at Dexter park, Brooklyn, on Sunday, April 22. Mac is concentrating on a win in that battle as he harbors the suspicion that the big city lads look upon his club as being composed of so many hicks.

McCormack broke through today with his line-up for the Brooklyn clash. Behind the fanning mill he will have Tracey, catcher for the Seneca Falls club in the Industrial league last year. Loghry, of Hobart college,e and Big Bill Segbers, Manchester's mound idol, will be there with the twirling stuff.

Eddie Quigley, the champeen stretcher of the Lehigh Valley, will be back at first with Neal O'Harrigan, famous Irisher, at second; Mort Fox, of year's Geneva team, at short, and Johnnie Kerins around the torrid zone.

Joe McKenna, that wonderfully developed president of the Sons of Rest, will be the main guy in the outfield with Tommy Kerins and Wirth as his side partners. Loghry or Segbers will also be available for garden work with Kid Cooley in reserve.

McCormack figures that his array of speed from the lively provinces will cause Brooklyn fans to realize that they surely reside in Hick Manhattan.

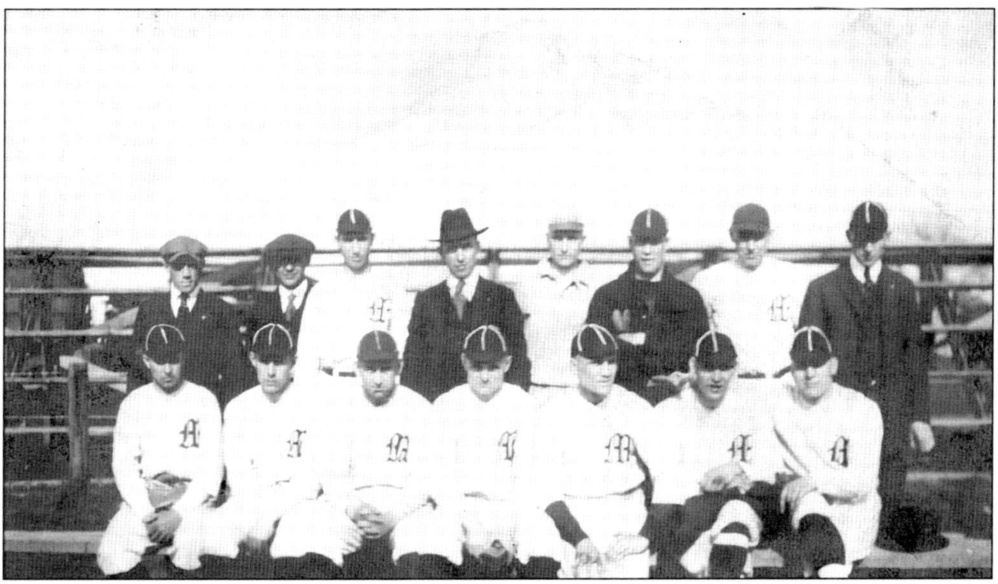

Nineteen seventeen was a year of change and a year of recognition for the Railroaders. New bleachers were built to accommodate 2,000 fans at King's Diamond and three of the four battles between the Railroaders and the Sayre Colemans went into extra innings, as each game was decided by one run. McCormick's Railroaders were Ontario County champs for the first time in their brief history.

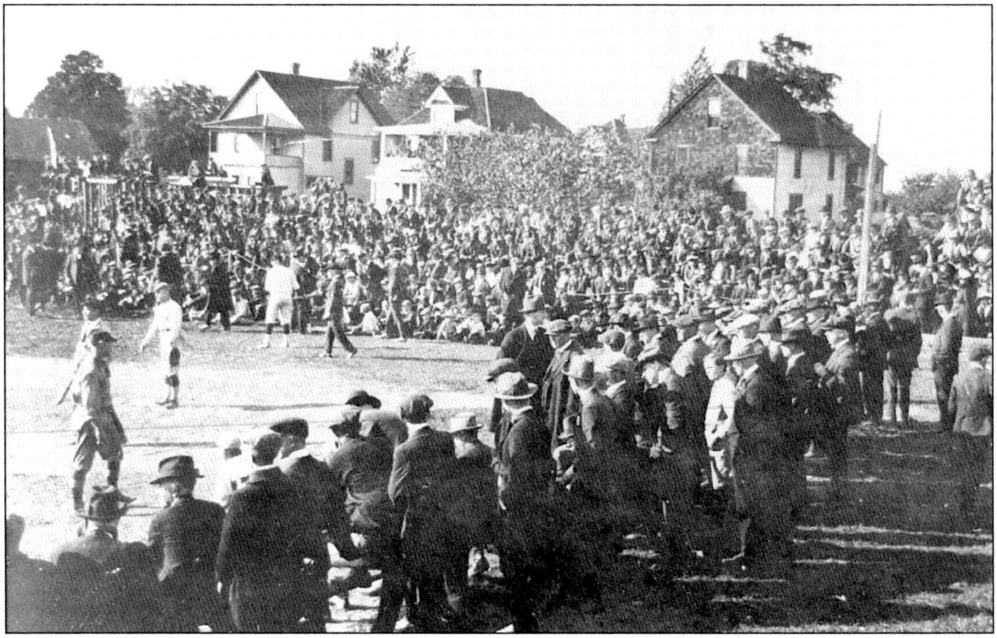

On September 17, 1919, Manchester lost at home to the Toronto Leafs of the international league 2-1 in 12 innings before a record crowd of 5,000 fans. Spectators used stepladders, rooftops, and balconies of surrounding homes (on State Street) to get a better view of the game. Manchester, Ontario County champions for the third consecutive season, posted a 17-7 record during the 1919 season.

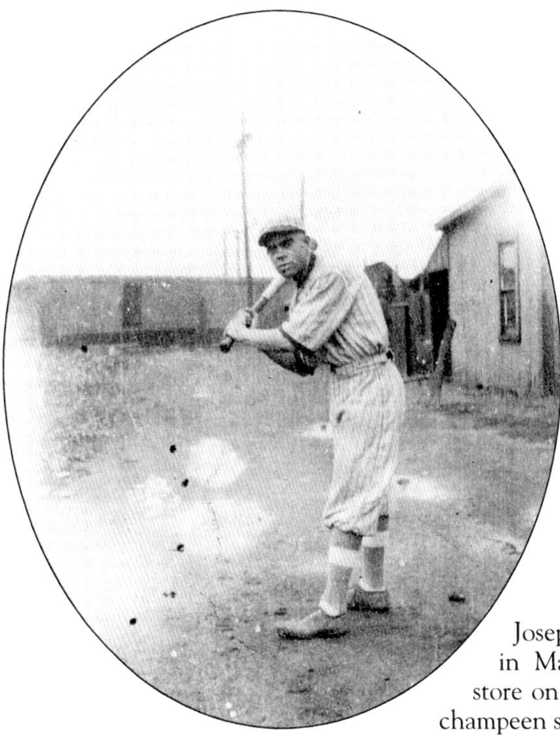

Joseph Mottelo poses near the rail yards in Manchester outside his mother's railroad store on Merrick Circle in 1919. Mottelo played champeen stretcher for the Railroaders.

During the 1922 season, Bill Segbers was pitching up to four times a week with different teams around the area under an assumed name. Segbers earned an extra $15 a game, an additional $60 more than the weekly railroad salary he received. McCormick was furious and gave Segbers an unconditional release. Segbers got even by pitching for the Auburn Lehighs in the next game, thrashing McCormick and holding his former teammates to one hit. McCormick and Segbers came to an agreement after the game and Segbers became a Railroader for good.

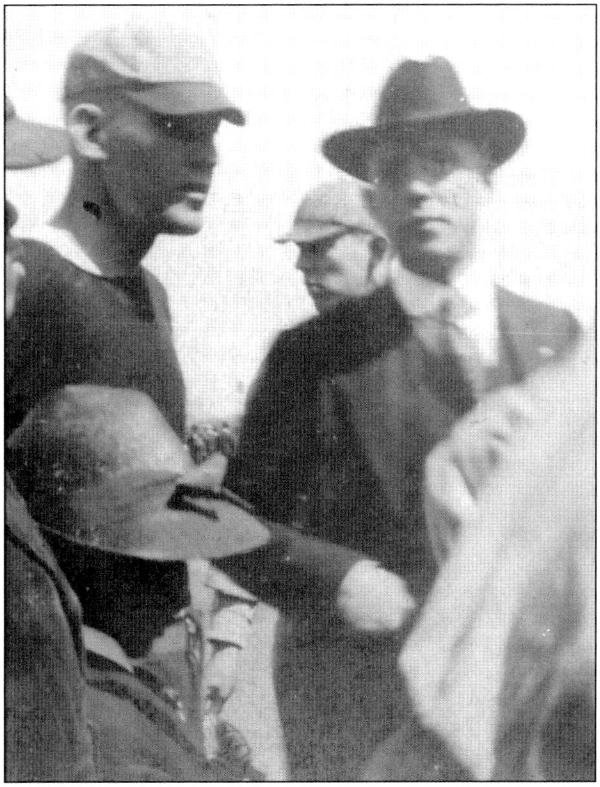

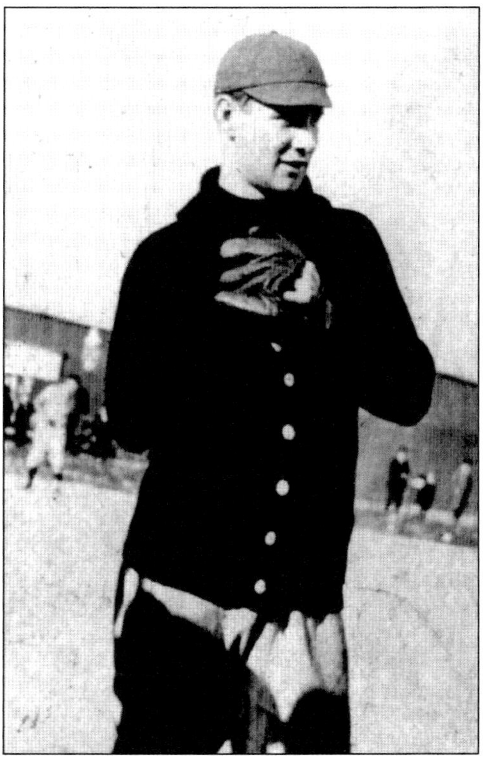

As one of Ontario County's greatest semi-professional pitchers, Segbers faced Boston Braves pitcher Al Mattern, Detroit Tigers ace John Bogart, and Chicago White Sox star Roy Wilkinson. Segbers, once a prep school star with the Lourdes Athletic Club of Queens, hit a home run at Ebbets Field to secure the prestigious A.G. Spalding Cup in 1910.

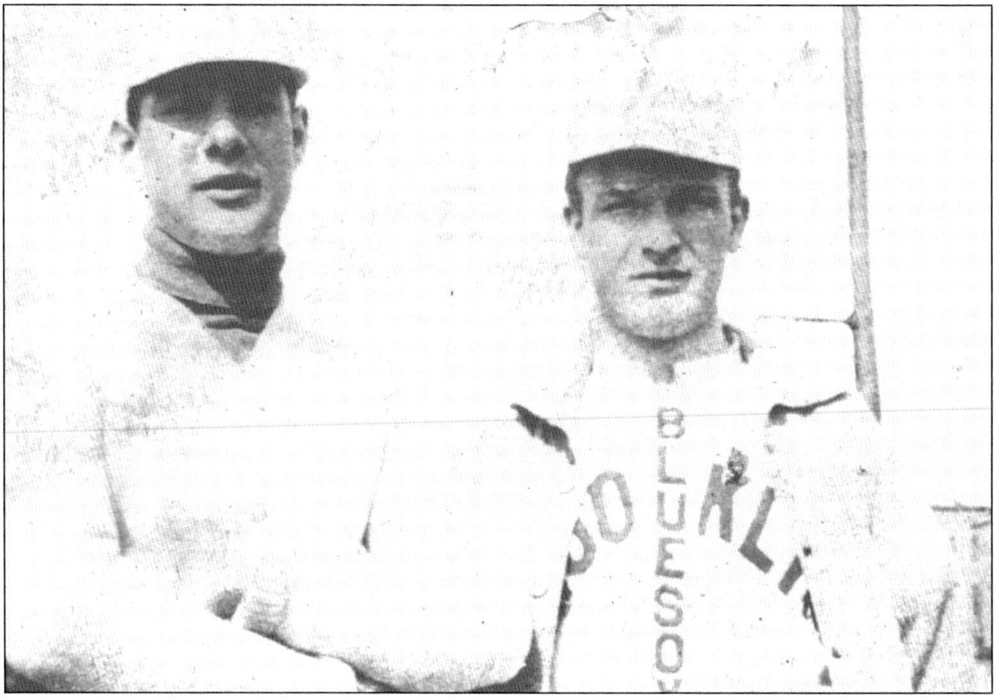

Segbers and Ed Quigley pose in uniform in 1914. Segbers played for one of baseball's greatest independent promoters, Max Rosner of New York, who boasted of such alumni as Lou Gehrig, Frank Frisch, Jimmy Ring, Hank Greenberg, Joe Judge, Tony Cuccinello, and Waite Hoyt.

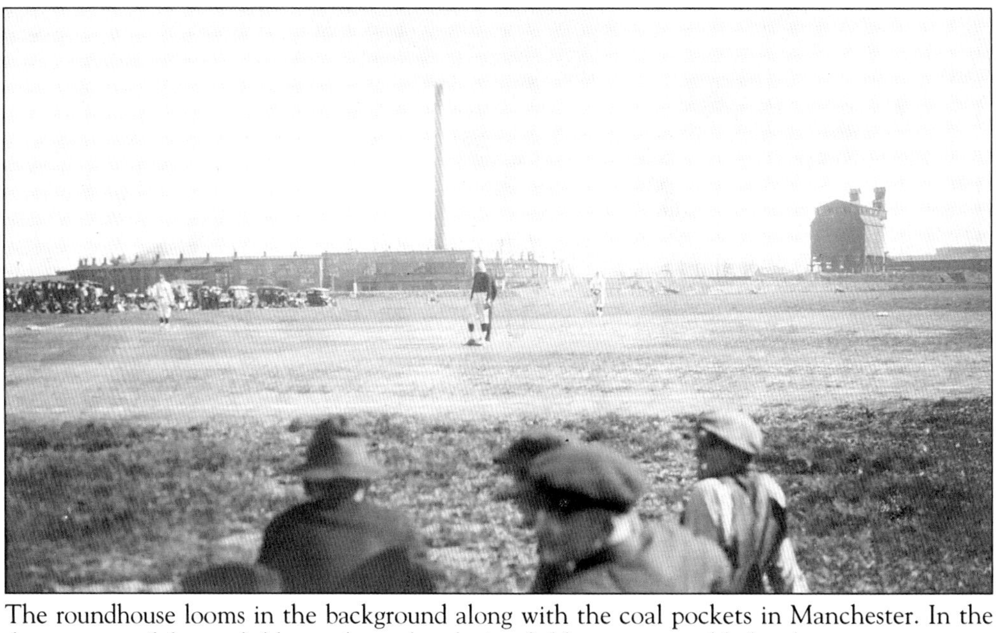

The roundhouse looms in the background along with the coal pockets in Manchester. In the deepest part of the outfield cows keep the playing fields at a reasonable level.

Between games one and two of the 1918 Labor Day double header against Canandaigua, Segbers keeps warm alongside his teammates. Six hundred union members participated and marched in a parade that began in Shortsville and ended at King's Diamond. The Labor Day parade still exists today and still ends at the baseball field now used for the local Little League games. At 10:30 a.m. the first game began. Segbers pitched a brilliant 10-inning performance, striking out 14 batters as Manchester defeated Canandaigua 4-3. The second game began at 1:30 p.m., and yet again, Segbers got the call. "Iron" Bill pitched nine innings, striking out 10 hitters. Manchester defeated Canandaigua for the Ontario County championship by a score of 5-2. In all, Segbers pitched 19 innings, striking out 24 batters without allowing a walk in either game.

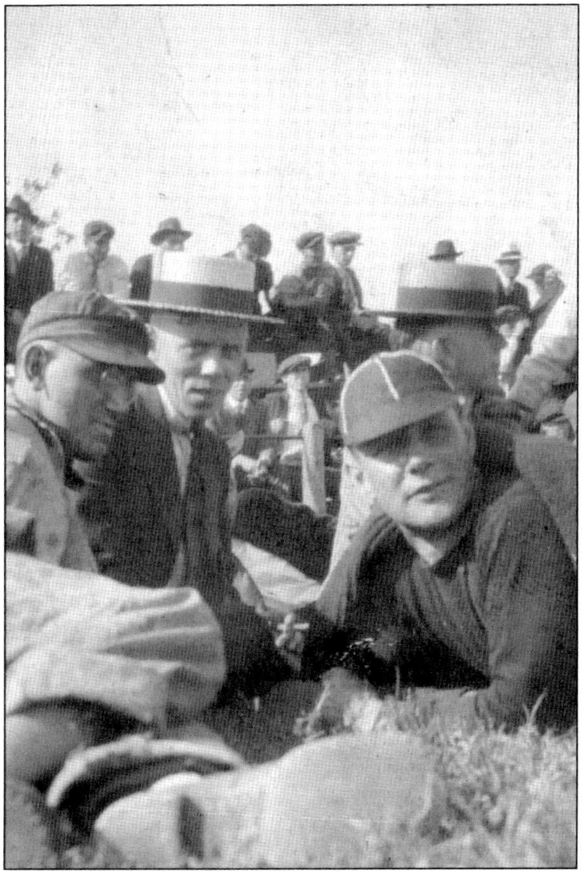

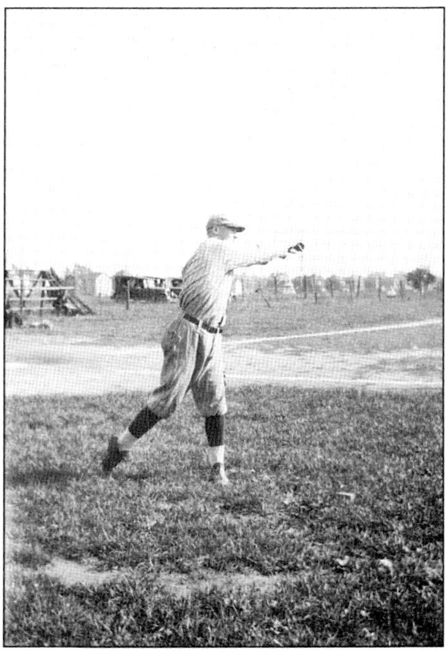

Mike Griffin played third base for the Railroaders and eventually took over the pitching duties from Bill Segbers. In 1929, three years after this photograph was taken, Griffin batted a .404 average for Manchester.

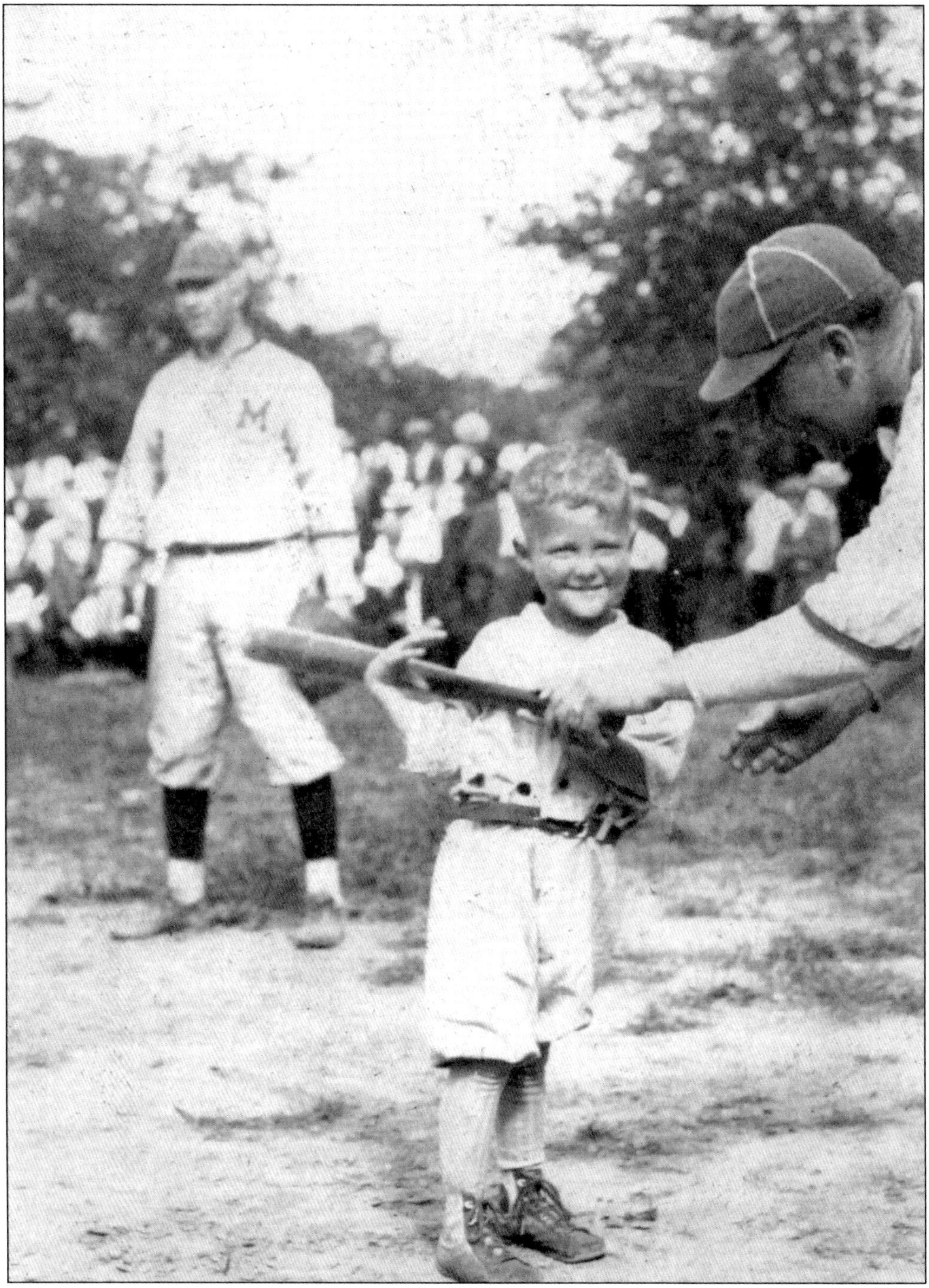

This photograph is a timeless monument to paternal guidance taken during the intermission of a 1920s game in Manchester. To keep fans occupied during the player's rest, an occasional field day was held for kids. Here "Big" Bill Segbers shows his son Jimmy how to swing a bat.

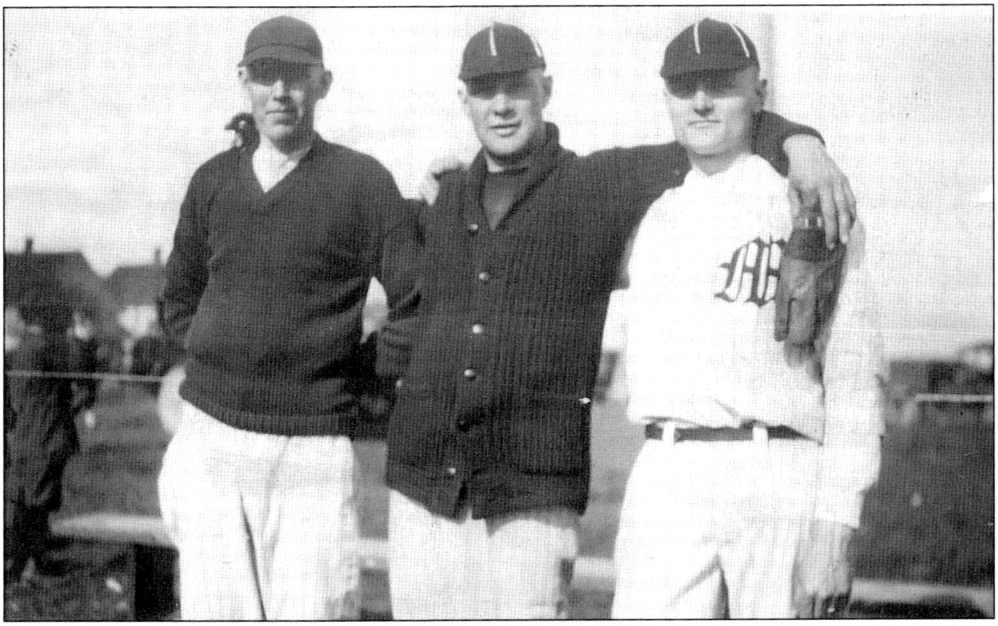

Three men, Potter, Segbers, and Cooley, made up Manchester's pitching staff in 1920. Pitchers were known as "twirlers," "tossers," and "diamond artists," while the act of pitching itself was known as the "offering." The ball was labeled the "spheroid," the "pellet," and the "leather." The feather duster, worn by Segbers in this picture, is a turtle neck sweater commonly used to keep the arms of pitchers warm.

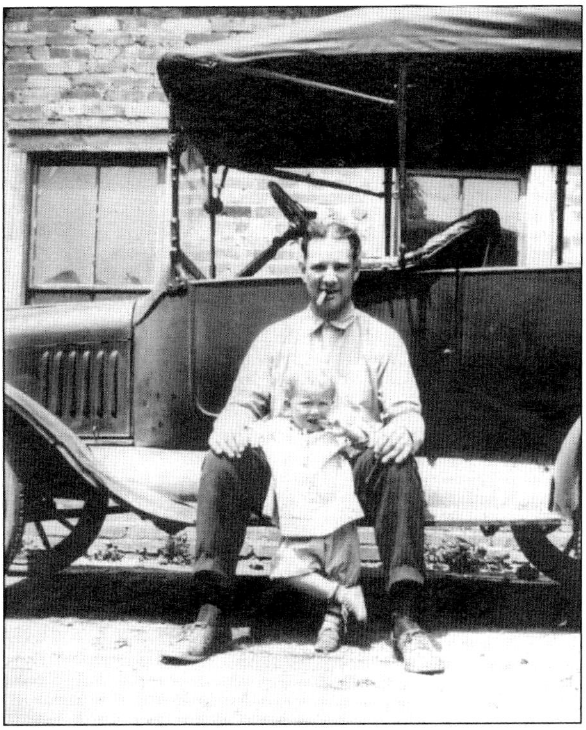

Bill Segbers and his son Jimmy sit on a running board of a Model T on June 15, 1923. Segbers was a dedicated father and husband.

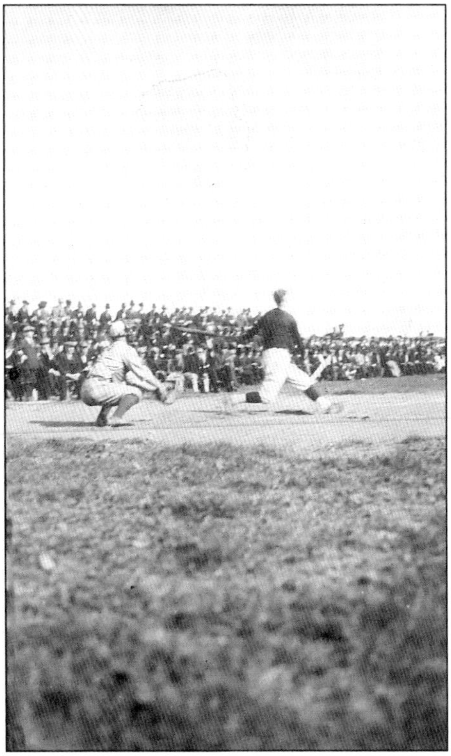

During a game against Geneva, Segbers hit a home run that cleared the street across from Gulvin Park, smashing into a parked Model T. During a tryout with the Rochester International League team in 1920, Segbers hits several balls over the fence and did not strike out. After hitting a home run against Rochester's ace pitcher, Segbers jogged to second base and sat down.

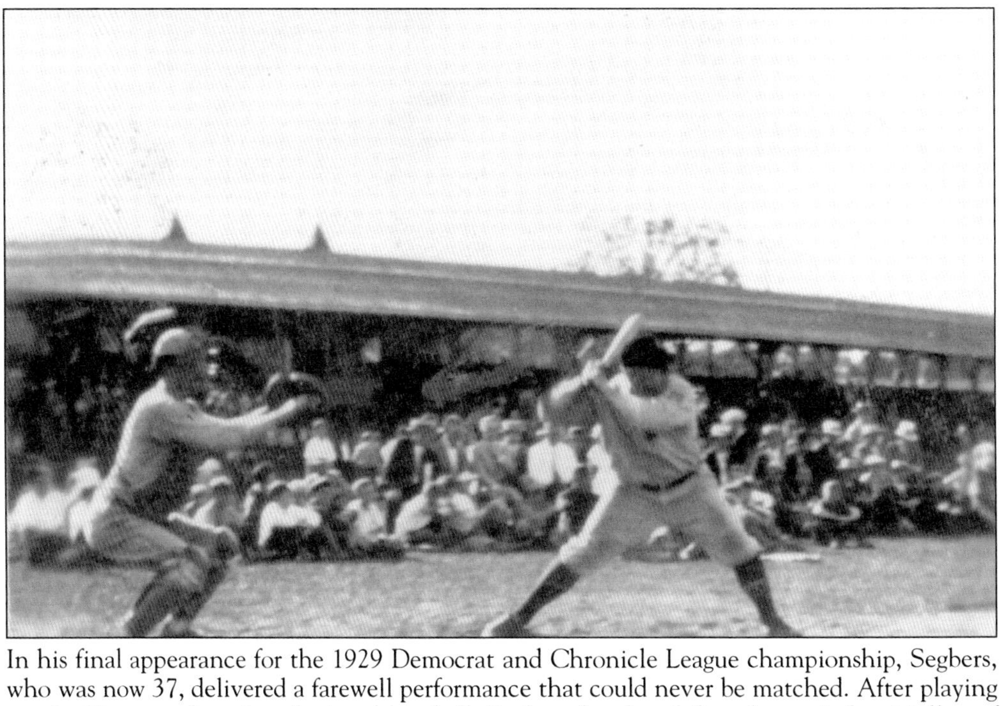

In his final appearance for the 1929 Democrat and Chronicle League championship, Segbers, who was now 37, delivered a farewell performance that could never be matched. After playing nearly 20 years of semi-professional baseball, Segbers faced undefeated ace pitcher Molloy of the Clyde Athletics and smacked a double in the 12th inning to knock in the winning run for Manchester. Clyde had not been defeated in two years.

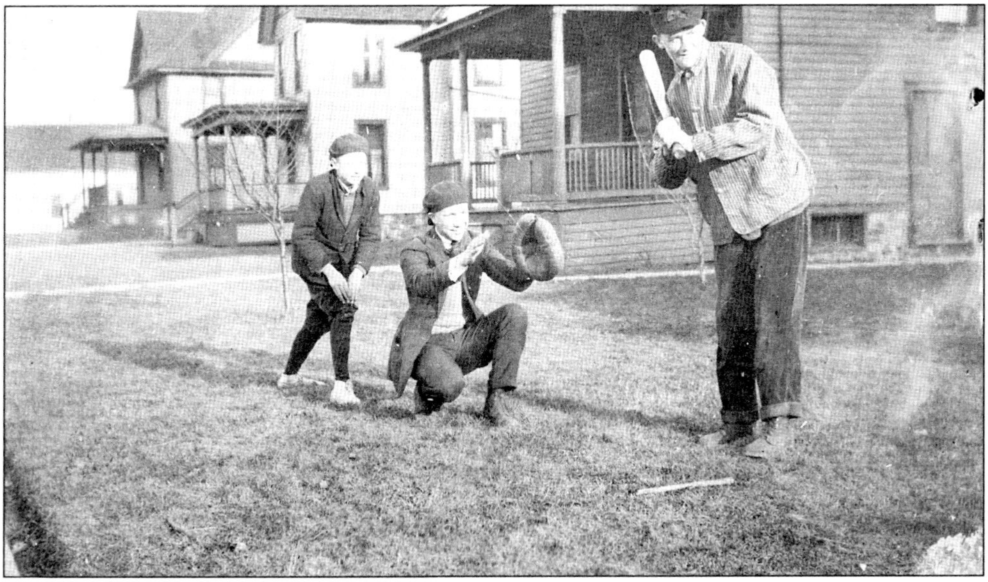

On October 1, 1892, soon after the arrival of the LVRR, Manchester established a set of ordinances and bylaws. Ordinance 13 read: "No person shall throw or play ball in said village; any person shall, for every such offense, forfeit the sum of five dollars." In this photograph, taken in 1920, Johnny Boardman (batting) and his friends play without concern for the petty ordinance.

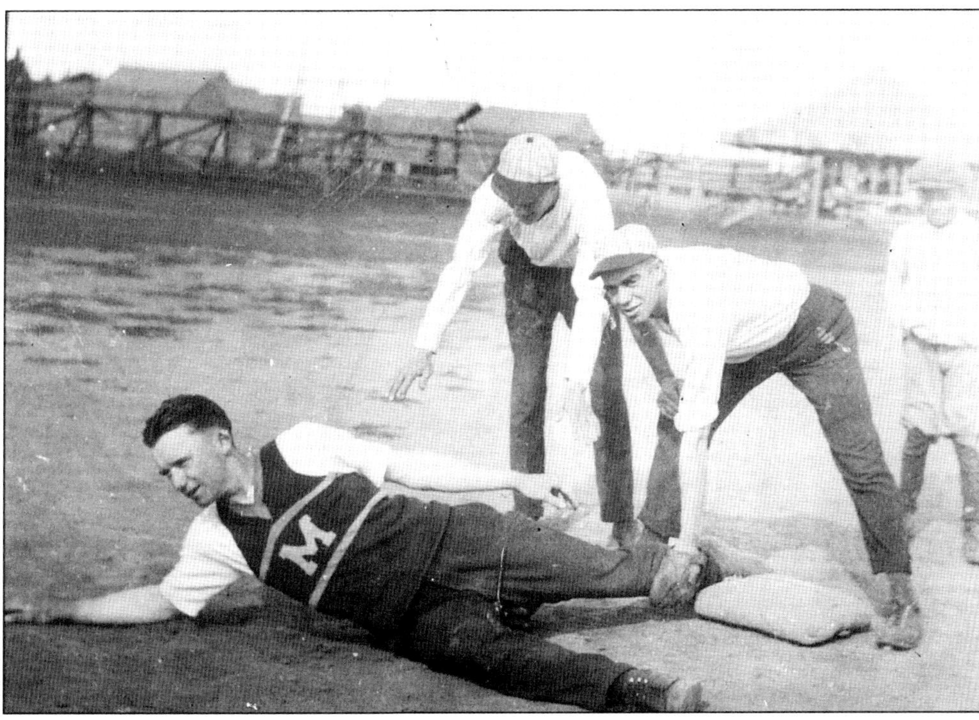

Joe Mottelo is shown here tagging out Johnny Boardman at King's Diamond in 1918. The annual fireman's carnival takes place in the area behind the field seen in this picture.

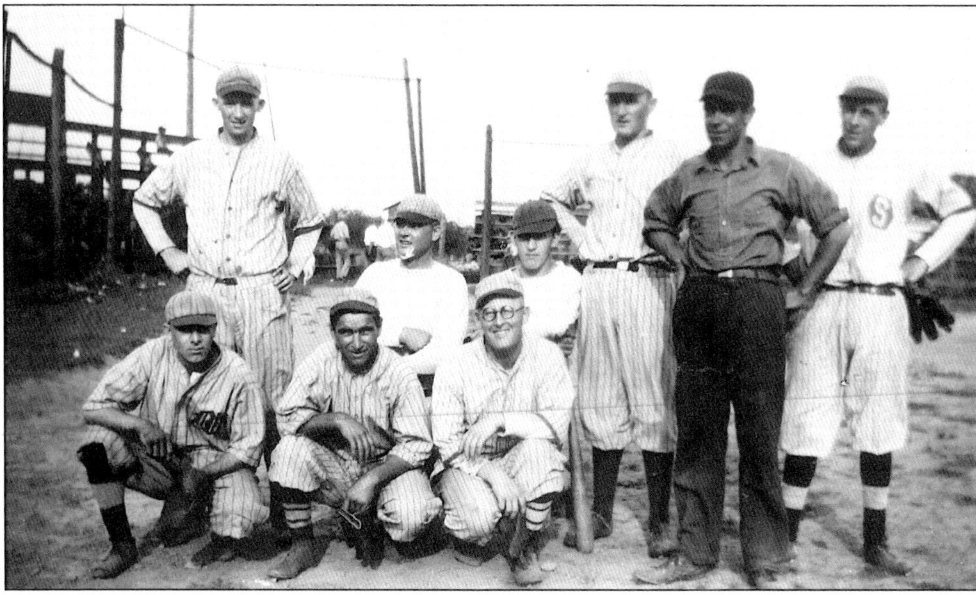

In this 1928 Manchester Railroaders team picture are, from left to right, as follows: (kneeling) Anthony Delgatto, unknown, Jack Childs (in bandage), Bubby Warner, and Harold Sprague; (standing) Johnny Boardman, Jake Murray, Joe Mottelo, and Ed Deflyer.

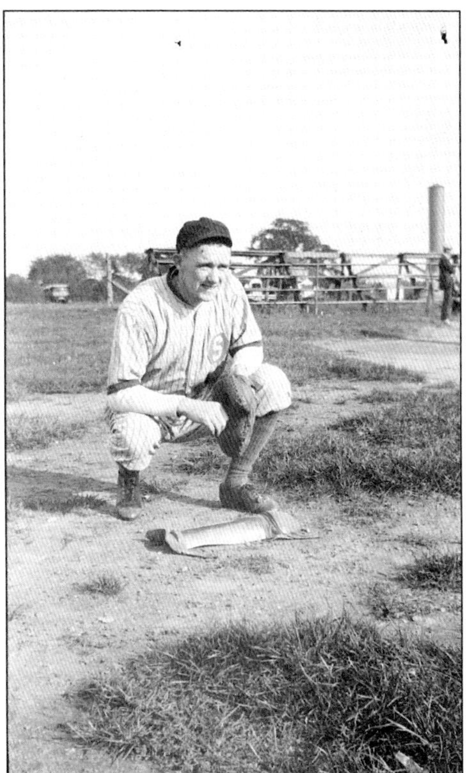

Boardman, seen here in 1926 wearing his old Hornell Shop team uniform, played many different positions as a utility player for the Railroaders. Boardman, whose father worked on the LVRR in Lockhaven, Pennsylvania, had considered working for a railroad in Chicago when his father received news that the LVRR was expanding into Manchester. The Boardman family then moved to Manchester to pursue further employment on the LVRR.

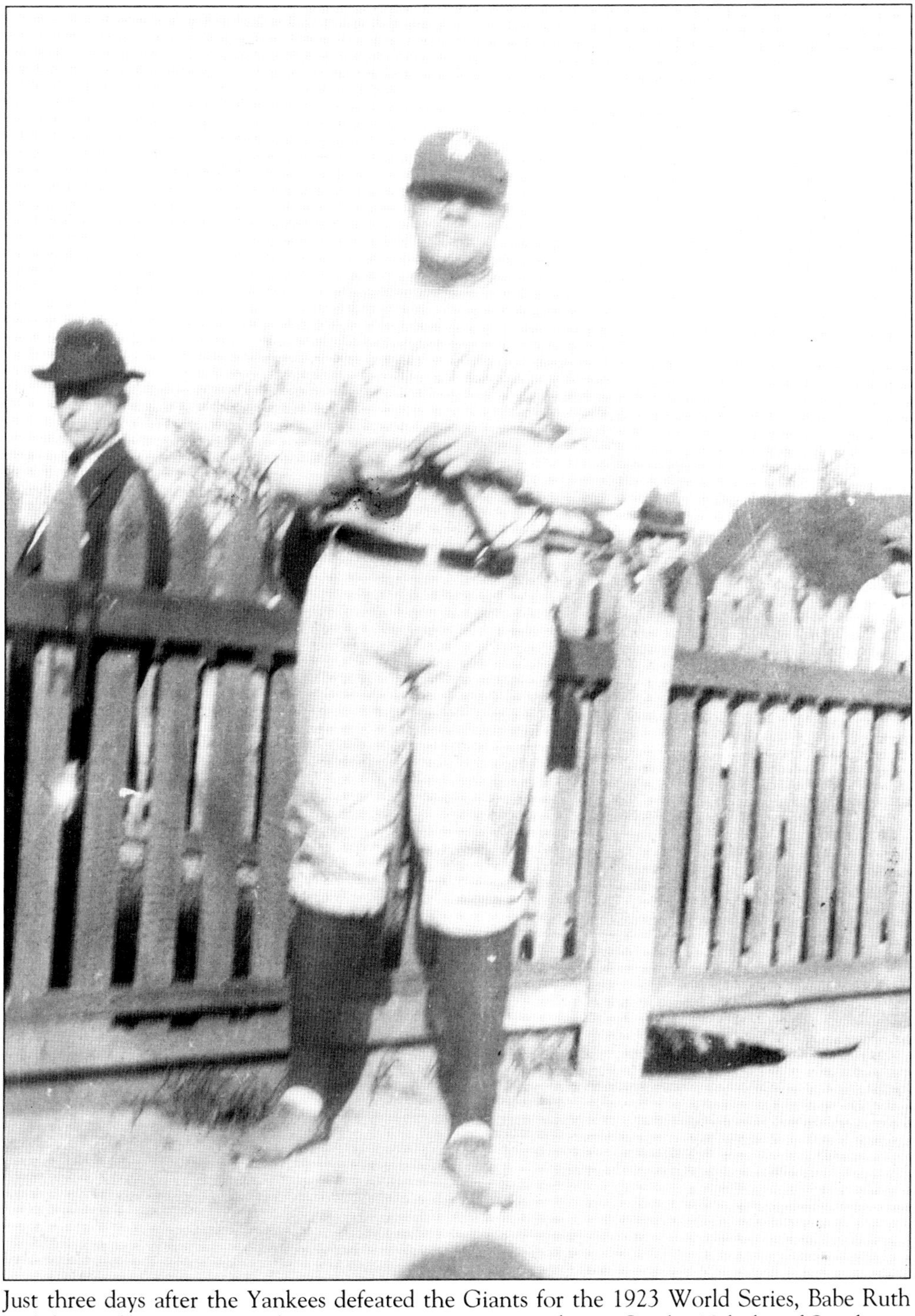

Just three days after the Yankees defeated the Giants for the 1923 World Series, Babe Ruth and the Yankees participated in a post-season promotional tour. On the 18th day of October in 1923, Ruth and the Yankees played exhibition games against the Erie Shop team in Hornell, New York. Like the 1923 season in which Ruth hit 41 home runs, Ruth delighted fans with a towering shot that cleared the fence and landed across the street.

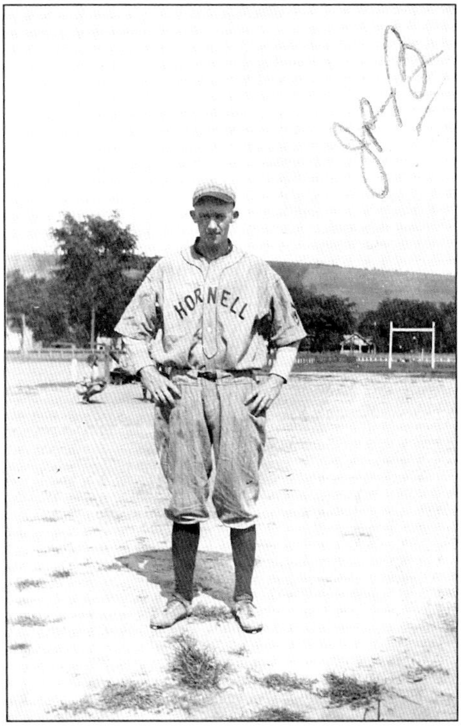

Pictured here in his Hornell Shop team uniform in 1925, Johnny Boardman played in the 1923 game against Babe Ruth and the Yankees. Boardman, a long time Manchester resident, would return to his old town after the 1925 season. As an Erie apprentice in 1924, Boardman earned 55 cents an hour, and in 1925 he earned about $4.13 a day. He was paid from $7 to $10 per game.

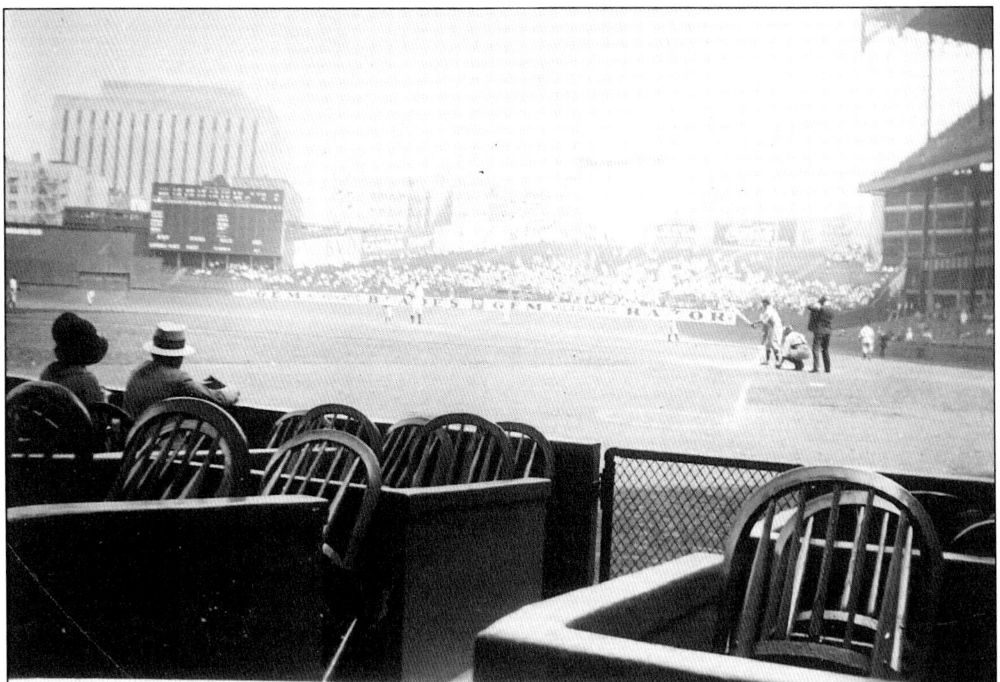

This photograph of Babe Ruth at bat during the seventh and deciding game of the World Series was taken on October 10, 1926. Mottleo took the picture just before Ruth hit his fourth home run of the series. Despite the fact that games one and two drew over 60,000 fans for each game, game seven drew a dismal 38,093.

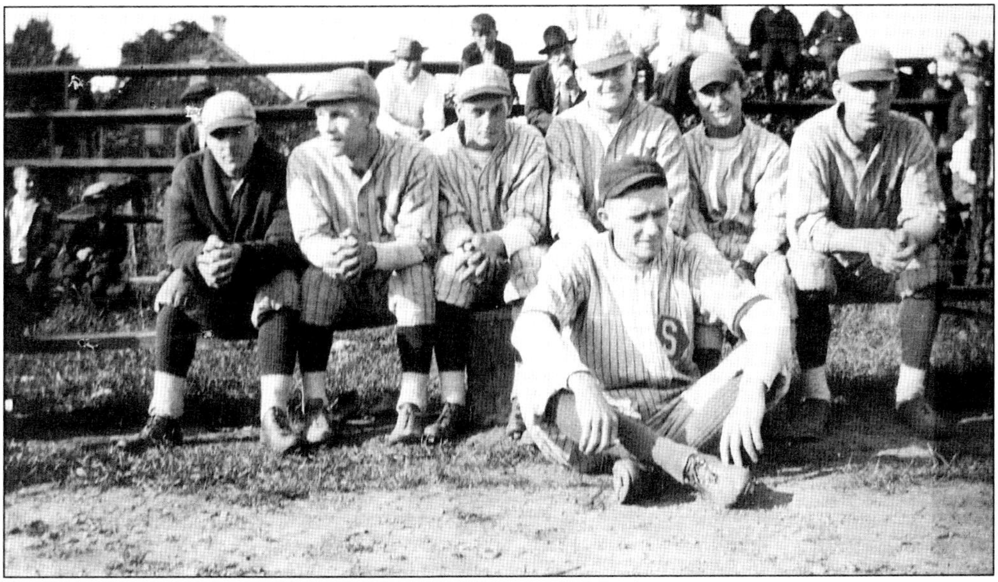

Six players from the 1926 Railroaders are pictured, from left to right, as follows: (seated) Bill Segbers, Johnny Boardman, Mike Griffin, Beans Cooley, Francis McShea, and Ed DeFlyer Sr. Boardman returned to the Manchester Railroaders in 1926 and once again obtained a job with the LVRR.

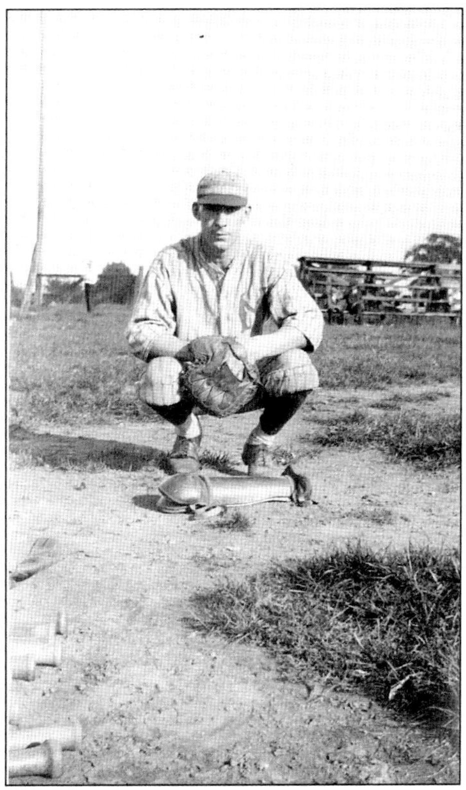

Ed DeFlyer Sr. became catcher for the Railroaders, replacing Francis Clary. Deflyer, a LVRR cop, had been an outstanding player for the Genesee Brewery Company in Rochester before coming to Manchester to settle down. Because of his unusual throwing power and balanced hitting, DeFlyer attracted several Major League scouts to Manchester; however, he chose to stay at home. He caught his last hard ball game at the age of 50. In 1990, he passed away at 92 years of age as the longest and last surviving member of the Manchester Railroaders.

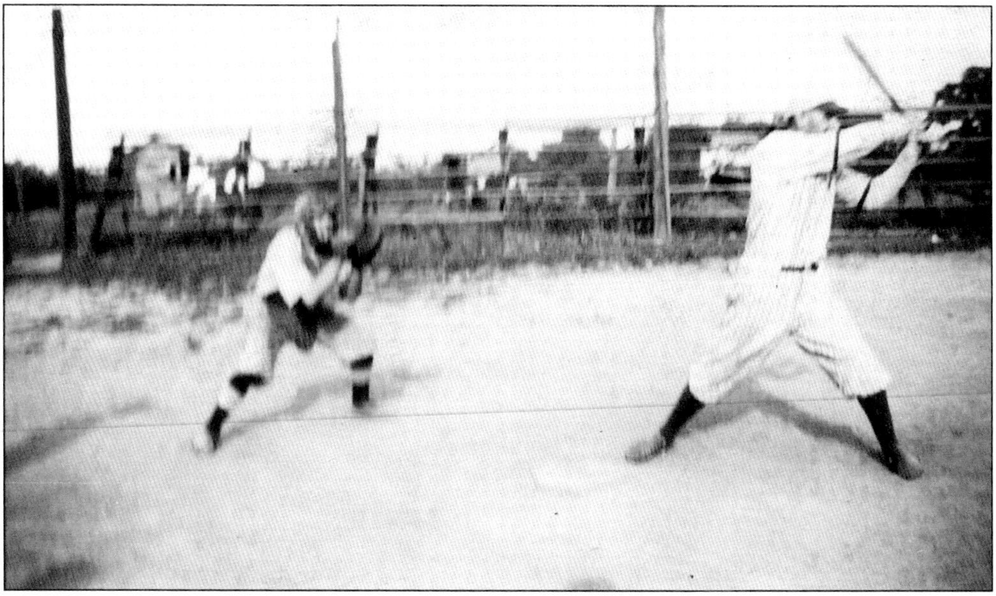

Manchester's Jake Murray takes a swing at King's Diamond in 1928. Murray traveled with Johnny Boardman to Hornell after losing his position on the railroad during the 1922 strike. Notice the distance between the catcher and Murray; many catchers were known to receive the pitch after one bounce.

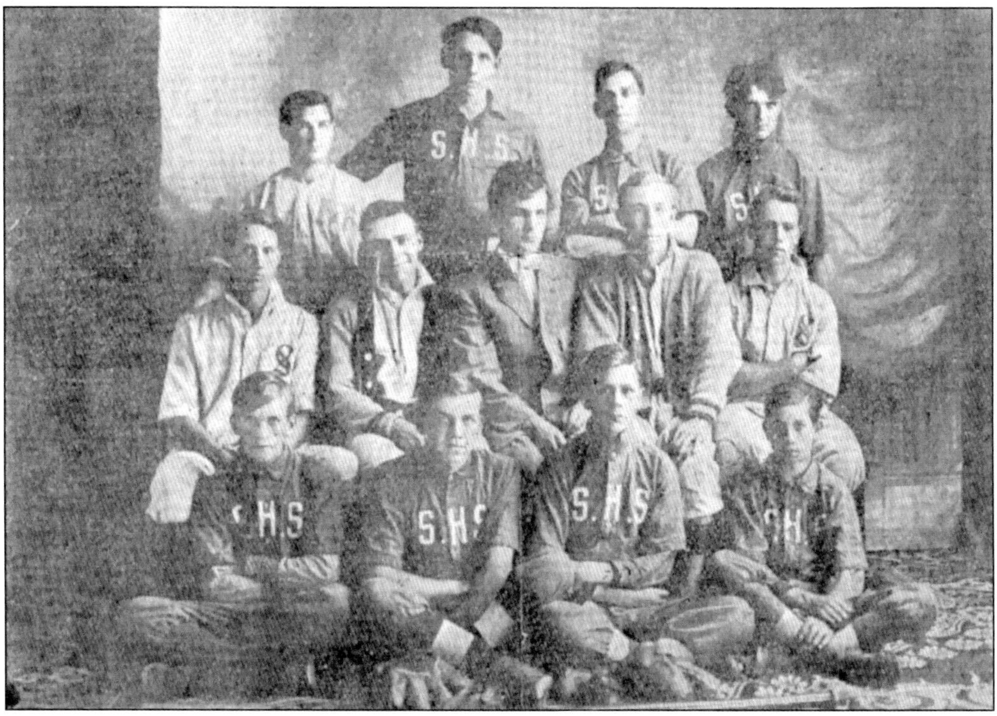

The members of the Shortsville High School baseball team of 1909 are, from left to right, as follows: (bottom) Dawson, Stoddard, Craig, and Curran; (middle) Kipp, Quinter, Coates, Dygert, and Packard; (top) Orlopp, Gillis, Bettz, and Delahunty. Stoddard and Curran went on to play semi-professional baseball for the Railroaders.

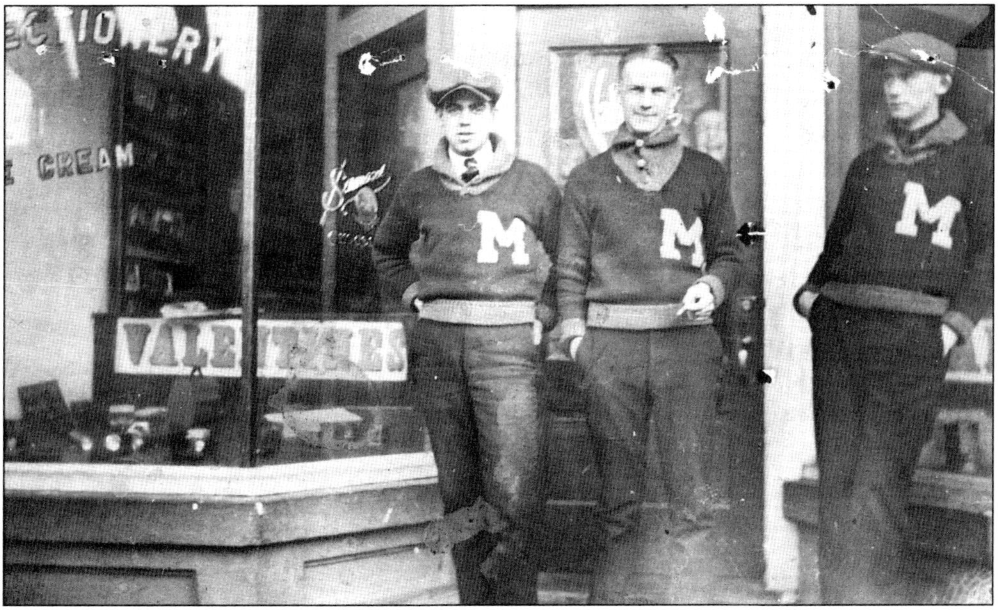

Although the form has modernized from letter sweaters to varsity jackets, the pattern and the value of brotherhood and comradeship hasn't been revised. In front of the "Gramma" Mottelo store in 1927 stand Joe Mottelo, Ray Rodney, and Clarence Fairchild. The Fines and Crowell feed mill now stands in the place of the old Mottelo store.

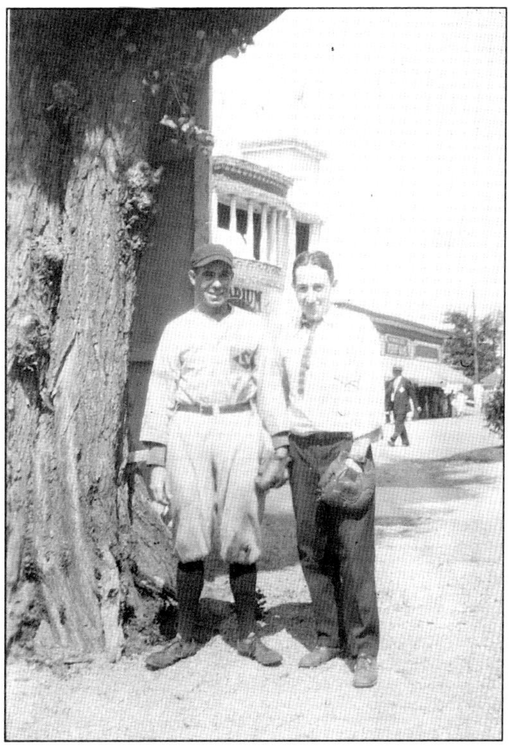

Shown here are Mottelo and Rodney standing outside the Crystal Beach Stadium and Amusement Park. Each summer the LVRR held a company picnic in which the main event was a baseball game between the Railroaders and the Crystals.

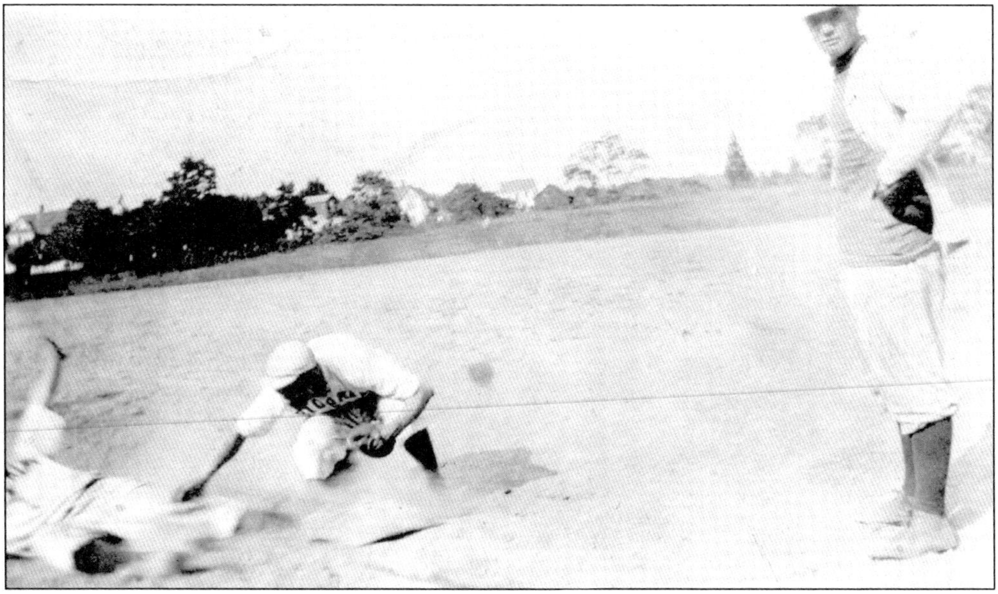

Action from the flat bush area of Brooklyn illustrates this umpire's failure to focus on the consequence at hand. Bill Segber's father, Joe Segbers, took this photograph in 1910. The Brooklyn Bushwick's chief rivals were the Bronx Giants. Unscrupulous umpiring was a major cause of dissension among the fans and players and, in some cases, an uproar would result, which in many cases disrupted the games to the point that they could not be completed.

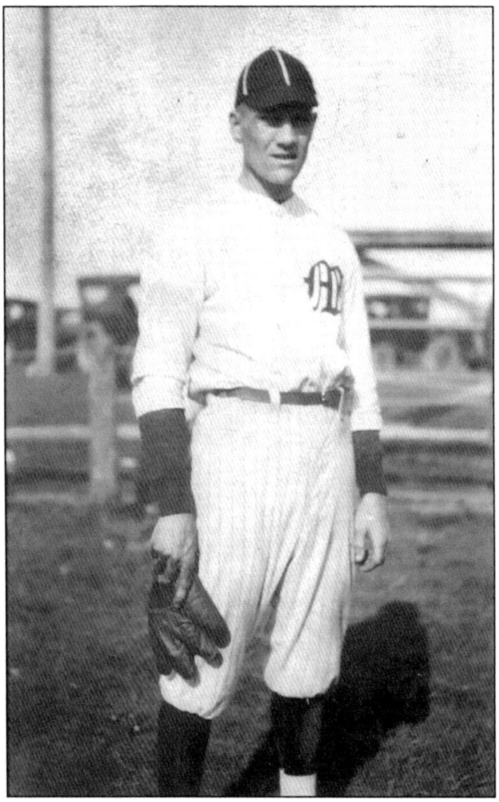

Irish brute Neal O'Harrigan, a timekeeper for the LVRR, played second base for the Railroaders for many seasons until becoming the manager of Manchester from 1924 until 1929. O'Harrigan, nicknamed "Midge," helped many Italians and Syrians with their citizenship papers and often received a bottle of wine on his porch for his generous service. O'Harrigan married Ester Hawkes, daughter of the proprietors of Hawkes Bakery.

Though very small in stature, Francis McShea was one of Manchester's fiercest competitors. For nearly ten seasons, McShea played shortstop for the Railroaders. For what he lacked in batting power, he made up in the "Torrid Zone" of the field. The "Torrid Zone" was the area located between third and second bases where frequent "daisy cutters" or hard hit ground balls were fielded.

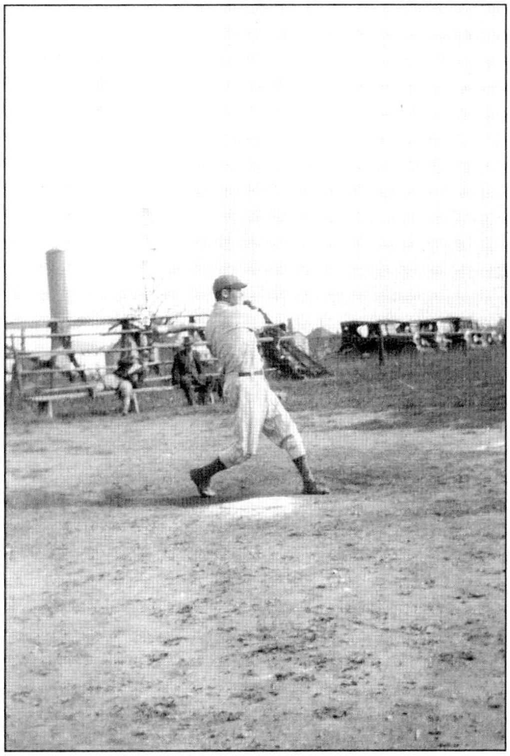

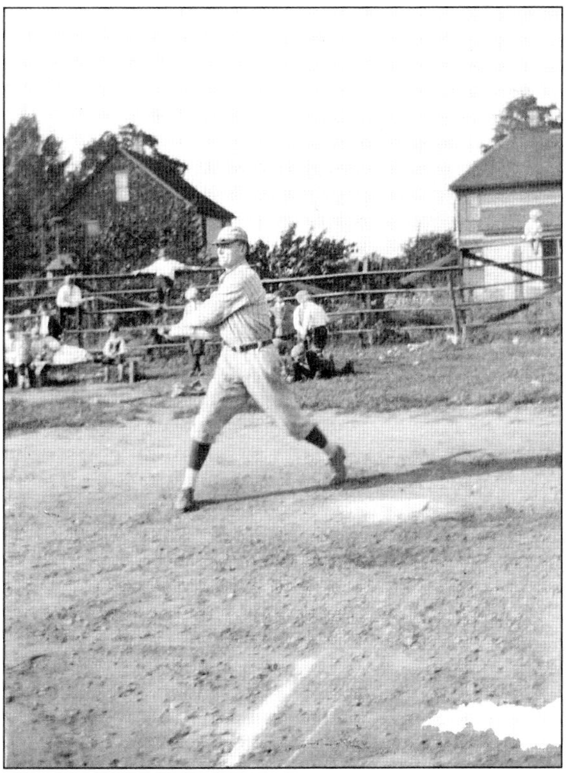

Leon "Beans" Cooley held the longest tenure of a Manchester Railroader, playing from 1914 to 1929. The lefty hit .268 in his final season and played four different positions in the field including pitcher, first base, right field, and left field. Cooley's grandfather, Hinman Shipman Smith, was the justice of peace for 50 years in Manchester.

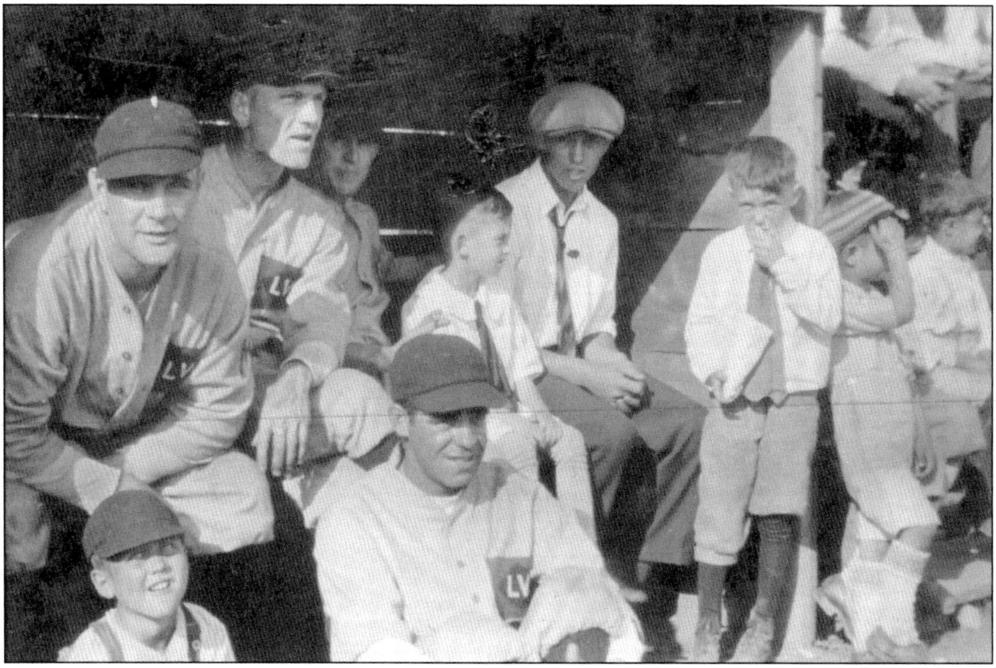

Segbers, Mottelo, and O'Harrigan (uniformed players) sit in the Stoco Lens Optical Co. dugout in Geneva, New York, in 1928. Several thousand fans attended the game that had been advertised as the "little" World Series.

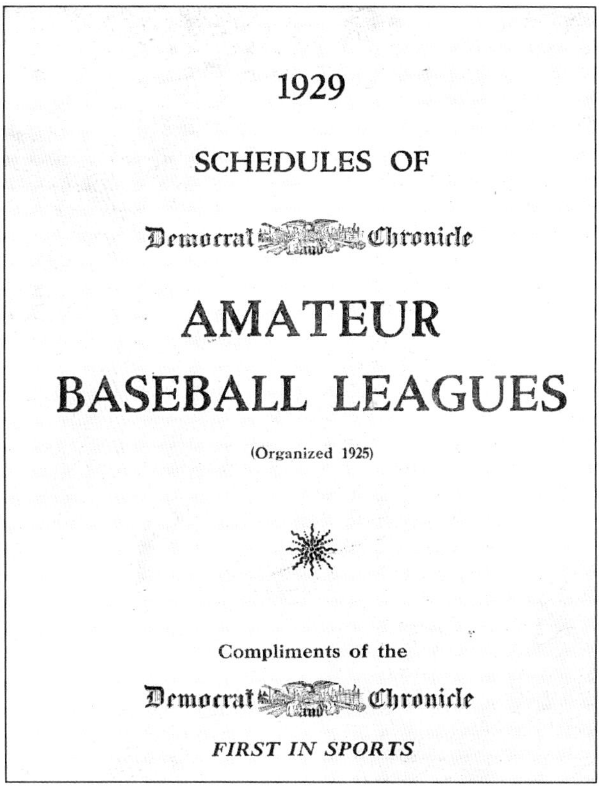

1929

SCHEDULES OF

Democrat and Chronicle

AMATEUR

BASEBALL LEAGUES

(Organized 1925)

Compliments of the

Democrat and Chronicle

FIRST IN SPORTS

In 1925, the *Democrat and Chronicle* organized and sponsored a baseball league made up of 44 teams from around the region. The league lasted from 1925 to 1929, with Manchester winning league titles in each season.

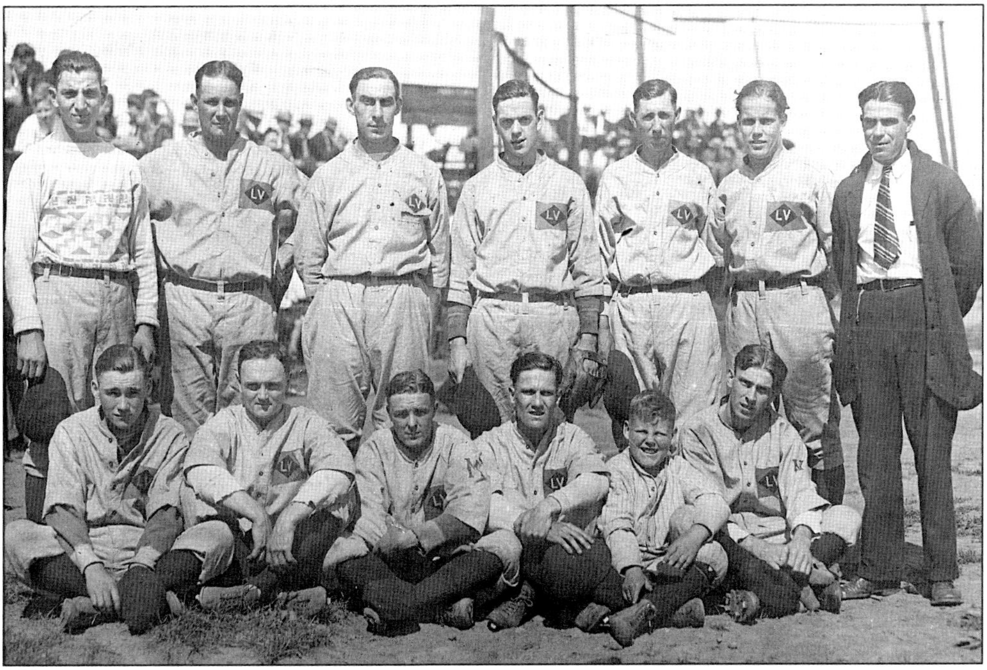

The 1929 Lehigh Valley Railroad Team from Manchester, New York, are pictured, from left to right, as follows: (sitting) Daly, Cooley, Griffin, O'Harrigan, Proechel, and Walters; (standing) Delgotto, Segbers, Deflyer, Bolan, Kerins, Nash, and Mottelo. Perhaps Manchester's greatest success came during the second game of the 1929 Democrat and Chronicle title series in which Manchester faced the Clyde Athletics. Clyde, after going undefeated for two seasons in 1927 and 1928, was defeated by Manchester 2-1 on August 11, 1929.

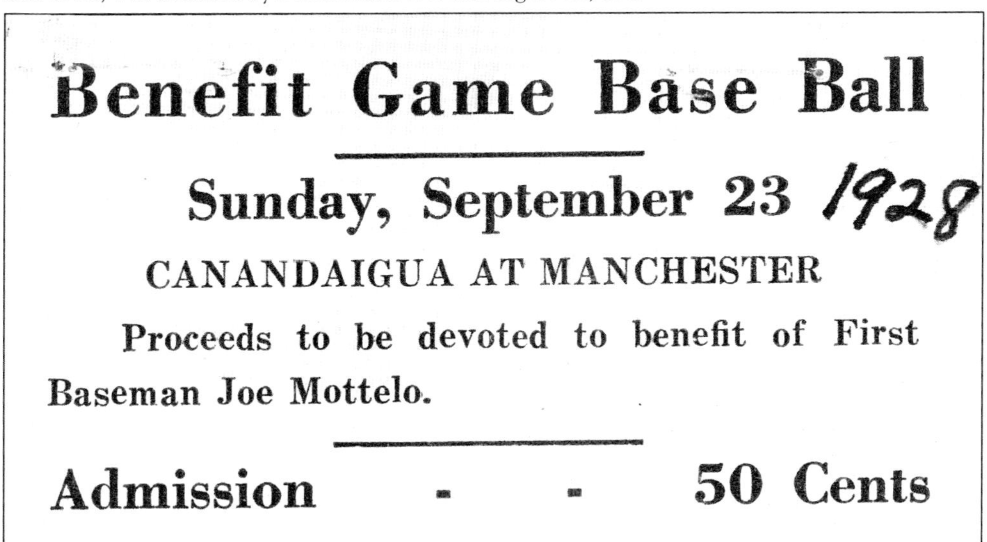

Benefit Game Base Ball

Sunday, September 23 1928

CANANDAIGUA AT MANCHESTER

Proceeds to be devoted to benefit of First Baseman Joe Mottelo.

Admission - - 50 Cents

In 1928, Manchester faced the Canandaigua Devil Dogs at King's Diamond. During the game, Mottelo took an inadvertent throw from Bill Segbers directly in the face. His eye was completely removed and Mottelo was taken to the Clifton Sanitarium for surgery. He lost his eye and never played again. This is a benefit ticket, which helped raise money for Mottelo's surgery.

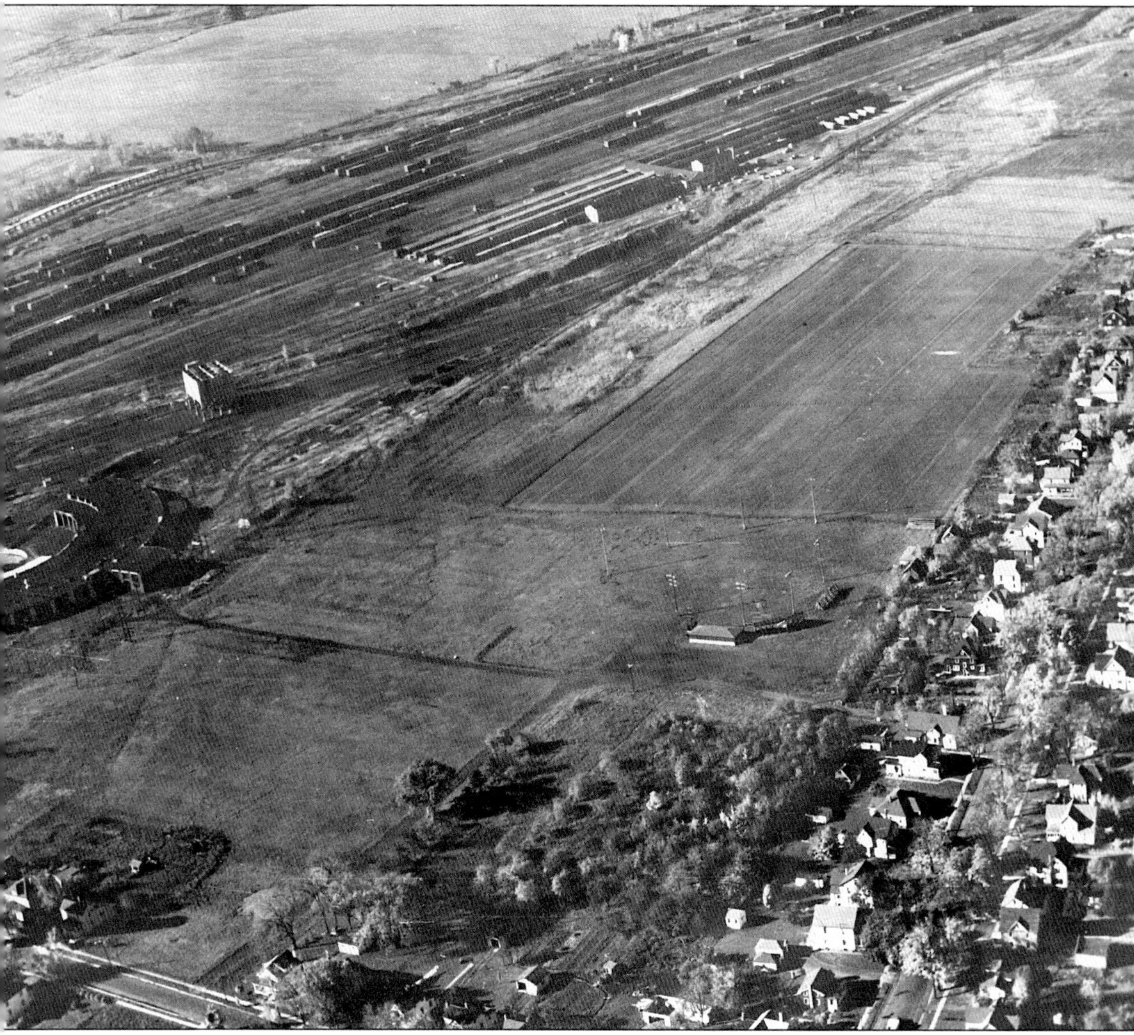

Manchester's "field of dreams," once known as King's Diamond, was constructed between State Street and Merrick Avenue, taking the place of an old Manchester farm. Note the close proximity of the transfer and the ball field where eight big leaguers competed at one time. Among them were Roy Wilkinson of the Chicago White Sox, Johhny Bogart of the Detroit Tigers, Al Mattern of the Boston Braves, Rip Collins of the St. Louis Cardinals, and Mosse Eggert of the Boston Braves who occasionally played for Manchester and was a Newark native. This aerial photograph was taken in 1955.

Five

Rivals

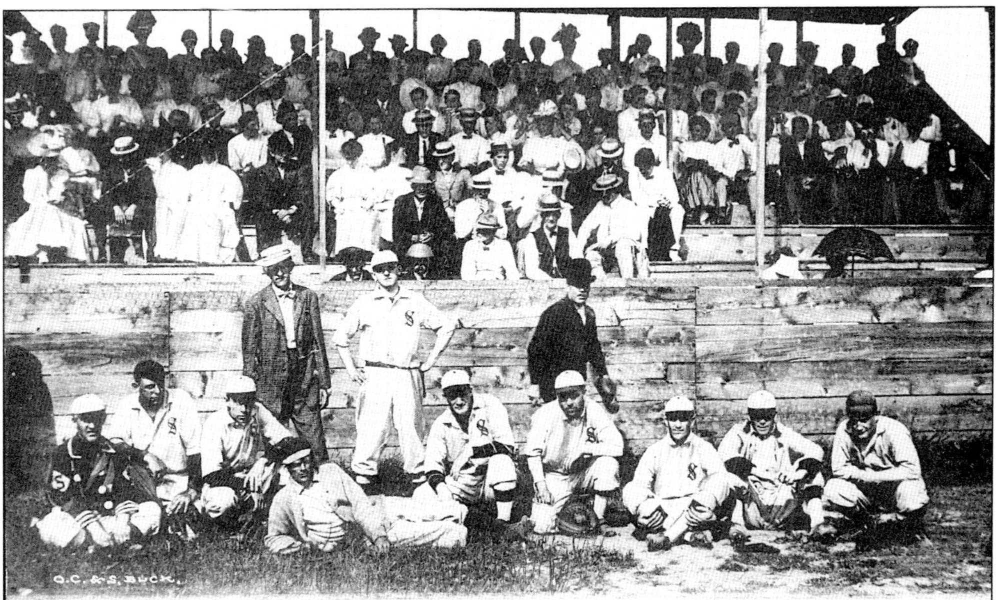

This photograph was taken in 1910 depicting Manchester's closest rival, zero miles away. The Shortsville Millmen were workers from various companies such as the Pioneer Thresher, Papec Machine, and Empire Drilling companies. The baseball games were known as the North versus the South, insinuating a miniature baseball Civil War.

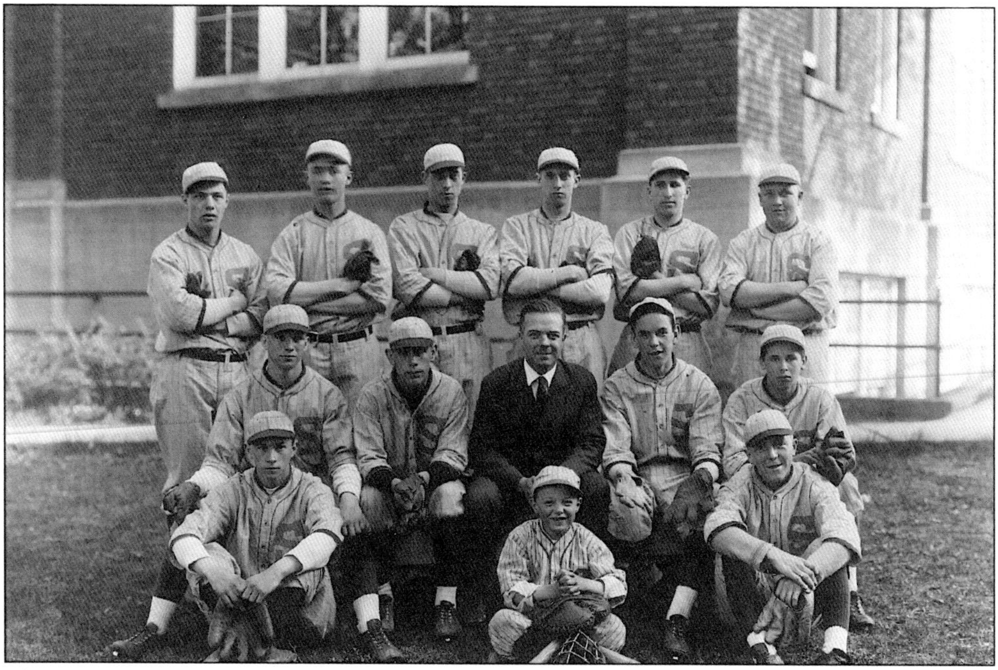

The 1924 high school team members of Shortsville are, from left to right, as follows: (bottom) Henry Broomfield, Gersbach (batboy), and Art Shaeffer; (middle) Paul Bullock, Buster Craig, Chapman (coach), Bill Bolan, and Parker Brown; (top) Gerald Gersbach, Jim Gersbach, Beecher, Pete Walborn, Harold Kipp, and Ernest Pitcher.

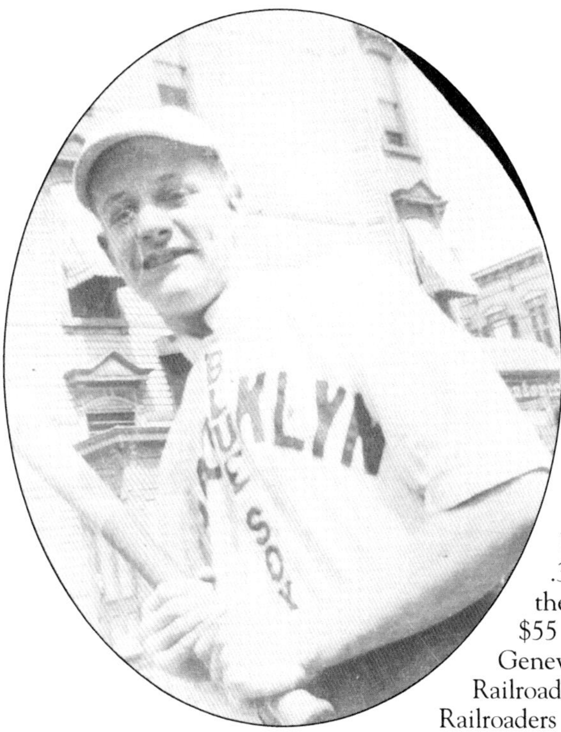

Ed Quigley, who later played first basemen for the Railroaders, carried a .309 batting average while playing with the Blue Sox in 1914. After being offered $55 a week by Stoco Lens Optical Co. in Geneva, which doubled his Lehigh Valley Railroad earnings, Quigley left the Manchester Railroaders in 1919.

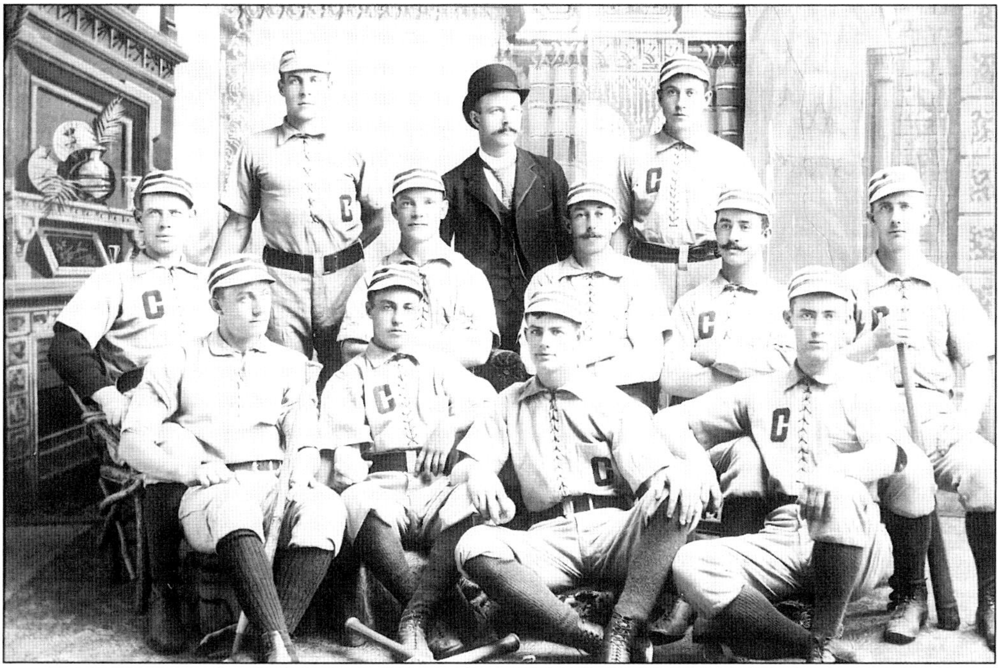

The Canandaigua Devil Dogs dominated the Finger Lakes for nearly 30 years of semi-professional baseball. By 1917, however, the Devil Dogs were dethroned by the little hamlet to the north known as Manchester.

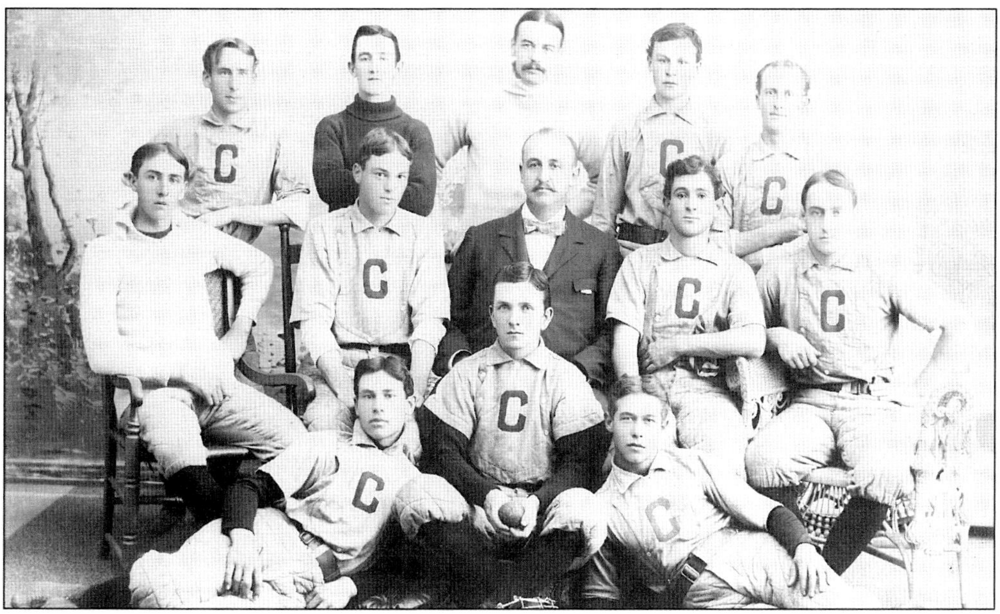

This antiquated masterpiece was taken at Crandall's Gallery over a century ago in 1895. The Canandaigua West Siders played near the boat launch in Canandaigua, New York. On a steamboat from Seneca point, Humphrey Bogart and his nanny would frequently travel to see the West Siders play. West Siders shown here are, from left to right, as follows: (bottom) Masseth, Fay, and Marks; (middle) Harris, Williams, Shangle, McNery, and Schofield; (top) Wilson, Fay Nichols, Hogan, and Dixon.

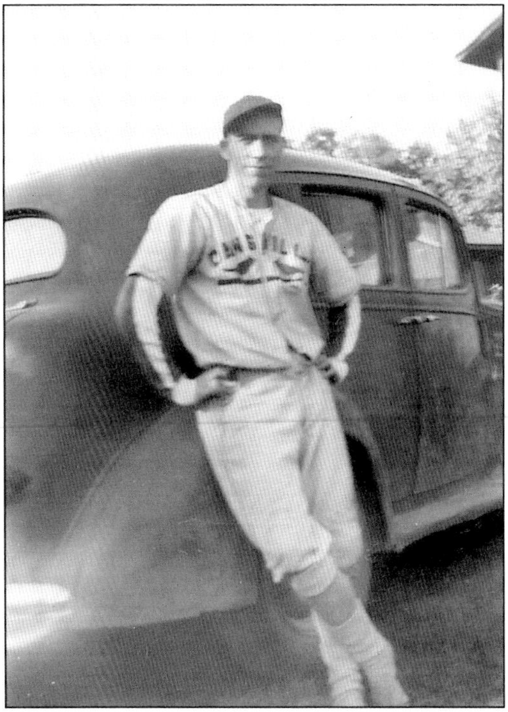

The Dansville Cardinals represented the Foster Wheeler steel plant in the New York State Industrial League. Pictured here is the legendary Charles W. Cowley Sr. On an errant pitch, he struck a batter in the head and because batters were not required to wear helmets, the blow was fatal. Sadly, Cowley left the game and never returned.

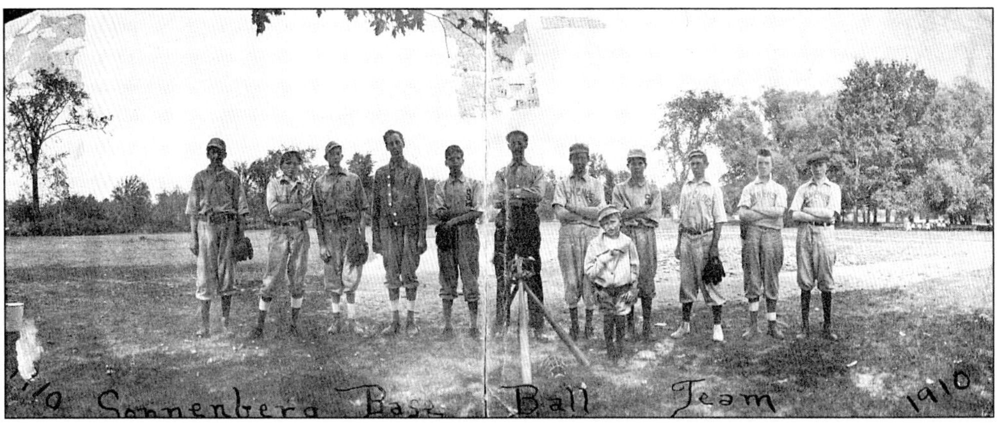

This photograph, taken in Sonnenburg in 1910, was of Roy Wilkinson (third from left), who would later pitch for the Chicago White Sox in 1919. Roy Hamilton Wilkinson was born in Canandaigua, New York, on May 8, 1893. After being drafted by the Philadelphia Nationals in 1917, Wilkinson signed with Columbus, Ohio, appearing in 43 games in 1919, and winning 17 of them. He was signed by the Chicago White Sox that year, and recorded a shut out and a complete game before appearing twice in the famed World Series against the Cincinnati Reds in 1919. In game five, he replaced Ed Cicotte, one of eight "Black Sox" banned from baseball for fixing the 1919 series. He then appeared in the eighth and final game of the series (the World Series was best of nine at that time because of post-World War I popularity of the game). Wilkinson received no decision in either game. Later he returned to his hometown of Canandaigua to face Manchester in the Ontario County Championship. He was defeated by the Railroaders twice and was shrouded by the Black Sox scandal and his poor pitching performance in the local games. Bill Segbers was the opposing pitcher for both Manchester victories.

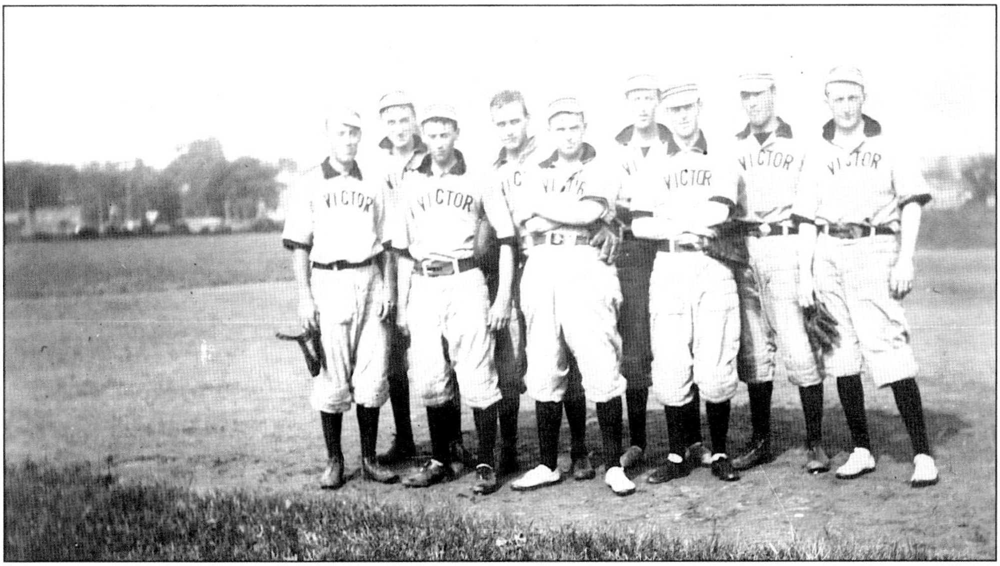

Victor, a strong Ontario County opponent 9 miles west, battled Manchester numerous times during the railroad era. The playing field was located on School Street, south of the Victor Coal and Lumber yard. The Black Diamond Hotel, adjacent to the Lehigh Valley Railroad station, is considered a landmark in Victor as it housed many baseball players and railroad workers through the years.

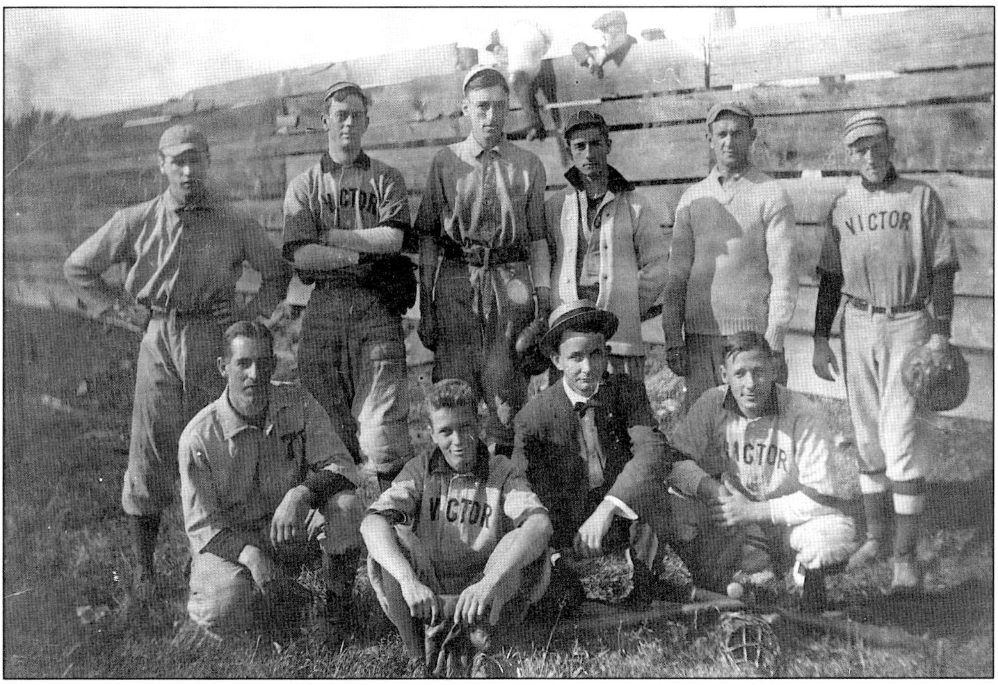

This team was employed by Locke Insulator in Victor. Irish families such as the Egans and O'Deas led the Victor team during early generations. John Egan owned a popular bar in Victor, which was also known as the Victor Hotel, presently located near McGhans "nearly famous pub." After Saturday ball games, many fans and players would gather at Egans to celebrate and trade baseball stories.

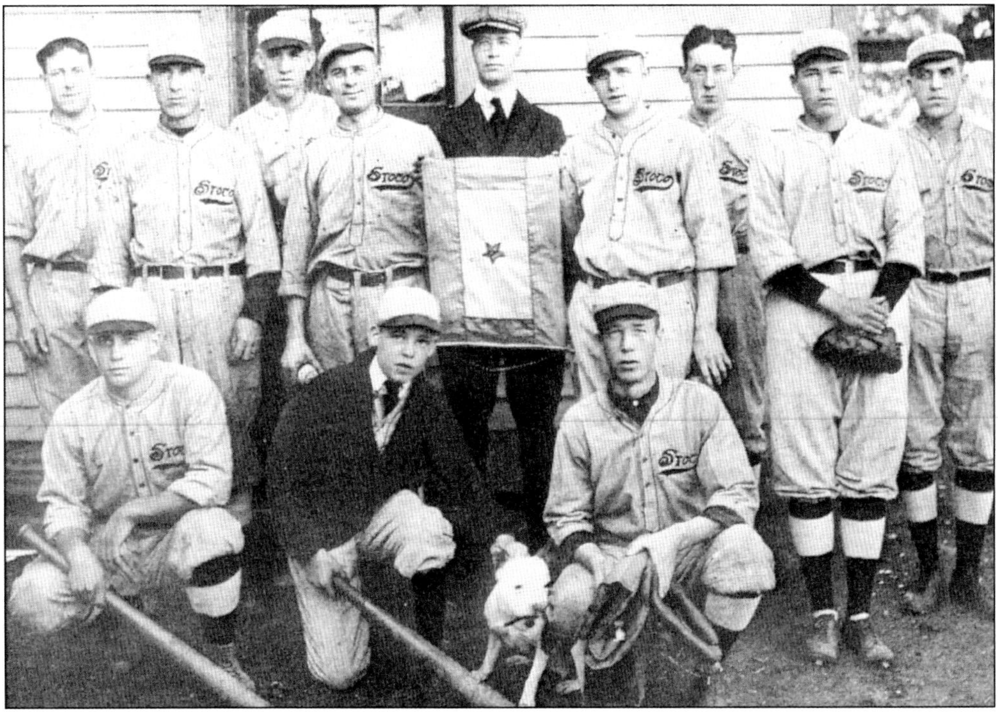

The Stoco Lens Co. team was a strong Industrial League rival from Geneva, New York. They were the first Ontario County Industrial League team to compete indoors at the local armory during the World War I era.

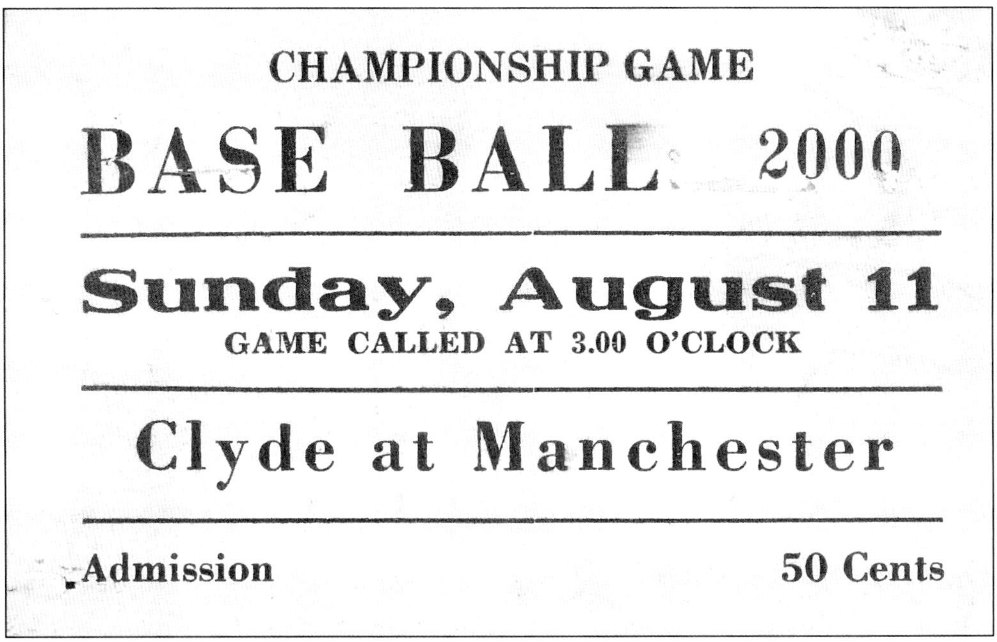

CHAMPIONSHIP GAME

BASE BALL 2000

Sunday, August 11

GAME CALLED AT 3.00 O'CLOCK

Clyde at Manchester

Admission 50 Cents

The popularity of baseball during the Depression was evident as shown here on this ticket purchased in 1929. This is ticket 2,000 of 3,500 tickets sold during the 1929 Democrat and Chronicle Championship game.

The Kay Pees of the Kodak Industrial League were big city rivals of Manchester. The Kay Pees hosted many of the games in Rochester, New York. In the 1930s, Kodak turned to softball, eventually becoming one of the top teams in the United States. Corporate management of Kodak believed that recreation was essential to promote company pride and worker morale.

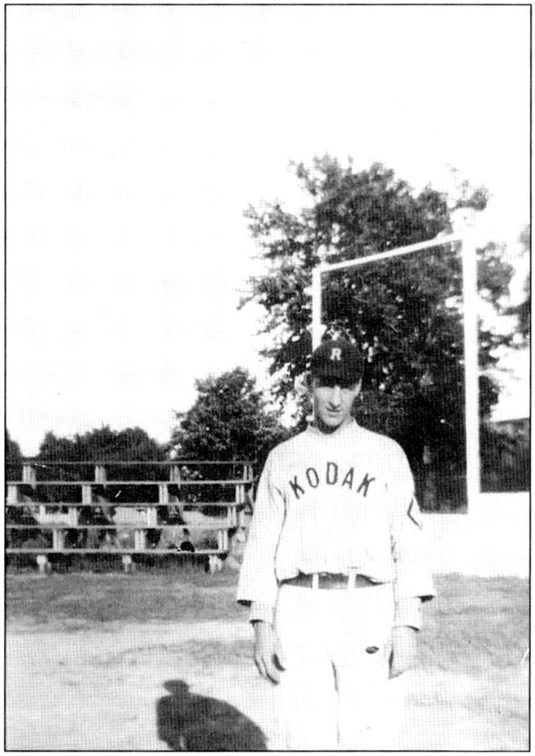

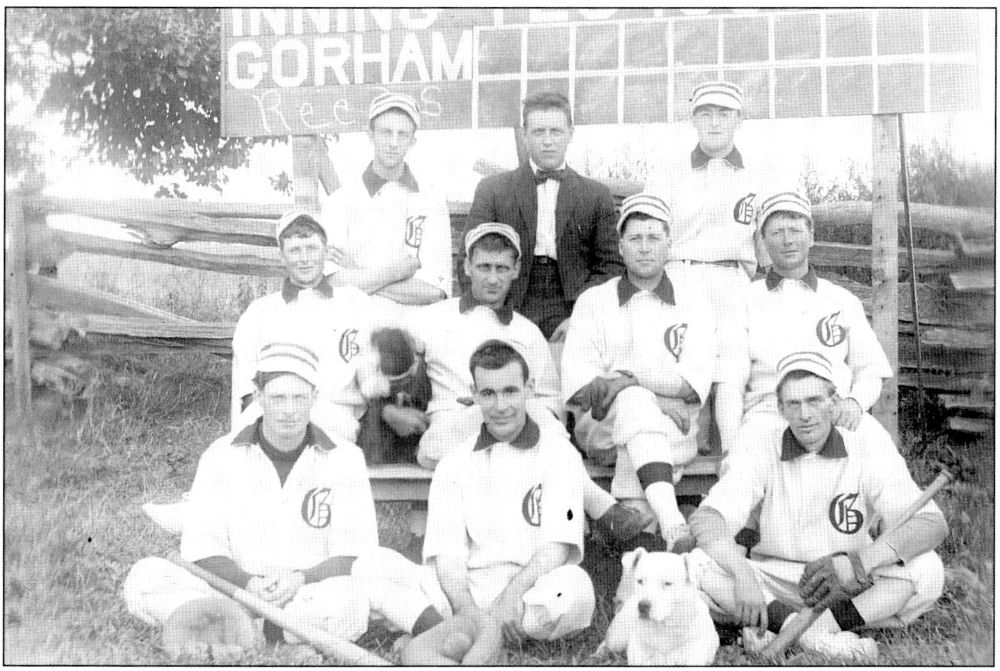

Shown here is the late 1800s Gorham team picture. Regardless of its size, this rural Finger Lakes community competed against towns much larger in population. The Gorham "aggregation," or team, consisted primarily of farmers and blacksmiths. Dogs were often used as mascots for baseball teams in the early 1900s.

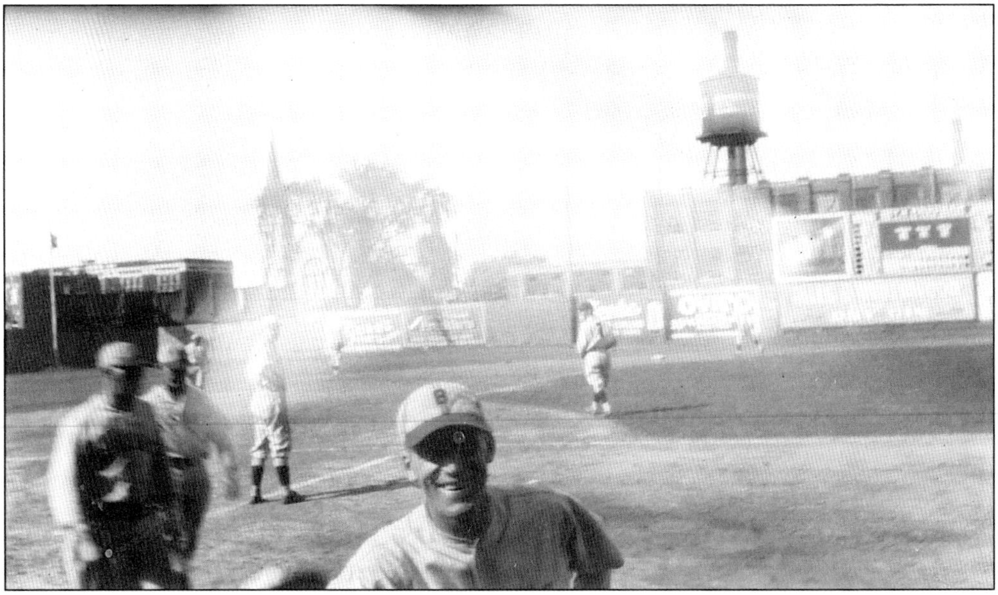

Many times throughout the 1920s, Manchester played against the Bisons from the city of Buffalo, New York. Buffalo's freight and passenger station was Lehigh Valley's "Grand Central" of upstate New York. The Bisons are an original charter member of the international baseball league and are the present day farm team of the Cleveland Indians.

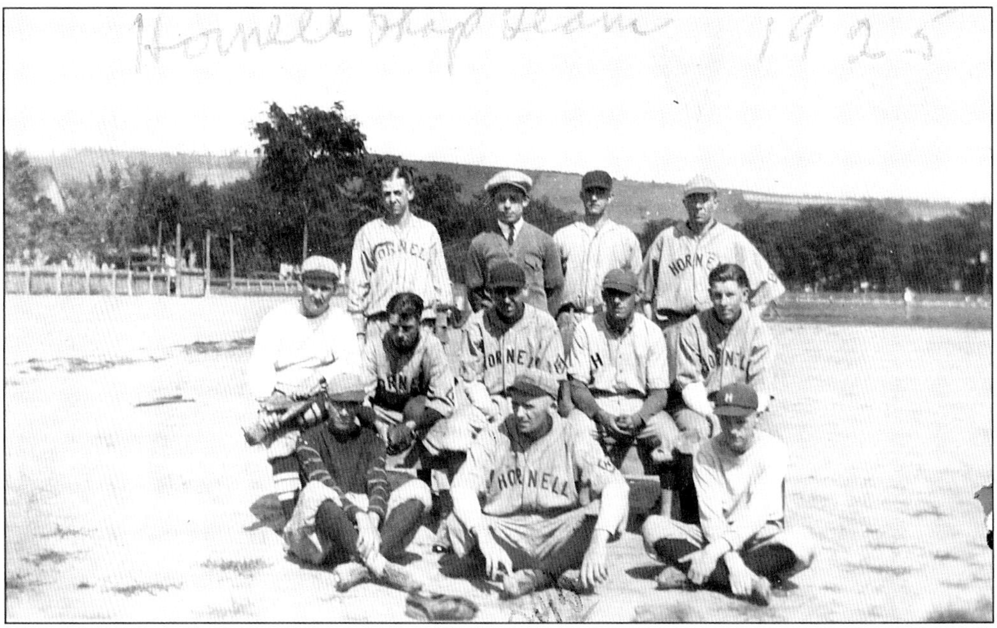

The 1925 Hornell Shop team represented the Erie Railroad at Maple City Park in Hornell. Hornell, located in a valley in Steuben County, played against Lehigh Valley and New York Railroads. Eventually, Maple City Park became the home field of the Hornell Dodgers, the farm team for the Brooklyn Dodgers. Yankees assistant manager Don Zimmer played shortstop for the Hornell Dodgers during the 1950s.

Seen here is a 1927 poster that advertises the famous Cuban Giants. Because of segregation the Giants couldn't play in an organized league, so they were known as a barnstorming team. They drew huge crowds based on their reputation for being the showmen of the baseball diamond.

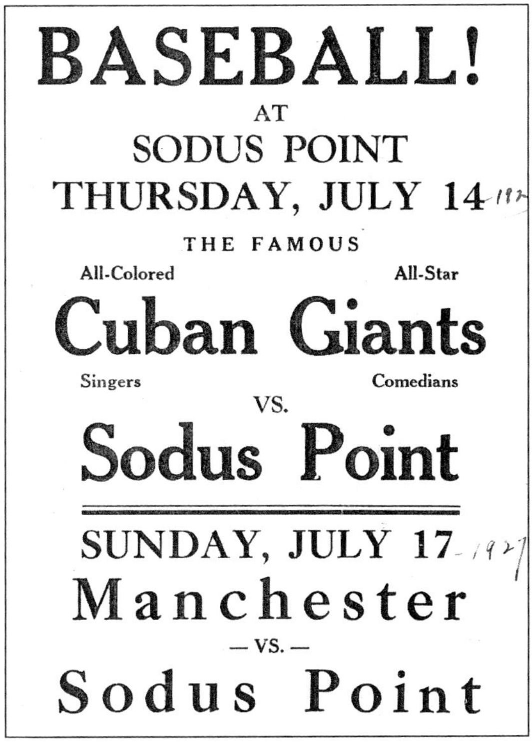

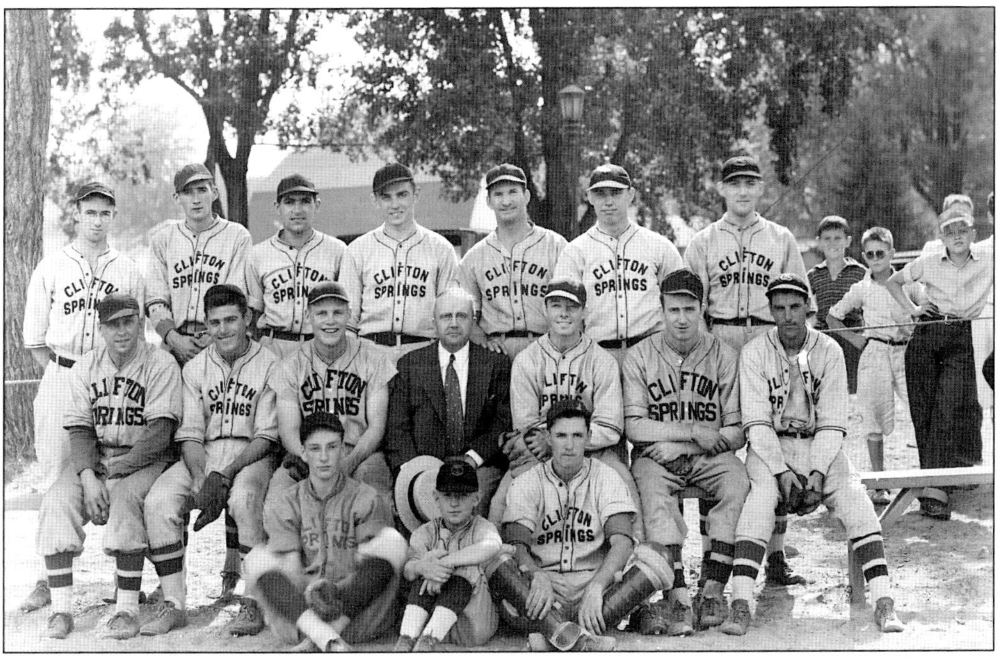

The Clifton Springs team was a familiar opponent of Manchester. Shown here is the 1936 team, from left to right, as follows: (bottom row) Dick Devereaux, Ken Walters, and Joe Boardman; (middle row) George Walters, Jim Perona, Dutch Proechel, Charlie Thomas, Peron, Paul Moulton, and Art Thompson; (top row) John O'Connell, Ed Daly, Don Smith, Thurston Smith, Art Bates, Gene Baker, and Asley McCumber.

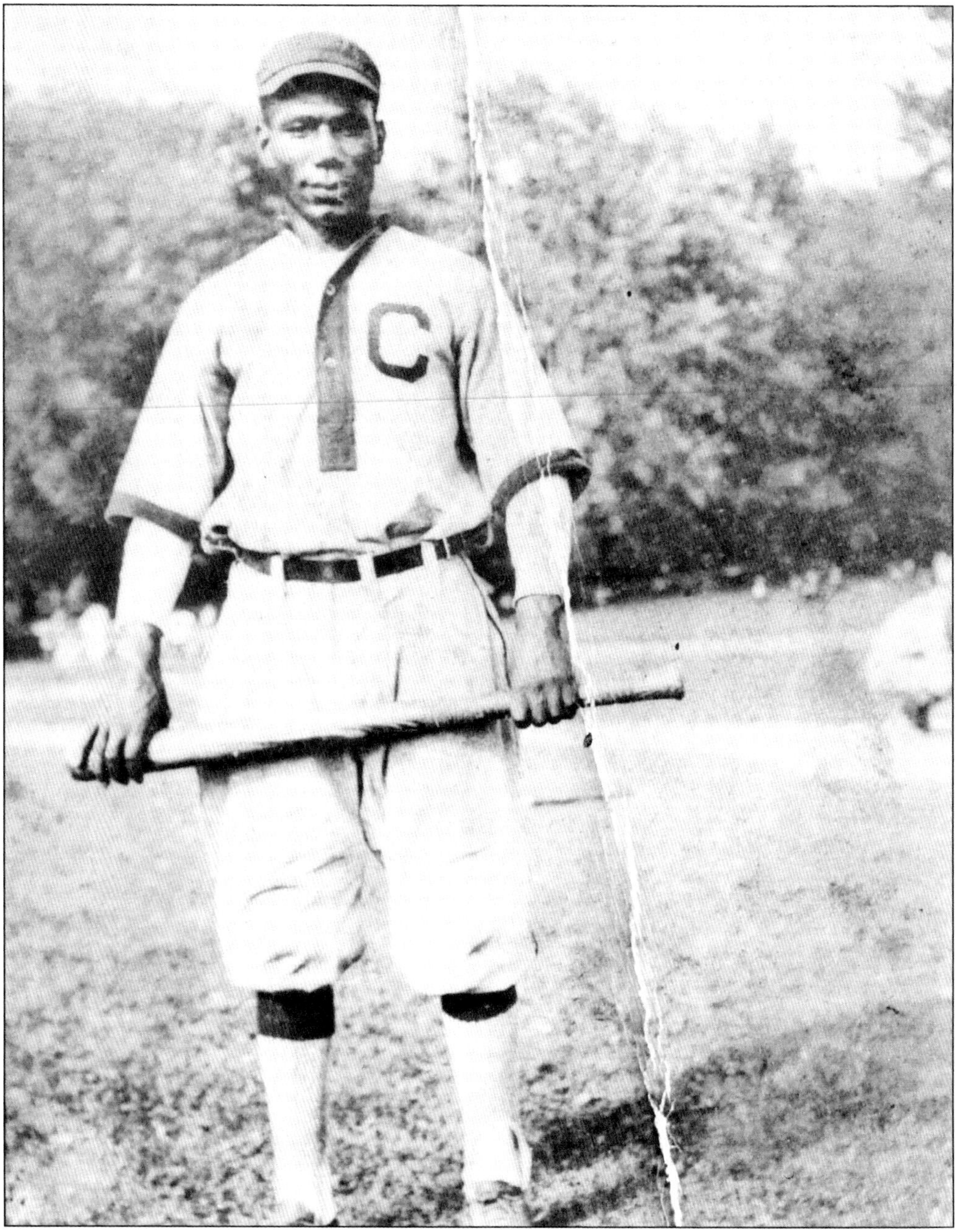

Henry McDonald, of Geneva, New York, became the first African American to sign a professional football contract with the Rochester Jeffersons in 1911 and later played with the Cuban Giants in the 1920s. Manchester faced McDonald and the Cuban Giants baseball team for several games during the Industrial League years. McDonald went on to umpire baseball for over 50 years in the Finger Lakes region, and his trademark for calling a strike was "It's a dandy!" McDonald was one of the first to be inducted into the Black Hall of Fame in 1973 along with other sport greats Jackie Robinson, Willie Mays, Jimmy Brown, and Buddy Young. He was the first African American to serve on a grand jury in Ontario County and the first African-American high school football coach in New York State.

Six

The Day No Games Were Played

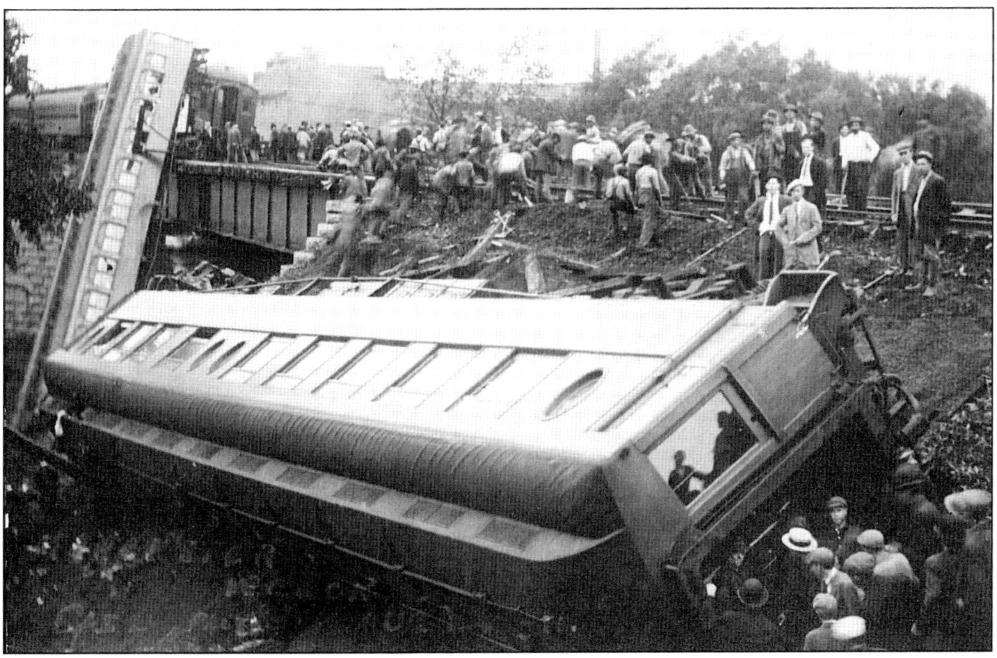

This is a rare photograph depicting the August 25, 1911 Lehigh Valley disaster in Manchester. The number four passenger train was the New York and Philadelphia Vestibule Express, one of the finest trains in the Lehigh Valley system. The train consisted of 14 coaches, which seated more than 530 passengers. In the picture below, the foreground shows the dining car, or the sixth coach. The car leaning off the tressel is the Washington Pullman car, or the eighth coach. The Philadelphia car, or the seventh coach, is not pictured.

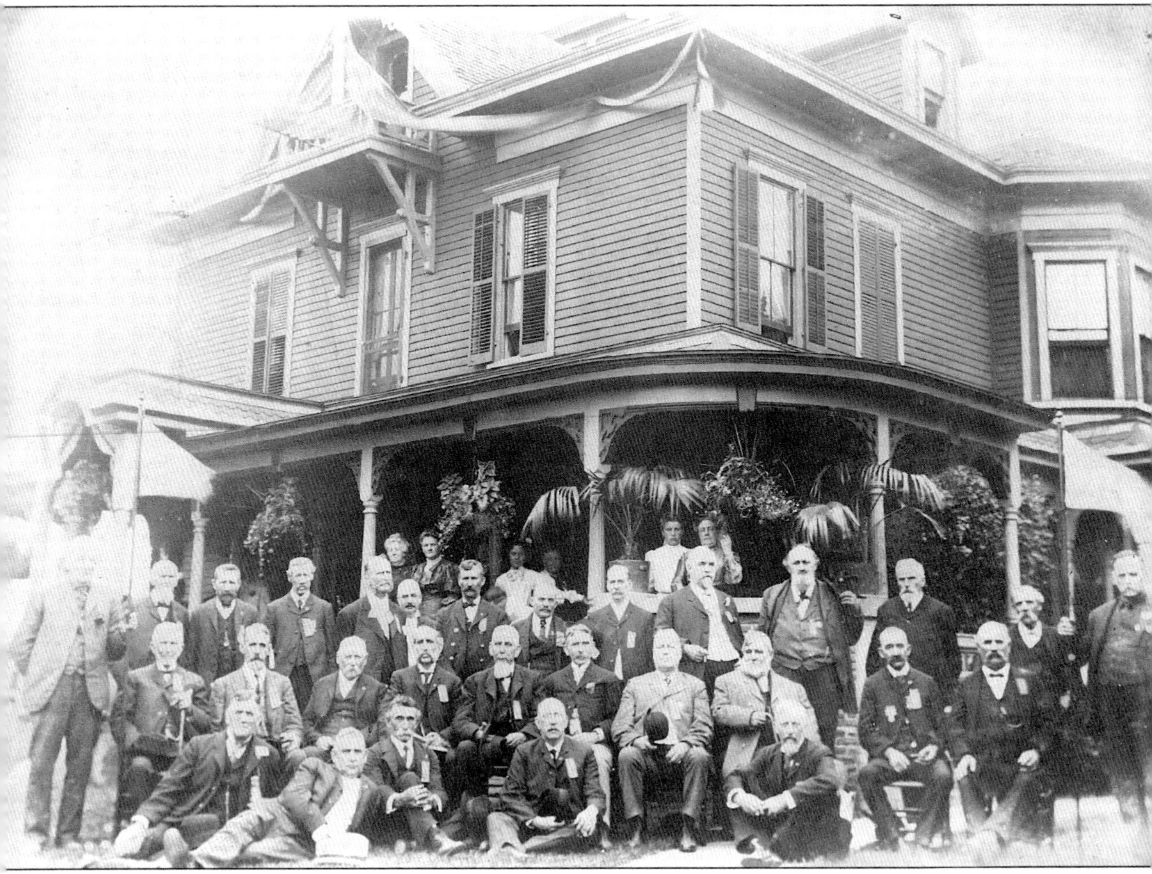

This photograph was taken at a Park Place Street home in Shortsville, where members of the Grand Army Reunion met in 1895. A similar meeting of GAR members took place in Manchester on the day of the crash in 1911.

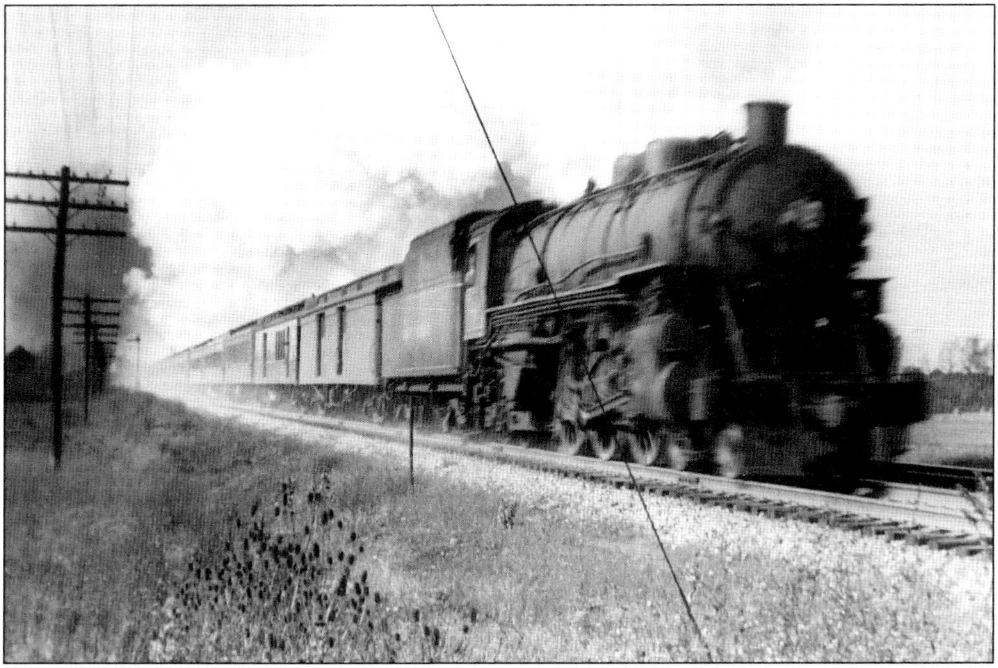

This is an early 1900 photograph of the Black Diamond that consisted of wooden coaches and traveled through Manchester daily as the premiere passenger train for the LVRR. Black Diamond express service began on Monday, May 18, 1896. The Black Diamond serviced 7.5 million passengers in 1918 and was referred to as the "handsomest" train for the LVRR.

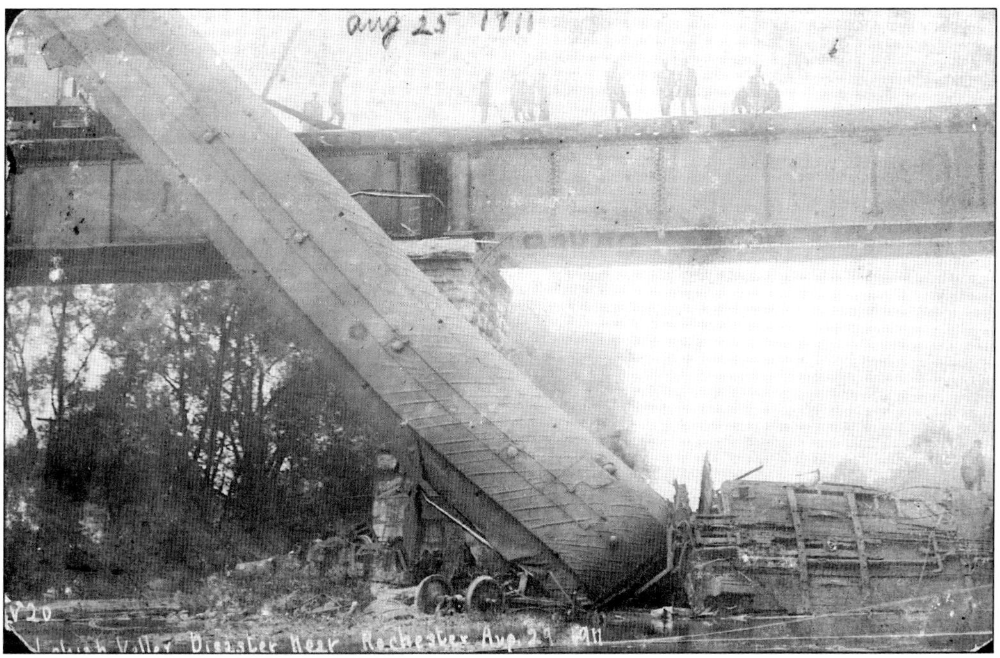

On August 25, 1911, a large passenger train derailed while crossing the Manchester tressel sending two coaches to the bottom and another off the tracks. The car hanging off the tressel is the Washington Pullman car. Amazingly, only one soul was lost in the Washington Pullman.

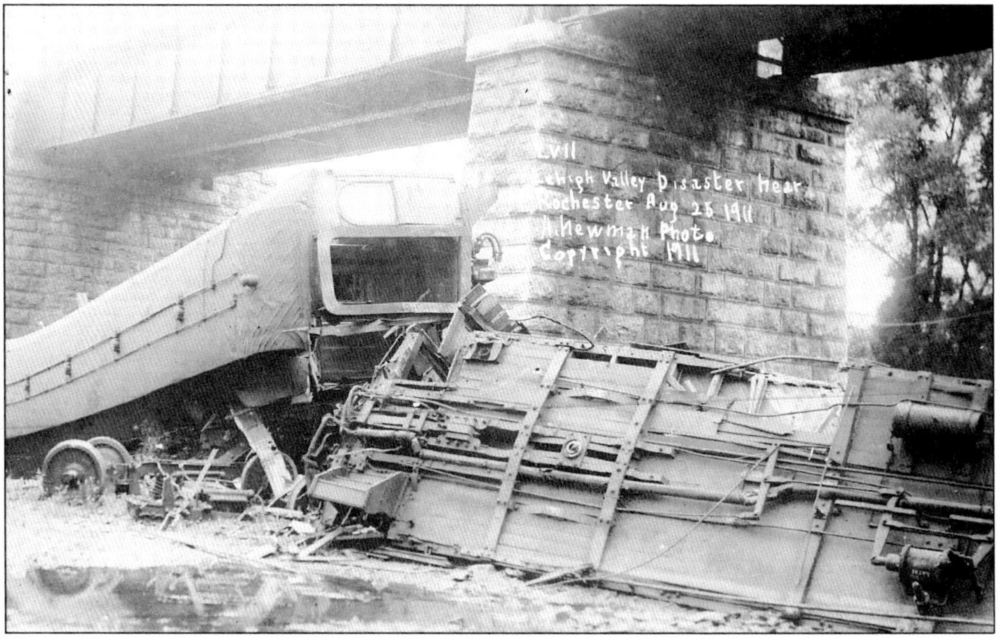

The seventh Pullman from Philadelphia fell 50 feet into the Canandaigua outlet, taking the lives of 23 men and women of the GAR. Many of the victims were Civil War veterans from Philadelphia.

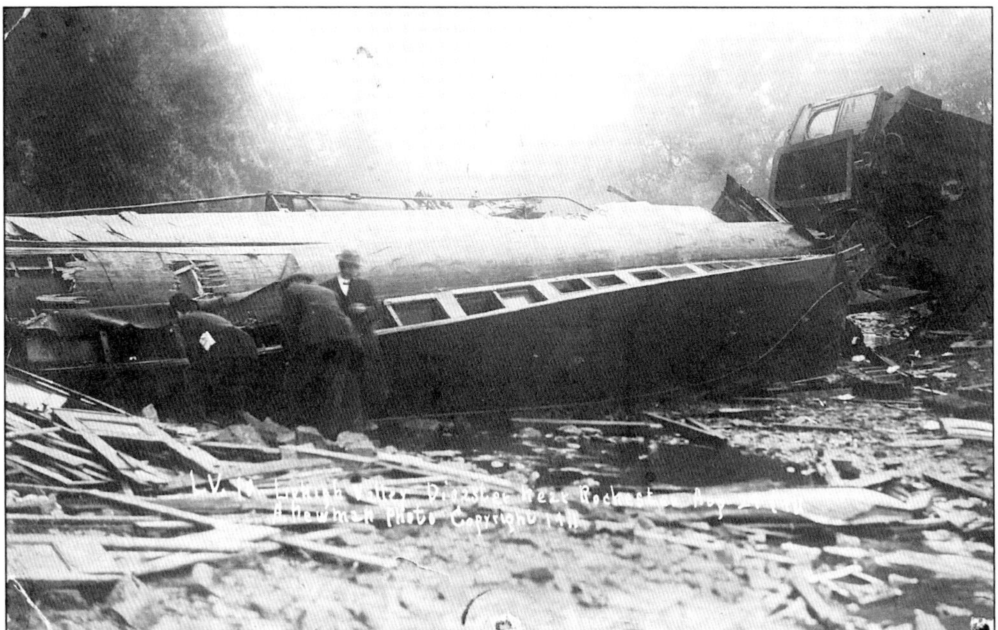

This is the seventh Pullman pictured from the opposite side of the tressel. In the autumn of 1910, gandy dancers re-laid the mainline through Manchester with 90-pound rails. One of the new rails laid near the tressel in Manchester was "riddled with transverse fissures," or internal defects. This was first internal defect of a rail found in U.S. history and helped lead to the current practice of X-ray or sound inspection of all rails.

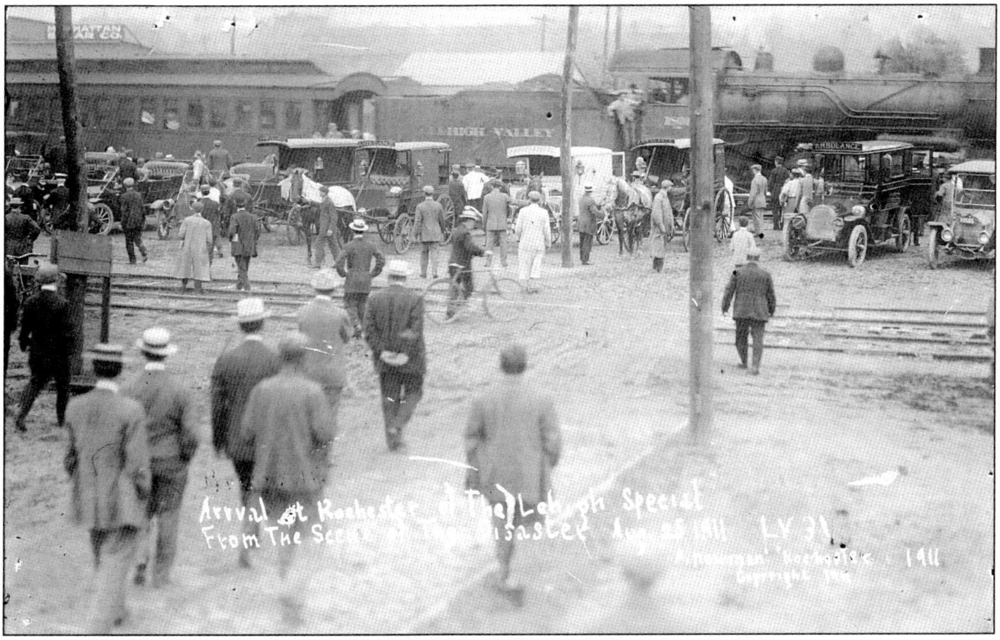

In the background of this photograph is the "Lehigh Special," a train dispatched following the wreck of 1911 to transport the injured to hospitals in Rochester, Canandaigua, Geneva, and Clifton Springs. Carlos Pierce Osgood, a local telephone and telegraph operator, arrived early on the scene and was instrumental in the notification of medical personnel. He summoned the Lehigh Special as well as other emergency services to Manchester to assist the community in the aftermath of the disaster.

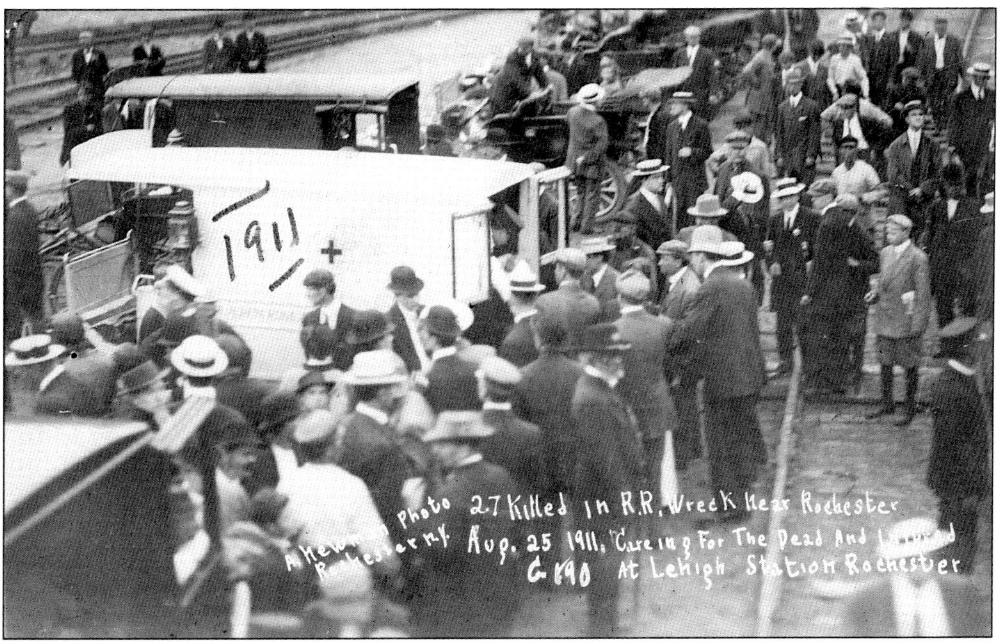

Horse-drawn and Model T ambulances from Canandaigua, Geneva, and Clifton, were summoned to help care for the remaining 62 injured. News of the crash spread far and fast as more than 10,000 curious outsiders flooded the small village.

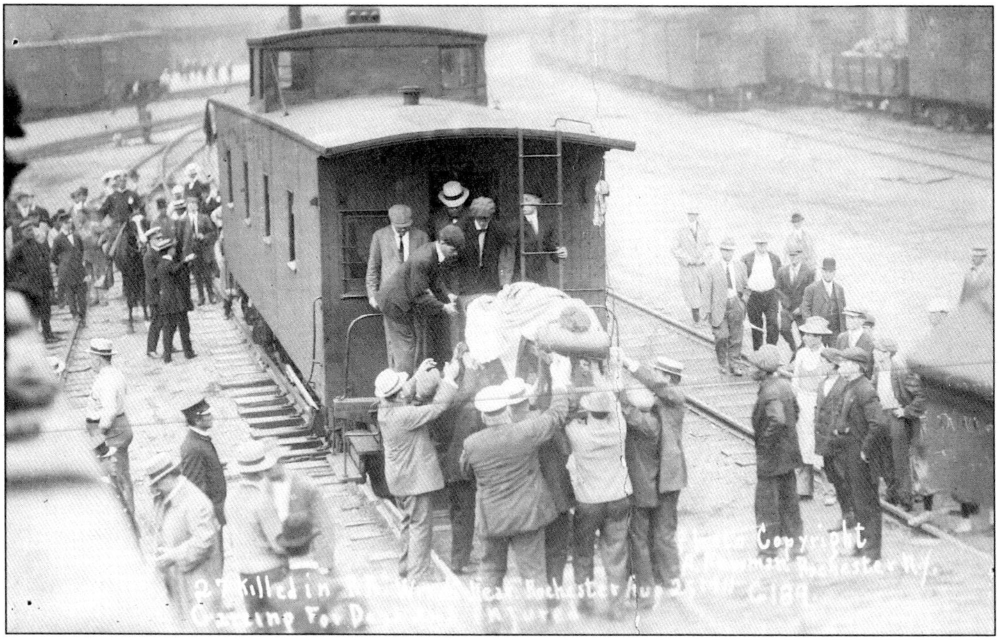

Workers lift an injured passenger aboard the caboose of the Lehigh Special. The dead were taken to the J.M. Stoddard Morgue in Shortsville which contained an elevator, water, and consuming furnace, in which the bodies were prepared for burial. The morgue could accommodate 35 bodies, and at the time was considered the largest morgue in the state within a 100-mile radius.

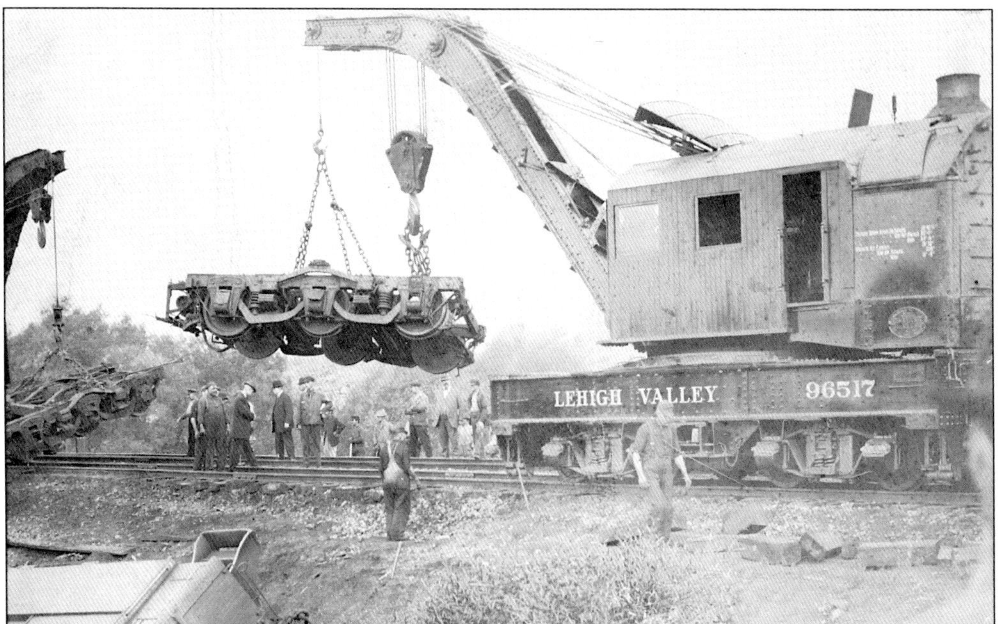

The cripple track crane number 96517 lifts the axles of the Philadelphia coach. The remainder of the wreckage was burned on site. In all, 29 people were killed and 62 were injured, making this the worst LVRR disaster since the tragic collision at Mud Run, Pennsylvania, in 1888.

Seven

THE ERA

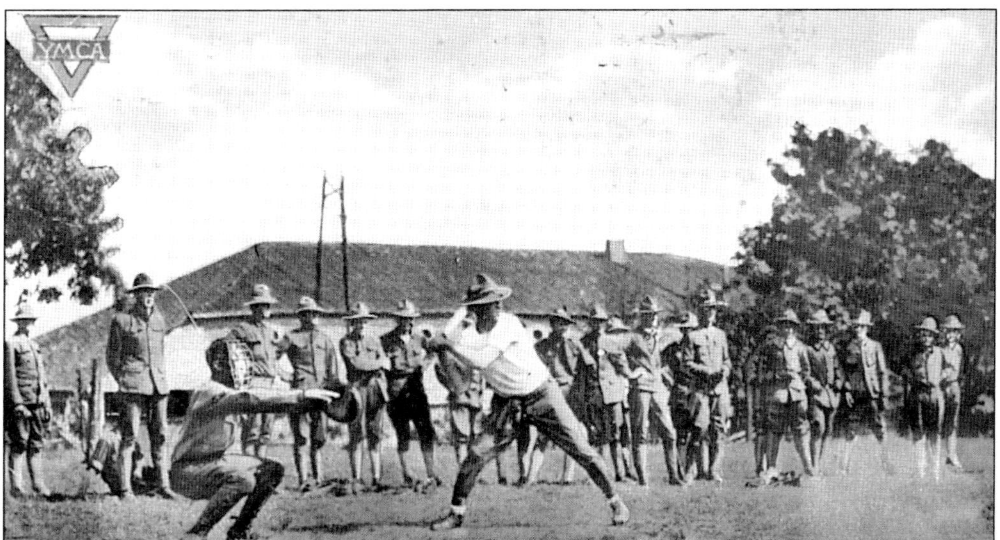

During World War I, many of America's finest played baseball for their respected services. Among these doughboys from Manchester were Bill Segbers, Johnny Kerins, and Francis Clary. Baseball was used to keep morale high throughout the war in Europe, as this 1918 postcard illustrates.

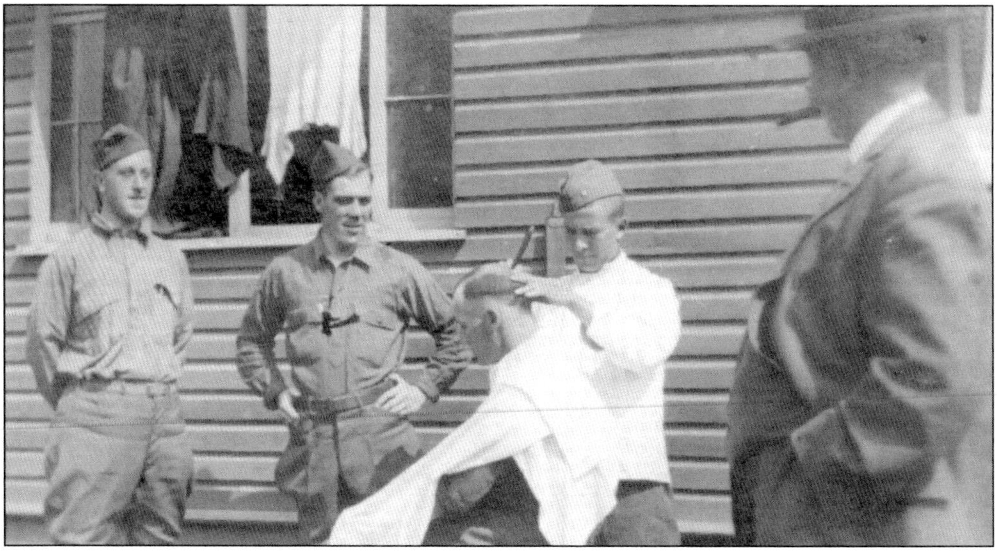

Bill Segbers, receiving his military haircut with his father, Joseph, looking over his shoulder during his stay at camp Devens, Massachusetts, volunteered for the army in 1918. Approximately 40 Manchester men served in the armed services during World War I. After receiving military training, Segbers was shipped to Europe where he spent time in Germany and France as a military policeman.

LETTER FROM WILLIAM SEGBERS

West St., Ayer, Mass.,
May 4, 1918.

The training we are getting here at Camp Devens will certainly be of much benefit to us. It will make better men of us all our lives.

I came here knowing that I would be placed under military discipline, but it has turned out to be not quite such a thing to be dreaded as I had supposed from my previous impressions. I have found that the officers in command over us are very helpful toward the men. They often take a personal interest in a soldier who is trying to do his best.

If a soldier makes a mistake or perform a duty wrong, his officers are fair and just in correcting him and in showing him how to do his work properly. I have been corrected in a very fair and understanding manner.

Of course, if a soldier deserves to be punished he should take his punishment like a man, but he comes to feel that it is just. This is putting the right spirit into me, and I think into the other boys.

We know we are here to learn how to be good soldiers and that is what we want to do. We cannot do this unless we all try, but it makes a lot of difference how our officers make us feel about it, and I have found that they do everything they can to help a fellow and to make him understand the necessity of discipline.

Kindest regards to all.

Sincerely,
Private William Segbers,
301st Military Police,
Camp Devens, Mass.

A letter written by Pvt. Bill Segbers of the 301st military police was published in the *Ontario County Times* on May 18, 1918. By serving his country during World War I, Segbers, in reference to his fellow soldiers, believed that "it would make us better men," and that military discipline and personal responsibility would hold merit throughout their lives.

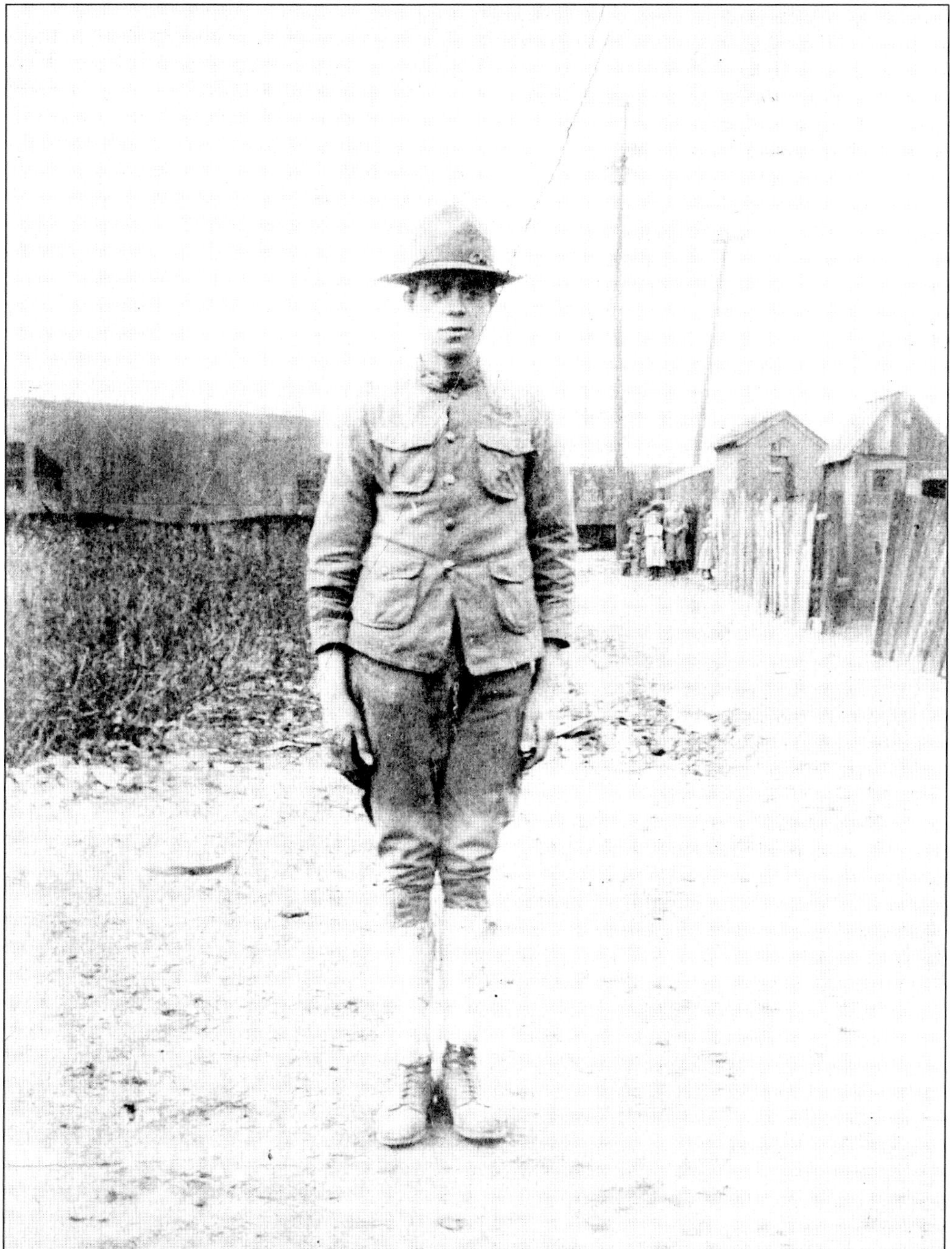

Joe Mottelo, wearing his 1918 Boy Scout uniform, stands in the Manchester freight yard. Boy Scout uniforms of this era looked similar to military uniforms, and many of the younger boys would emulate the activities of the doughboys of World War I.

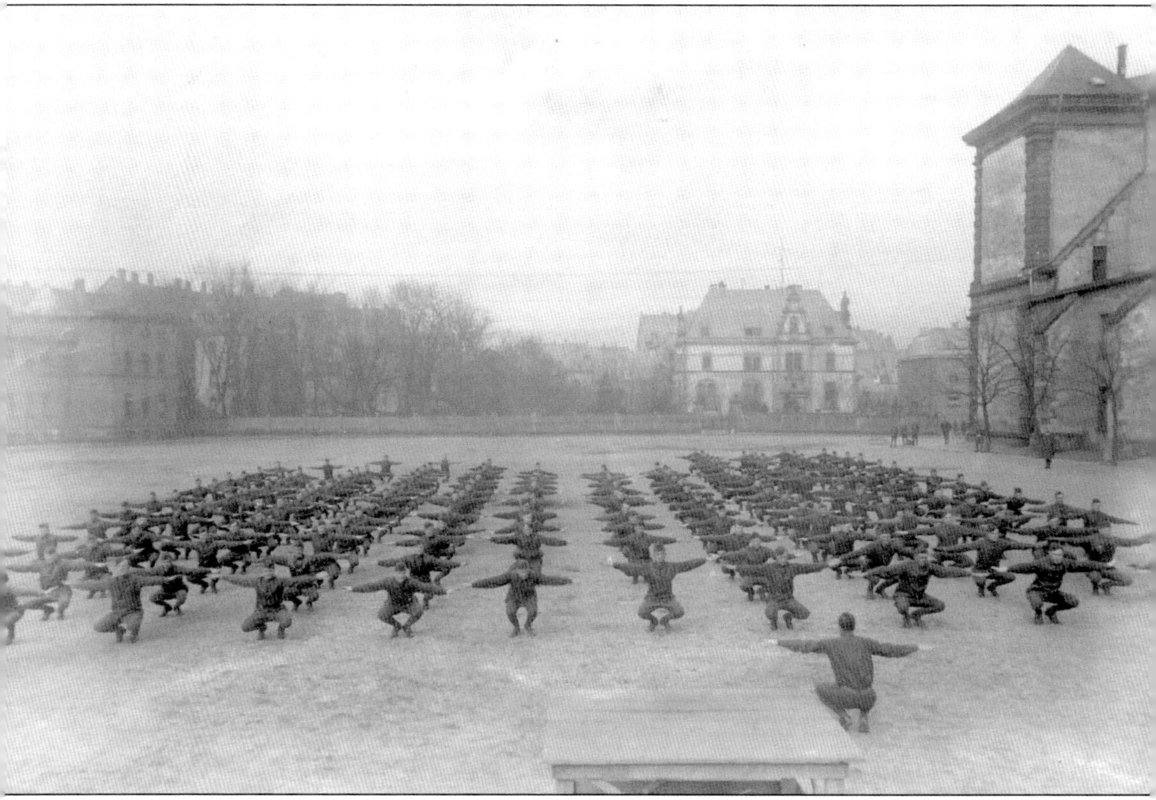

Members of the 301st division prepare for morning calisthenics in a German courtyard. This panoramic photograph was taken in the early morning hours one day in 1918. It was essential to keep the soldiers unified and in superior physical condition during World War I, as foot soldiers often had to overcome the physical demands of trench warfare.

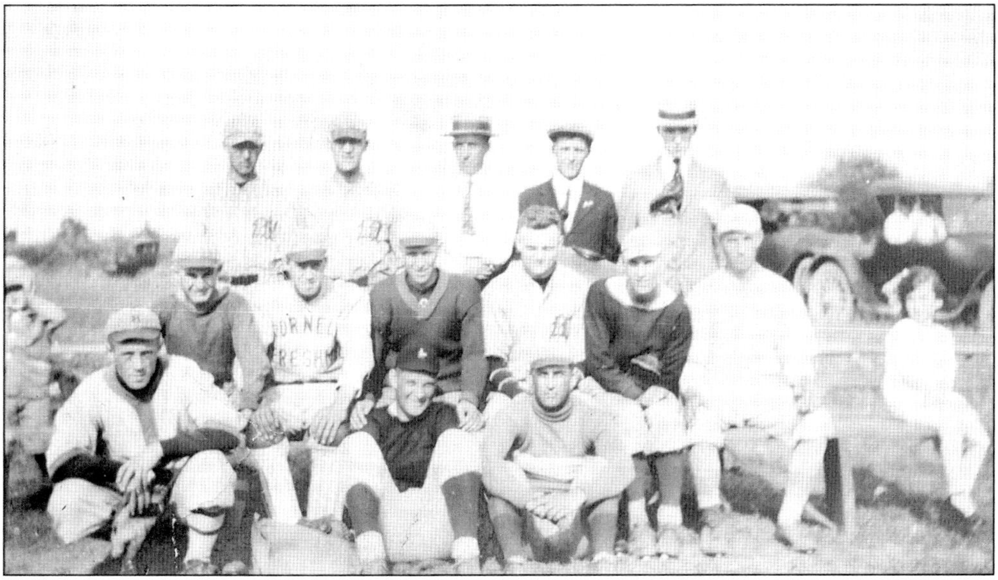

Shown here is the last picture of the 1918 Railroaders before several members joined the war effort in Europe. The hatless player is Lawrence McNally. McNally, the brakeman and hero of the July Fourth game that year, became a casualty of war in the yards of Manchester where he fell between two boxcars. His legs were severed and he eventually died of his injuries.

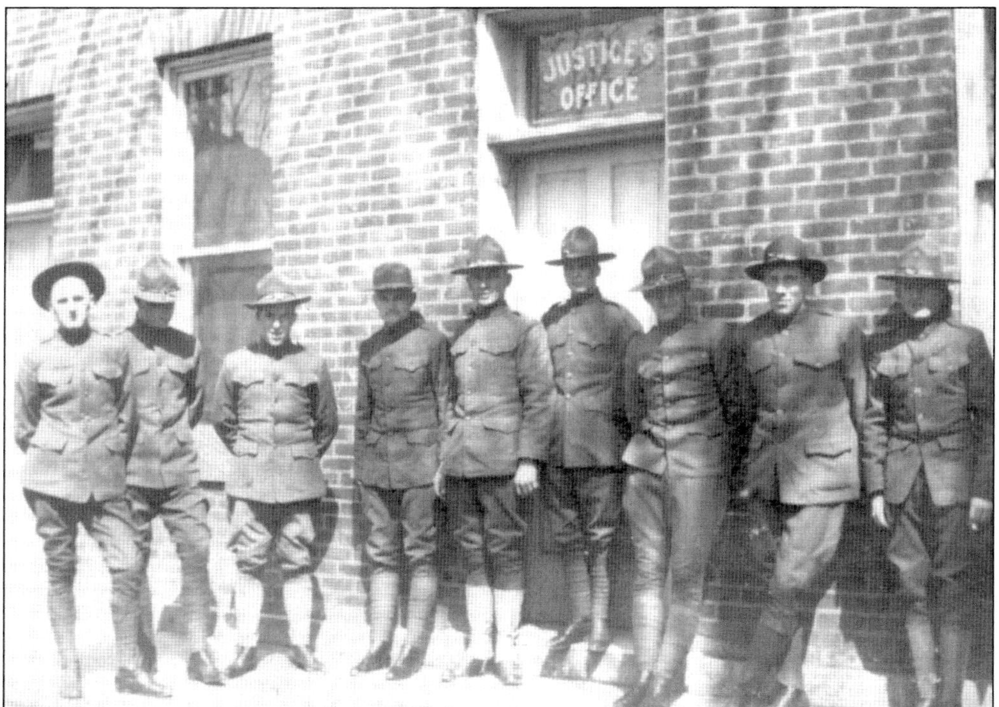

This photograph was taken in front of the old Manchester village hall on Armistice Day in 1919.

M. P.'s Cop Contest From Hospital Gang

Trier, May 24.—The 1st M. P. Bn., G. H. Q., yesterday afternoon defeated the team from Evac. Hosp. 19, by the score of 8 to 6, in a good game. The teams are in the Trier League and previous to yesterday's contest the Hospital eleven had a clean record and the M. P.'s had lost one game.

Score by innings:

		R.	H.	E.
Evac. Hosp. 19	....230 000 010—	6	15	3
M. P. Bn.	.........302 010 02x—	8	15	2

Widespread popularity of baseball allowed soldiers a brief liberation from the battlefields of war in Europe during World War I. Bill Segbers participated as pitcher for the M.P.s in France during the war.

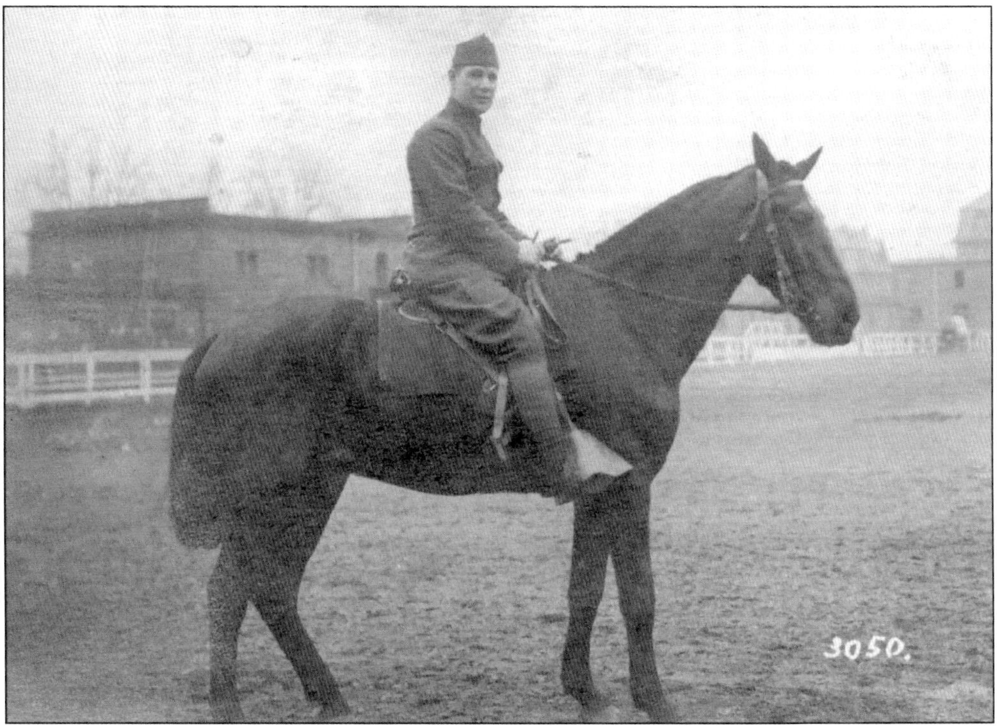

Segbers was a member of the mounted patrol in the 301st division in 1918. Military policemen encountered various confrontations with combat soldiers outside the battlefield during furlough periods. Segbers, a native of Queens, first encountered horses in Europe and mastered the form of riding in a short period of time.

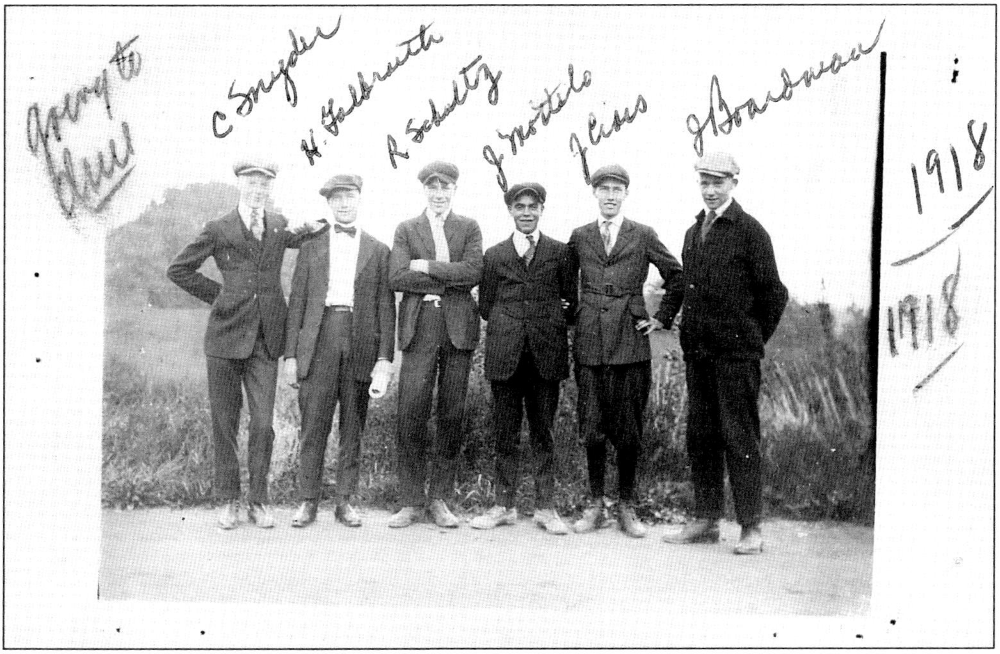

This group of teenage Boy Scouts would drill in front of Mink's homestead on Saturdays, like this one in 1918, preparing for the call of battle. The Boy Scouts, from left to right, are Charlie Snyder, Homer Gailbraith, Roger Shultz, Joe Mottelo, John Cross, and John Boardman.

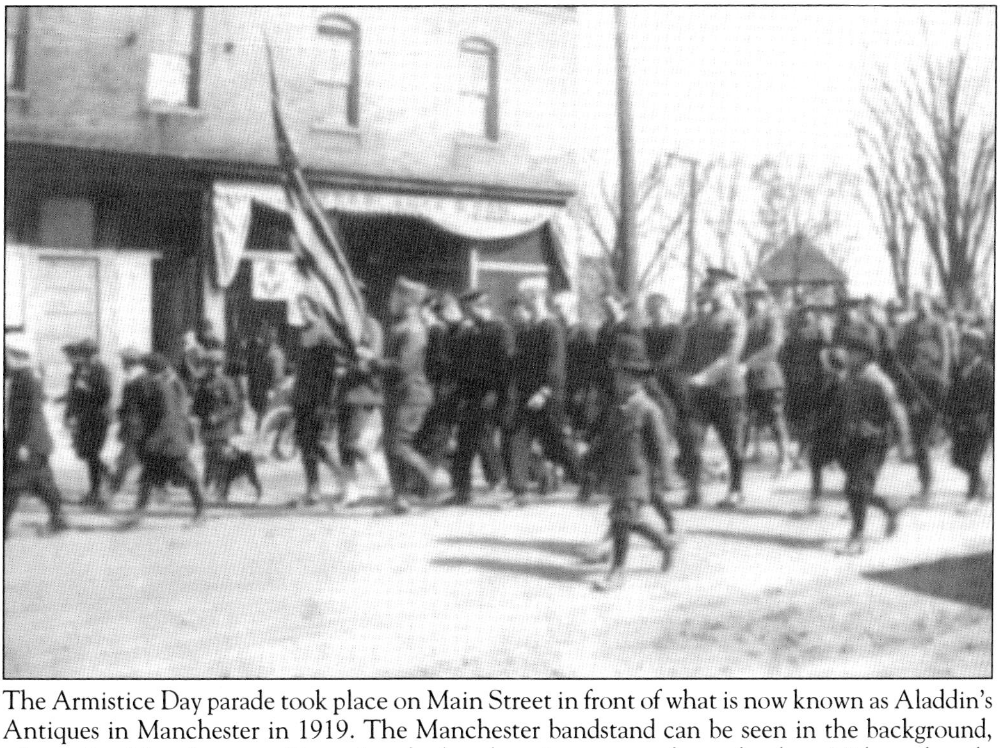

The Armistice Day parade took place on Main Street in front of what is now known as Aladdin's Antiques in Manchester in 1919. The Manchester bandstand can be seen in the background, where the Manchester military band played various songs from the late 19th and early 20th centuries.

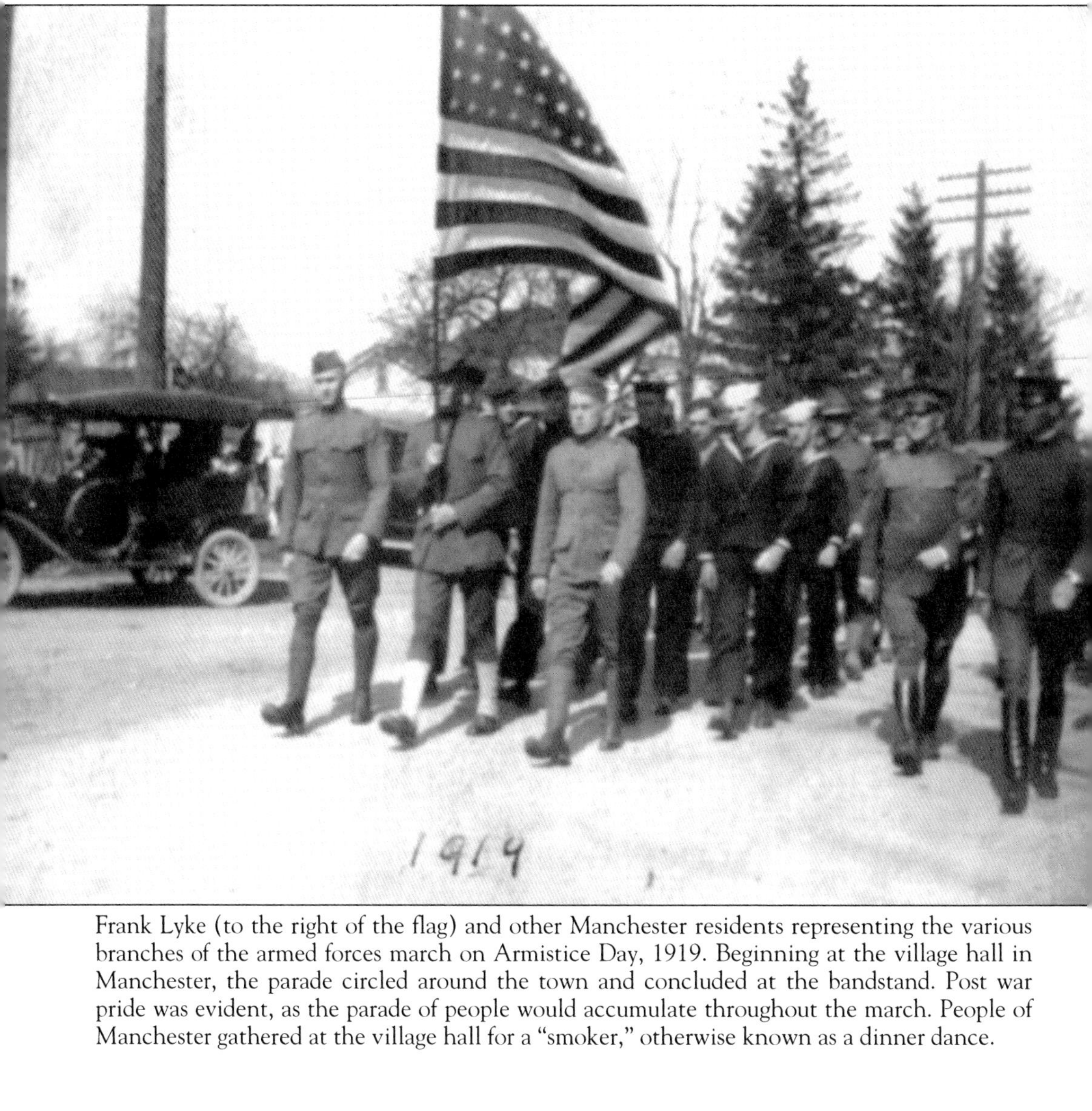

Frank Lyke (to the right of the flag) and other Manchester residents representing the various branches of the armed forces march on Armistice Day, 1919. Beginning at the village hall in Manchester, the parade circled around the town and concluded at the bandstand. Post war pride was evident, as the parade of people would accumulate throughout the march. People of Manchester gathered at the village hall for a "smoker," otherwise known as a dinner dance.

Eight

WOMEN OF THE RAILROAD

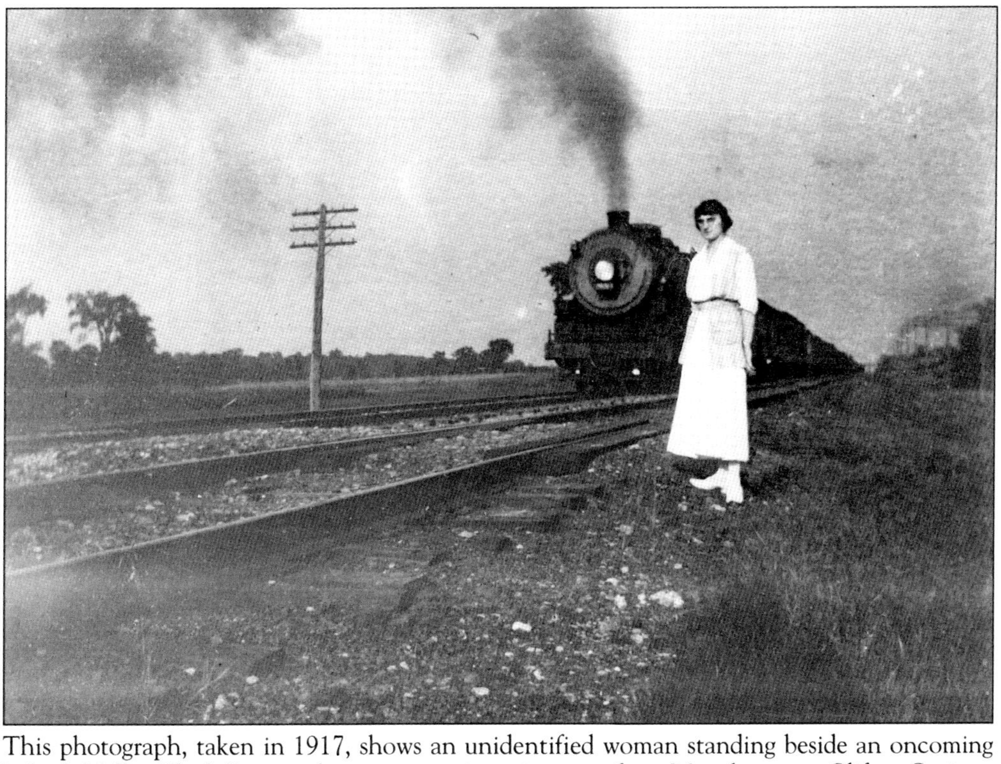

This photograph, taken in 1917, shows an unidentified woman standing beside an oncoming Lehigh Valley Black Diamond passenger train as it passes from Manchester to Clifton Springs. The Black Diamond was known as the "crack passenger" train of the LVRR. It was commonplace for people in Manchester to gather and watch the exquisite train pass through.

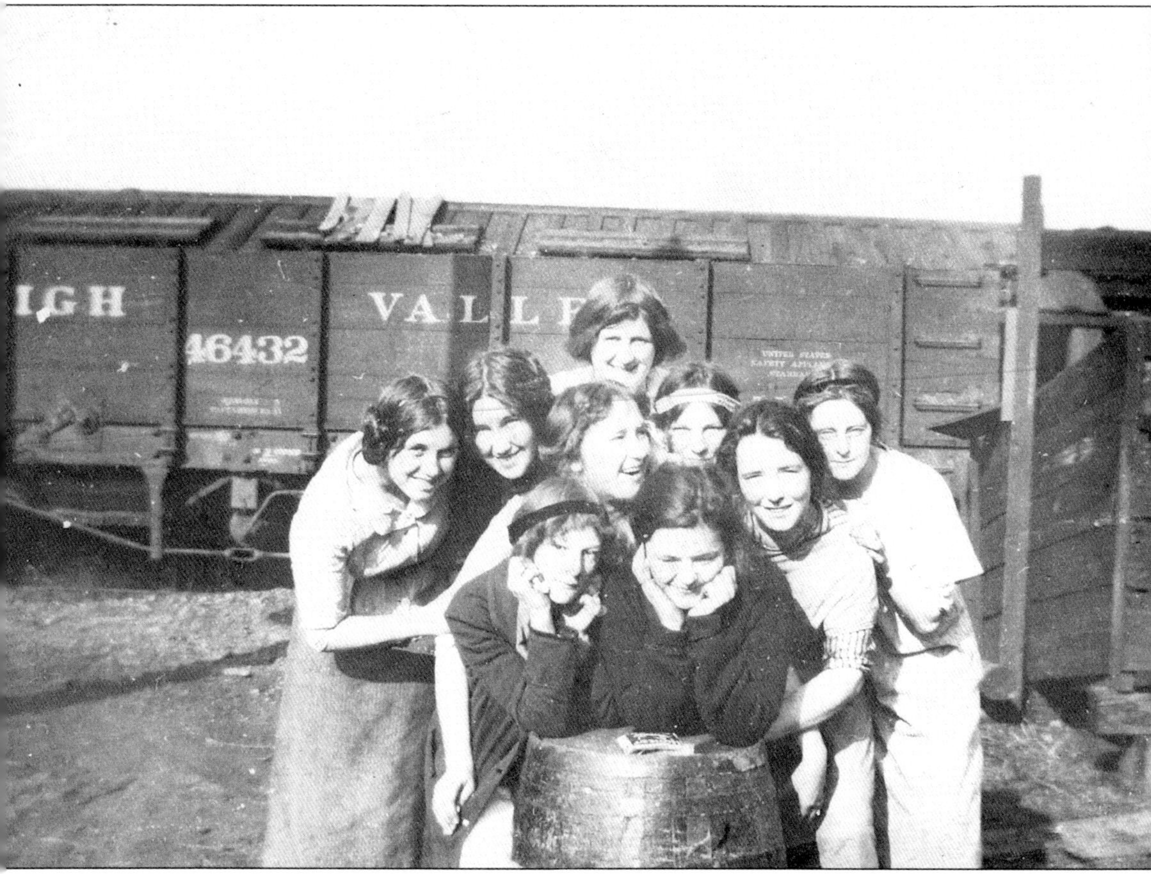

Adjacent to the coal pockets in Manchester, a group of Manchester women pose in front of a Lehigh Valley coal car in 1918. Many of these women were wives of State Street and Merrick Avenue railroad workers. Women had to be aware of the changing wind directions when hanging laundry because the air emitted from the transfer was hazardous and coal dust and ash accumulated around the area.

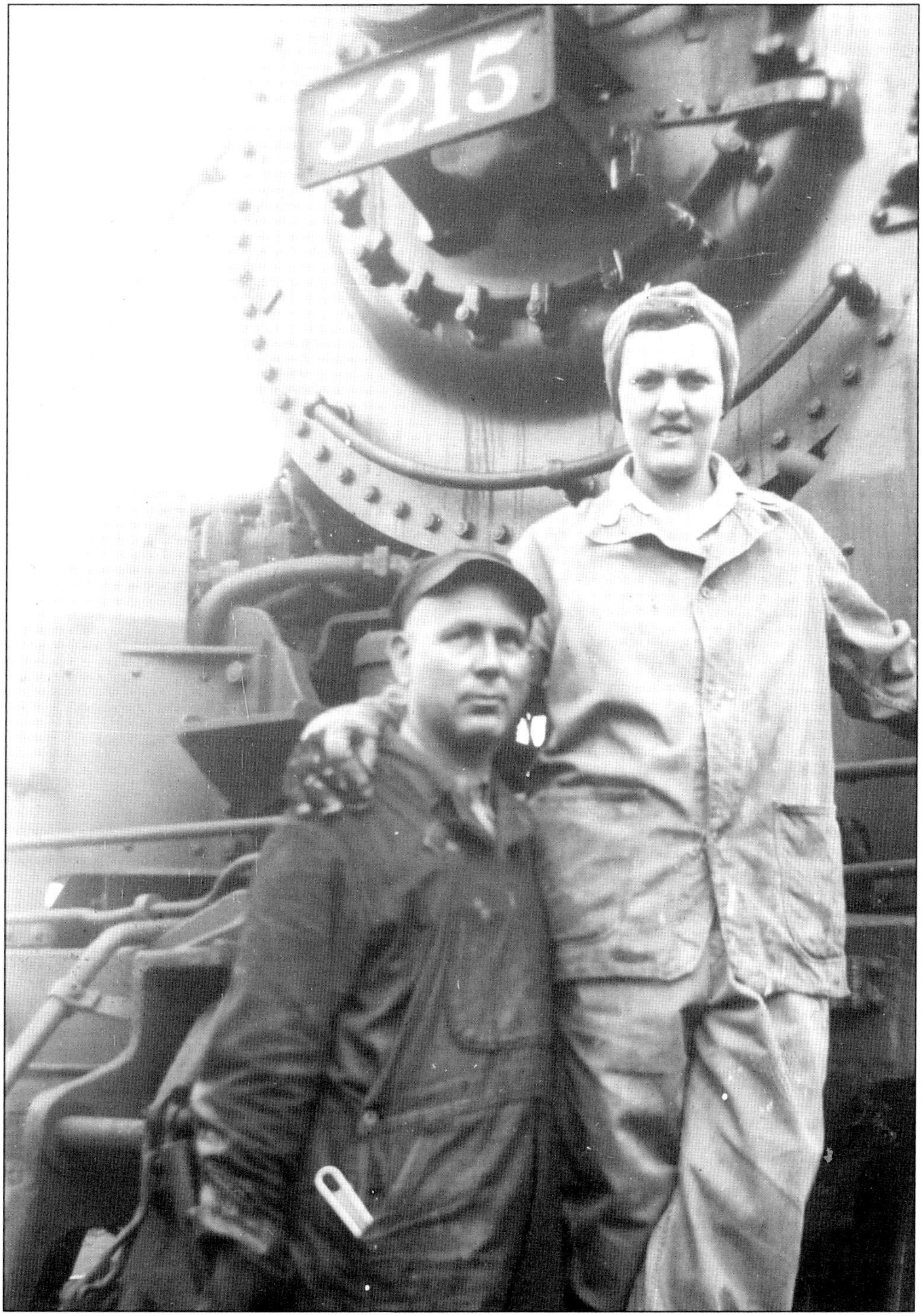

Maintenance mechanics Ike Vanderwall and Theresa Diazio pose in front of locomotive 5215 during World War II. Diazio helped Joe Mottelo in the warehouse during the 1940s and washed the large freight engines after trips. Hot steam was used to degrease the engines, and train inspectors from Buffalo would inspect the trains to ensure the engine was properly maintained.

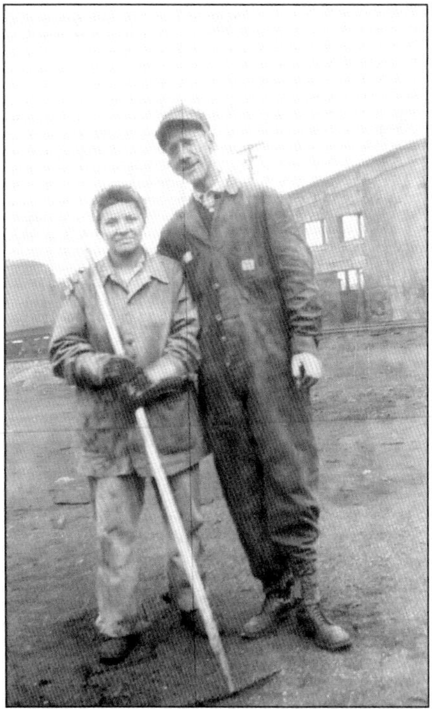

Florence Angeline, a Lehigh Valley worker, and Mike Corcoran, the foreman of the engine house, stand in front of the roundhouse in Manchester in 1943. Corcoran lived on State Street in Manchester. Angeline, a daughter of an Italian immigrant, was a niece of former Manchester Railroader Joe Mottelo.

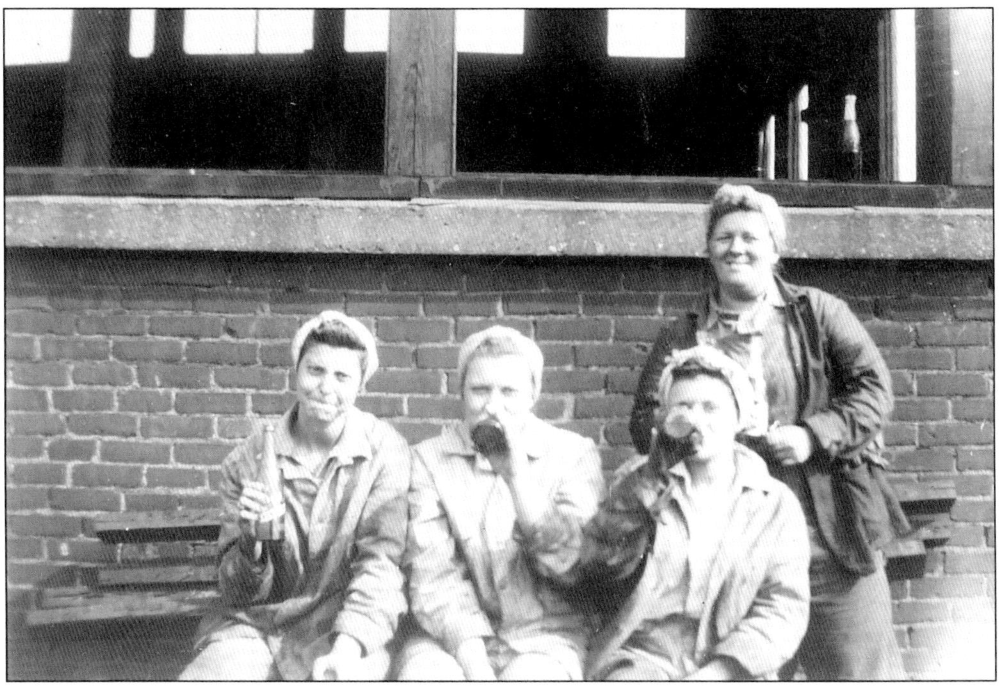

This photograph depicts women taking a soda break in 1943 at the roundhouse in Manchester. The women were required to wear turbans, safety shoes, overalls, and gloves to protect them from the dangers of the cleaning process. Women worked as early as 1914 on the railroad. Shown here, from left to right, are Anna DeDonto, Theresa Diazio, Louise Angeline, and Anna Haak.

Louise Angeline and Cora Griffin are seen here standing in front of a locomotive in 1943. During World War II, women held clerical and maintenance positions on the LVRR, temporarily replacing the men in service.

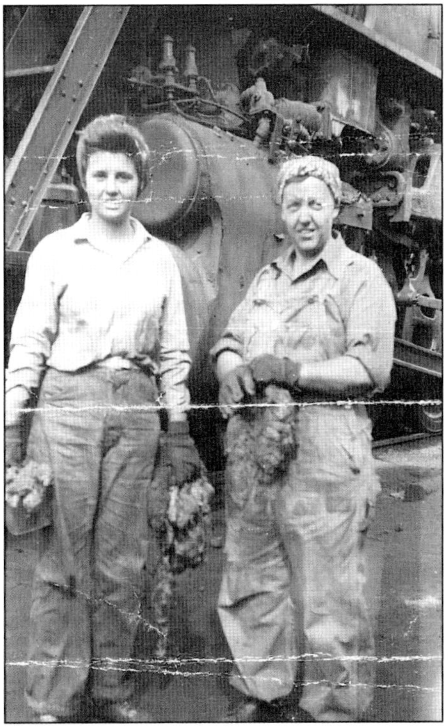

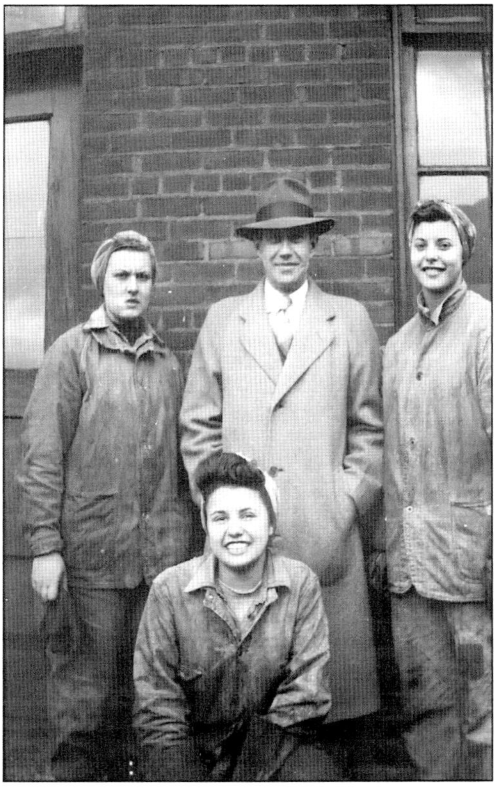

Theresa Diazio, Mr. Barth (master mechanic), Anna DeDonto, and Louise Angeline pose in front of the engine house in 1943. While a high school student at Manchester, Angeline spent her early evenings and summers working on the railroad. Angeline is currently the chairman precinct judge for the Republican Party in the county of Dallas, Texas. Sen. "Ike" Harris of Texas issued Angeline credit for providing respite care for the mentally disabled in 1988.

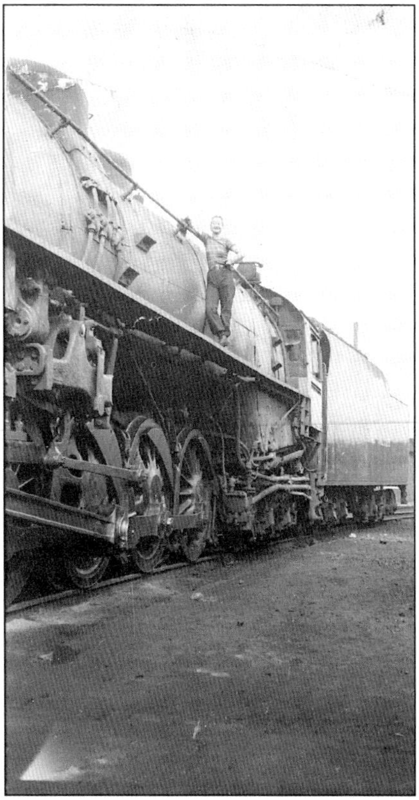

Rita Walters from Shortsville works on a T class 4-8-4 Wyoming, the workhorse of the LVRR. Its principle job was to handle the heavy freight traffic during World War II. Women were also known to work on the transfer, which was considered to be a job exclusive to men.

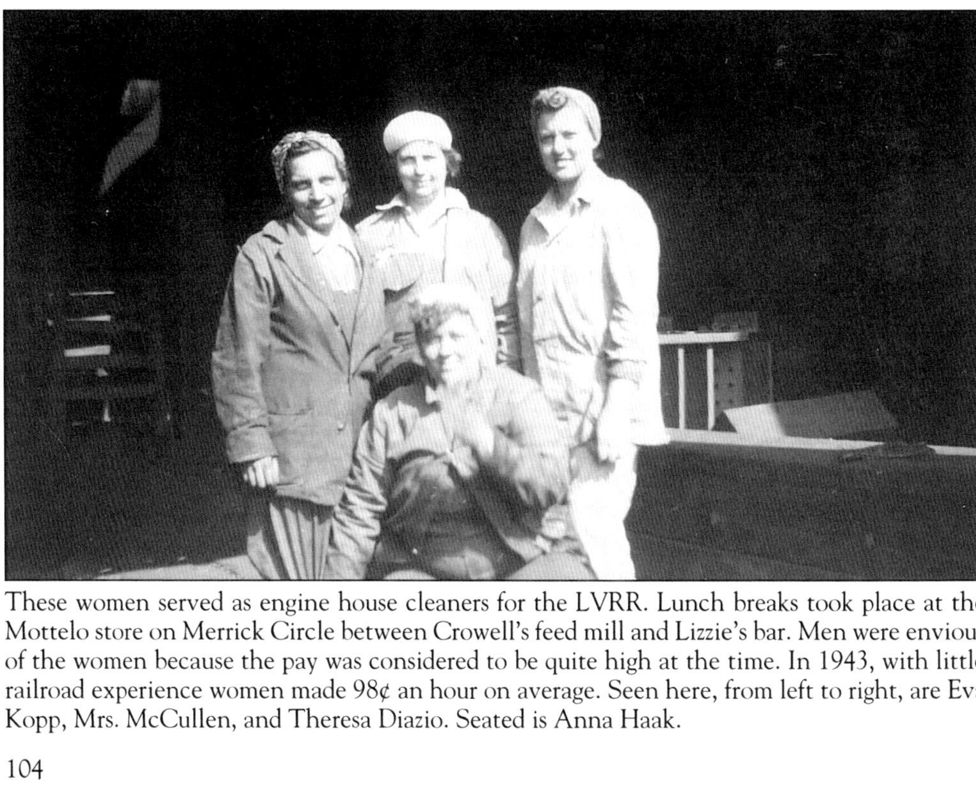

These women served as engine house cleaners for the LVRR. Lunch breaks took place at the Mottelo store on Merrick Circle between Crowell's feed mill and Lizzie's bar. Men were envious of the women because the pay was considered to be quite high at the time. In 1943, with little railroad experience women made 98¢ an hour on average. Seen here, from left to right, are Eva Kopp, Mrs. McCullen, and Theresa Diazio. Seated is Anna Haak.

Nine

THE PEOPLE

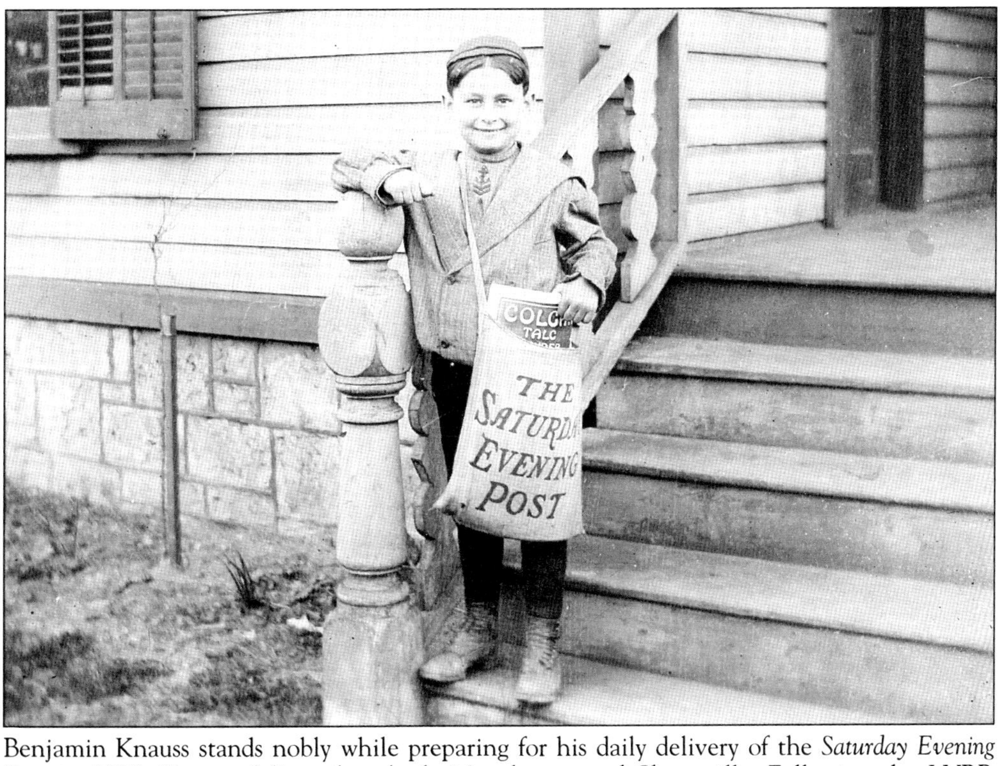

Benjamin Knauss stands nobly while preparing for his daily delivery of the *Saturday Evening Post* in 1905. Knauss delivered to both Manchester and Shortsville. Following the LVRR arrival in 1892, Manchester had only 365 residents. By 1915, following the transfer expansion, Manchester's population exceeded 1,000 people. Nicknamed "transfer town," many immigrant families migrated from Pennsylvania and New York City to seek work in Manchester.

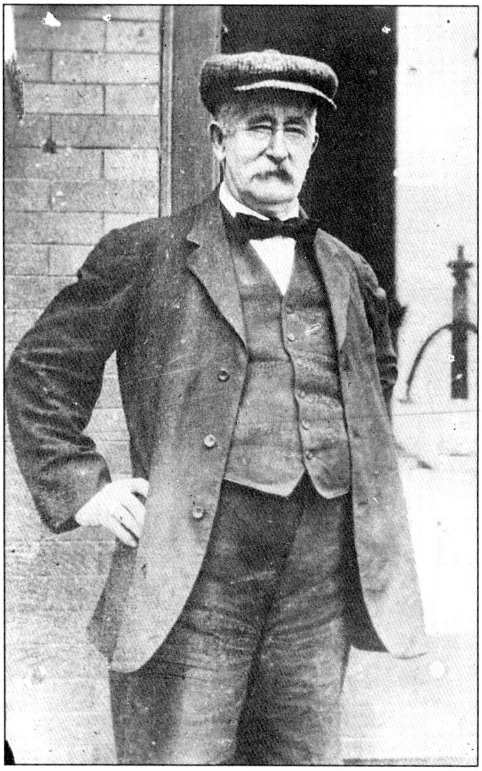

Carlos Pierce Osgood is shown here posing outside the Red Jacket Telephone and Telegraph Company in 1929. Over a quarter century prior to this photograph, Osgood organized and incorporated the Red Jacket Telephone Company, the first independent telephone company in New York.

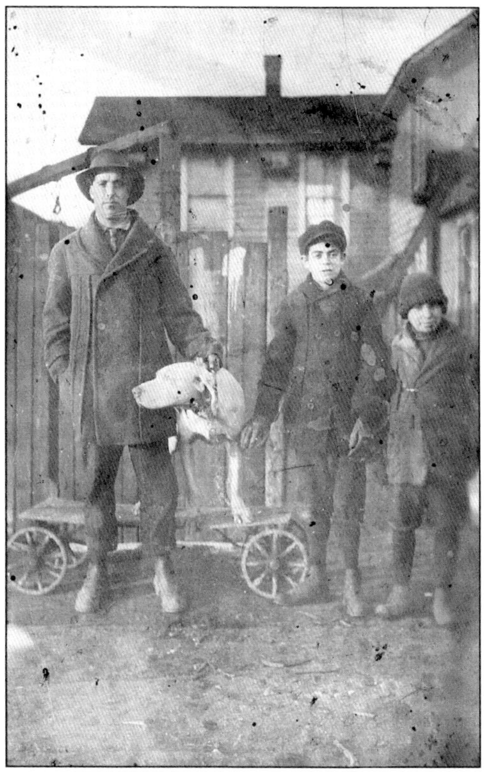

Papa, Joseph, and Preasa Mottelo stand before their home in 1910 near the present-day Steakout restaurant. The Italian immigrants settled in Manchester looking for work on Lehigh Valley Railroad.

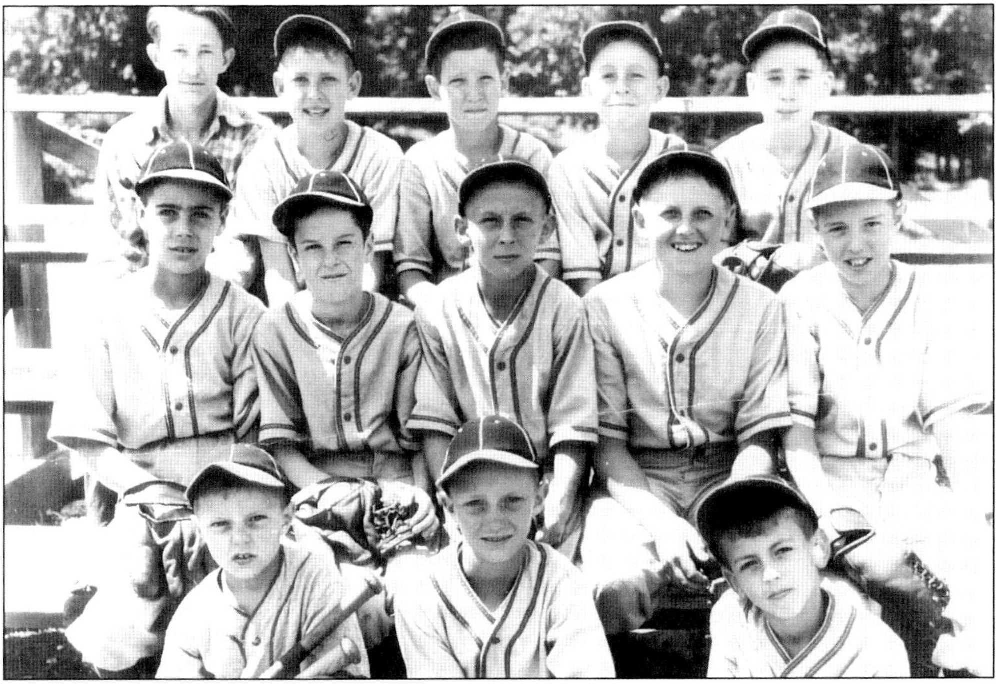

Seen here are the Shortsville "Champs" of 1947. The young boys shown in the picture organized the "Champs" in 1946. Their ages ranged from 9 to 11 years old. Little League baseball had not entered the area and did not appear in Ontario County until many years later. Two of the players, Dan O'Donnell and Whitey Williams, signed professional baseball contracts when they completed high school. From left to right are as follows: (front row) Dick Shaeffer (batboy), Richard "Whitey" Williams, and Jim Farrell; (middle row) Elwin Wasson, Mickey Bolan, Bob Vanherpe, Francis "Cap" Walker, and Russ Williams; (back row) Melvin "Pee Wee" Skyner (coach), Dan O'Donnell, Carl Romeiser, Herb Sadler, and Neil Hogan.

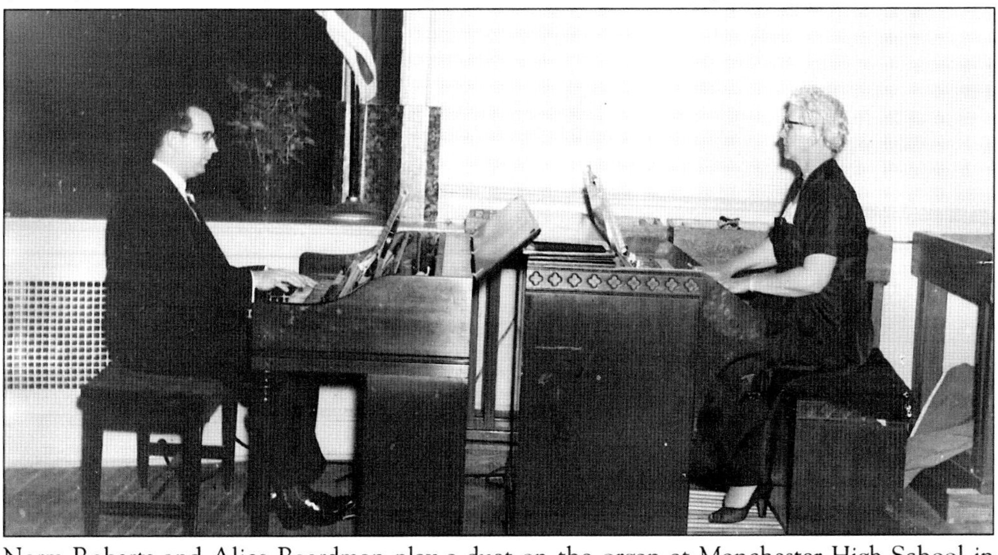

Norm Roberts and Alice Boardman play a duet on the organ at Manchester High School in 1954. Alice was St. Dominic's organist for many decades and also performed for the silent movies at the theater in Manchester.

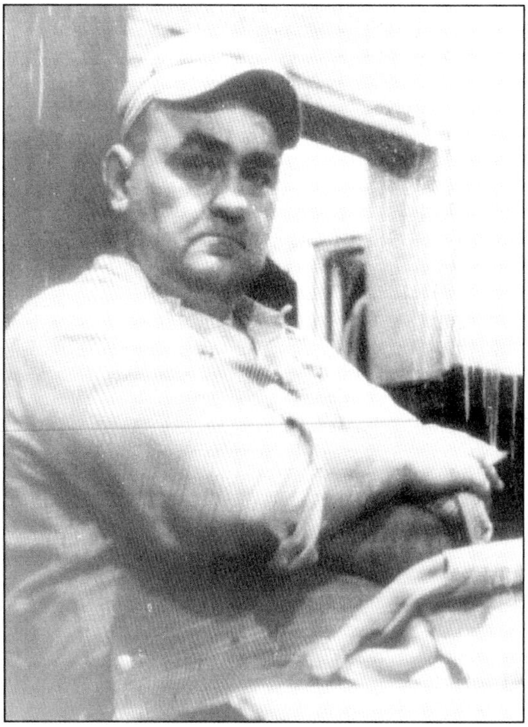

Longtime Lehigh Valley engineer Bill Stambach, a Shortsville native, served the LVRR for over 40 years. Stambach's father, Stanly, also worked as an engineer for the LVRR. Stambach married Minnie Lautz, and they had seven children. Stambach's great grandson Bill Bayno is the current basketball coach at University of Nevada, Las Vegas.

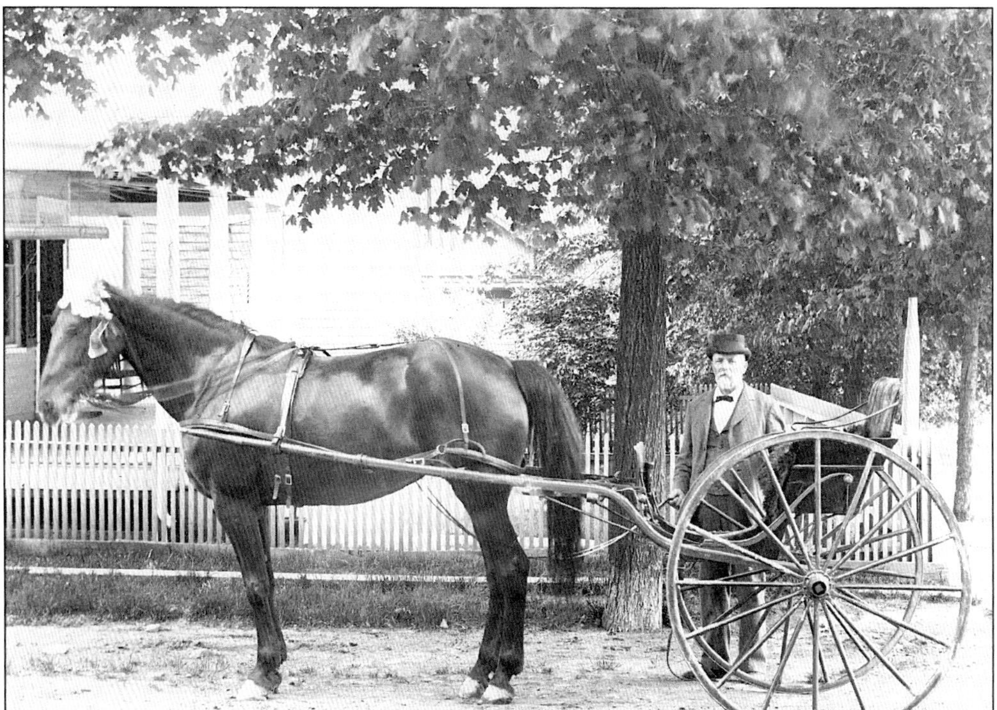

John Eddinger, a wounded Union soldier in the Civil War, carried fuel oil to people by horse for many years. Eddinger came to Manchester from Pennsylvania, and his legacy accounted for three generations of engineers and conductors on the LVRR.

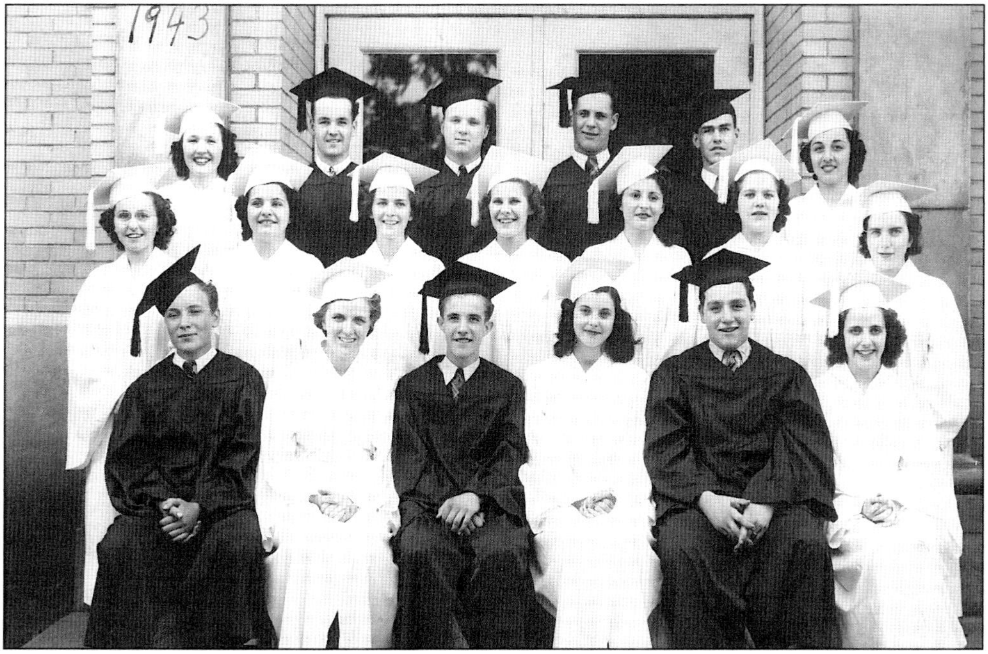

These 1943 Manchester students are, from left to right, as follows: (bottom row) Fred Record, Clara Tuttle, Bill Ross, Anna DeDanto, Casto Zona, and Althea Deyo; (middle row) Althea Wooden, Florence Angeline, Ruth Fish, Ann Evancho, Jean Sementelli, Ruth Dubler, and Mary Jane Rosa; (top row) Monica Hill, Curt Shultz, Clyde Henry, Bill Segbers Jr., Howard Vienna, and Antoinette Diazio.

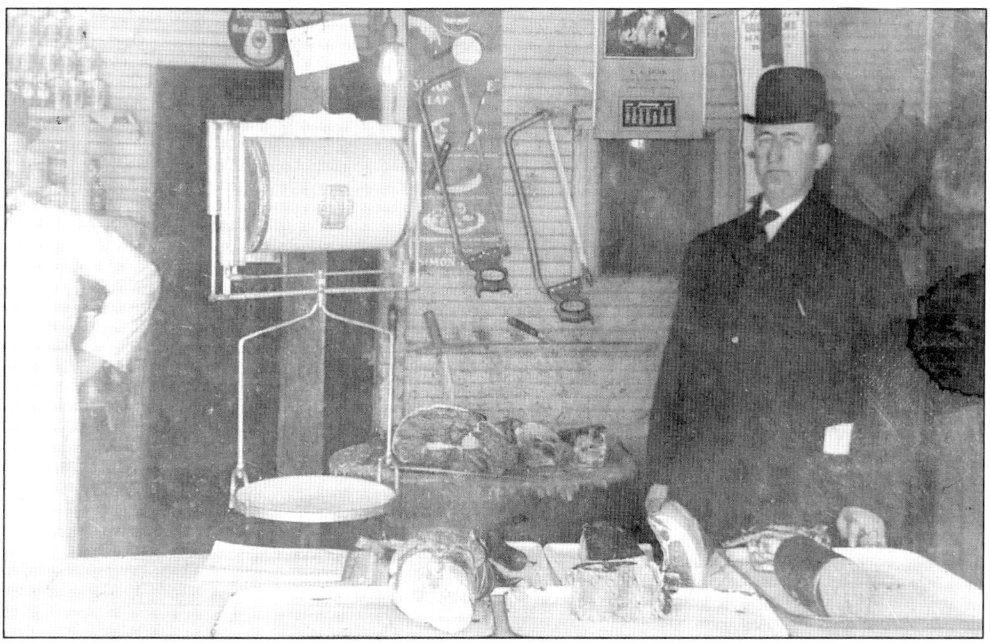

Proechel Meat Market in Manchester is currently Marie's Restaurant. Proechel's son George "Dutch" Proechel was the mascot for the Railroaders in the 1920s and went on to be a county player in the 1930s.

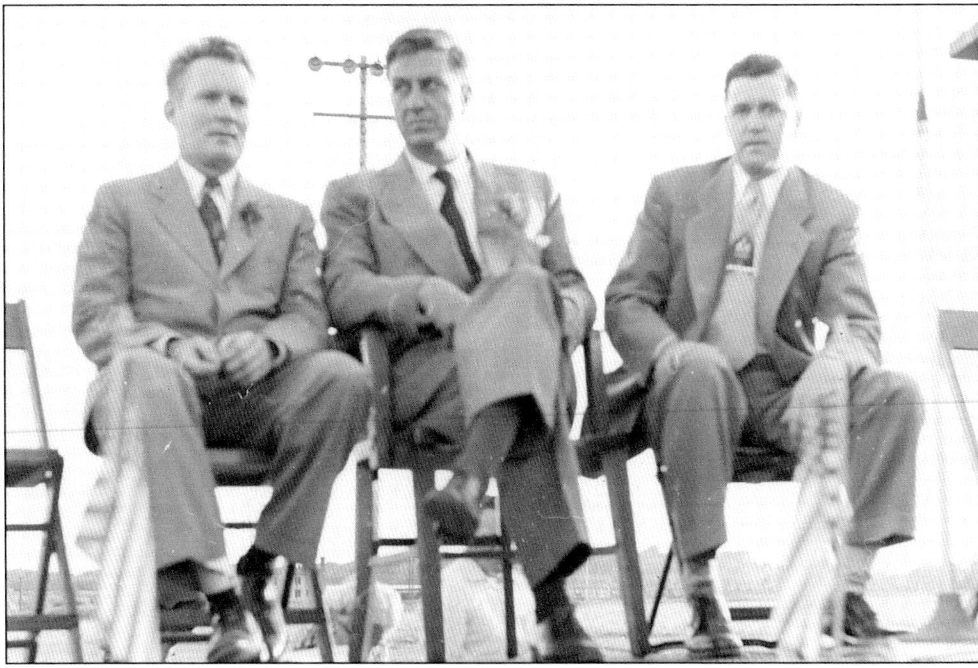

At King's Diamond in Manchester, Mayor Reggie Lush and Francis Boardman converse with Franklin Delano Roosevelt Jr. (middle) during a 1950s election year. Despite the small town size of Manchester, their support was influential as a union railroad town with strong democratic ties. Roosevelt's visit coincided with the completion of exit 43 for the New York State Thruway.

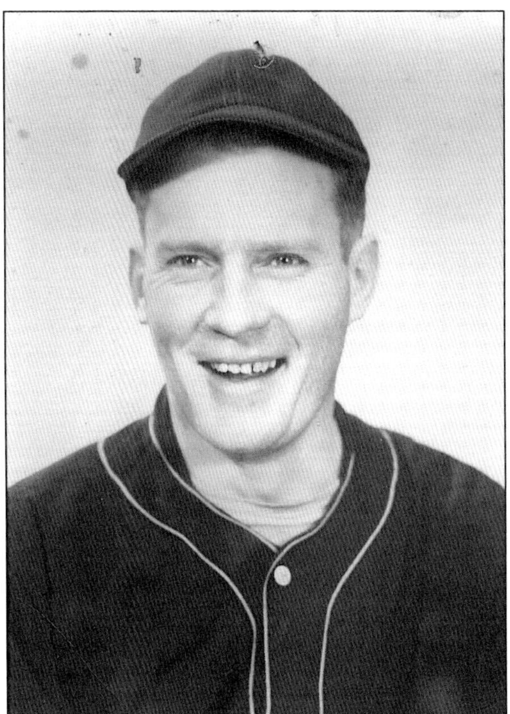

Reggie Lush is shown here in his 1949 Manchester Fireman fast-pitch softball uniform. That year, Manchester won the state Industrial League championship. During the season they played and defeated the Joe Louis Punchers of Detroit, the Chicago Hot Top Ten, the Oklahoma City Cowboys, and the Gruman Long Island Yankees. Reggie showed great spirit by playing catcher with a wooden leg, which was amputated after a train accident while working in the freight yards.

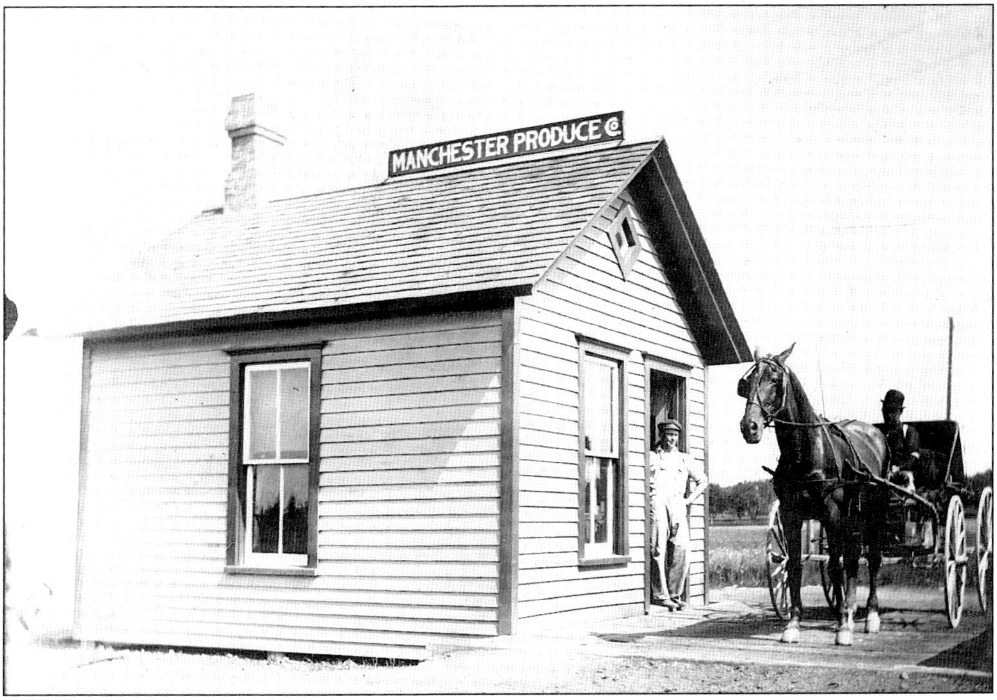

Manchester's produce building is shown here in the late 1890s. Manchester is one of the largest cabbage producing areas in the United States. Farmers maintained their produce by keeping perishables in an icehouse. The ice was harvested from the outlet in the winter and many families maintained produce cellars in the banks of the Canandaigua outlet.

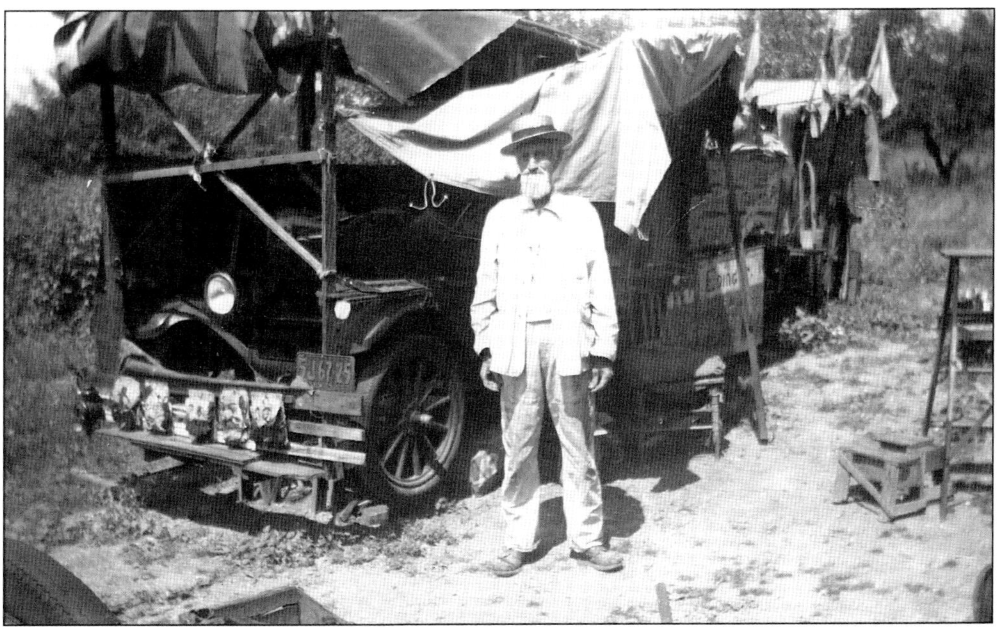

William "Horse" Eddinger I was born on February 4, 1867. As shown here in 1938, he hitched a wagon wheel trailer behind a 1926 model T Ford and invented a makeshift summer home. Eddinger was a conductor for the LVRR in Manchester.

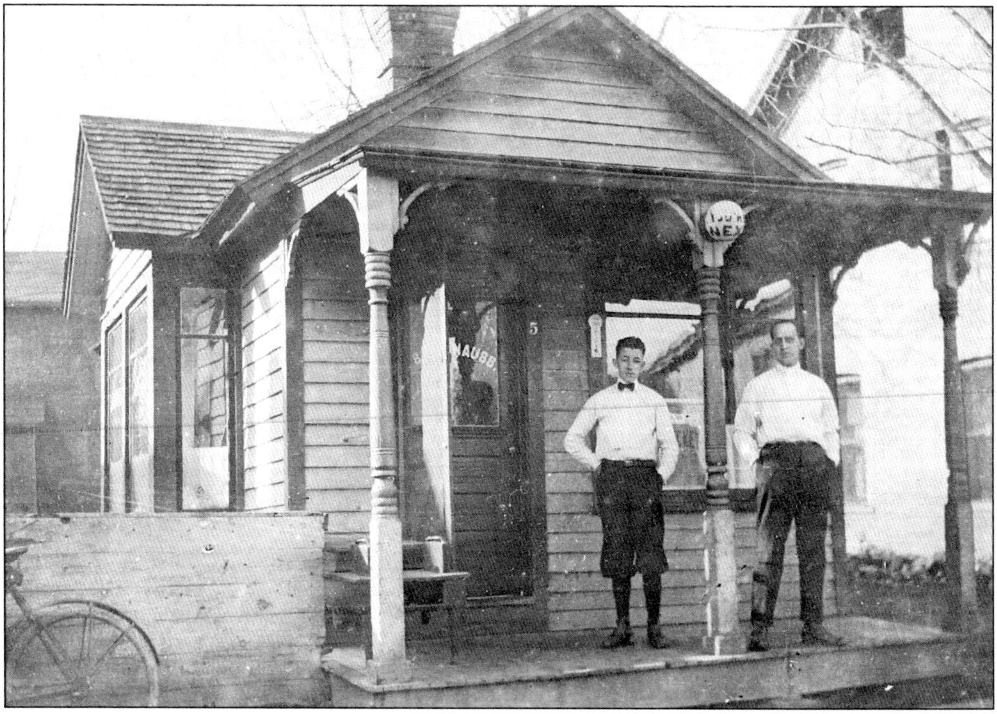

This 1910 photograph is of the former Knauss barbershop located on Water Street, Shortsville. Sidney Knauss (right), a Canadian, later opened a barbershop in Manchester. Many people from surrounding towns and cities would come to Knauss's barbershop by train for a special cut and shave.

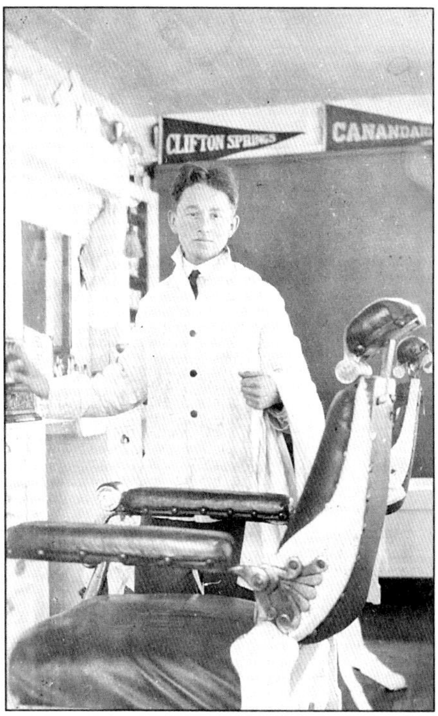

Ben Knauss, shown here in 1916, pauses in the barbershop. Ben apprenticed briefly in the barbershop before deciding to work for the LVRR in Manchester. Ben's mother, Effie, played piano for the picture shows, and her father owned the famous blacksmith shop in Shortsville.

Two Manchester boys fish in the Erie Canal near Palmyra, New York, in the 1920s. Irish immigrants dug the canal in the 1840s in order to transport merchandise and other various materials. The canal was a popular site for swimming, fishing, and ice skating for many area people.

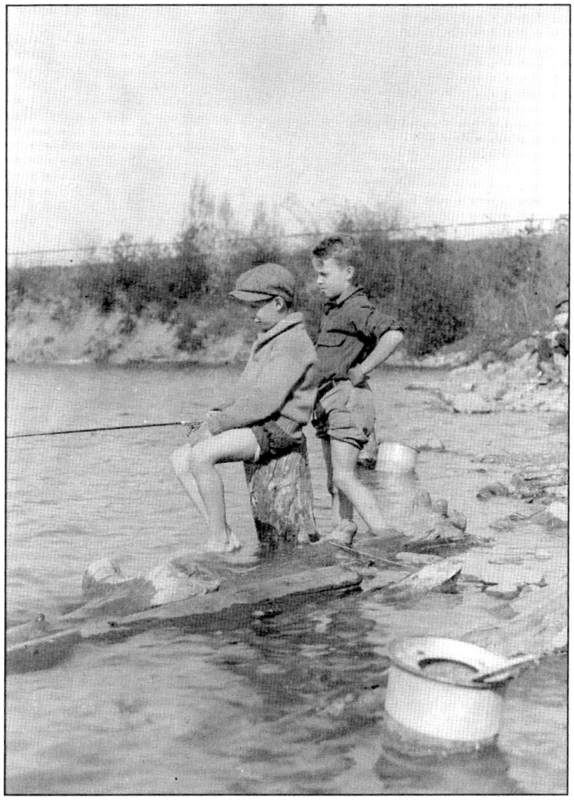

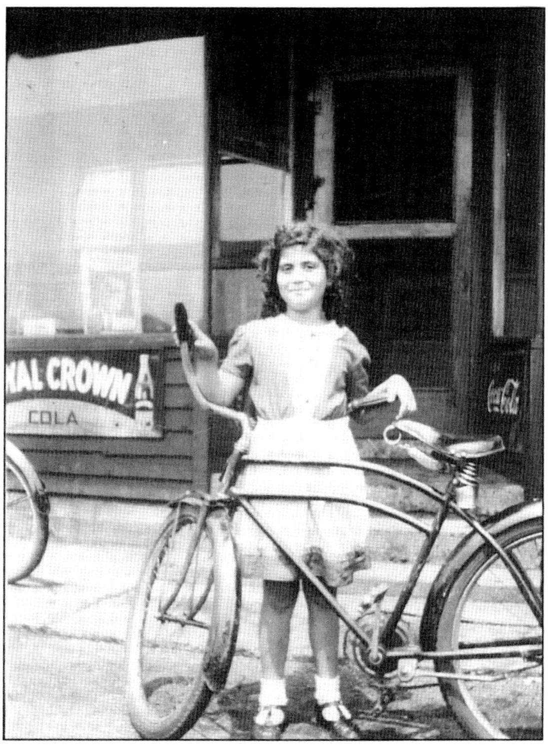

Lucy Angeline stands before the Mottelo's store in 1947. The youngest daughter of an Italian immigrant, Angeline, like many children of Manchester, would flock to the Mottelo's store to buy candy, taffy, and baseball cards. Ice cream was a favorite in the summer days.

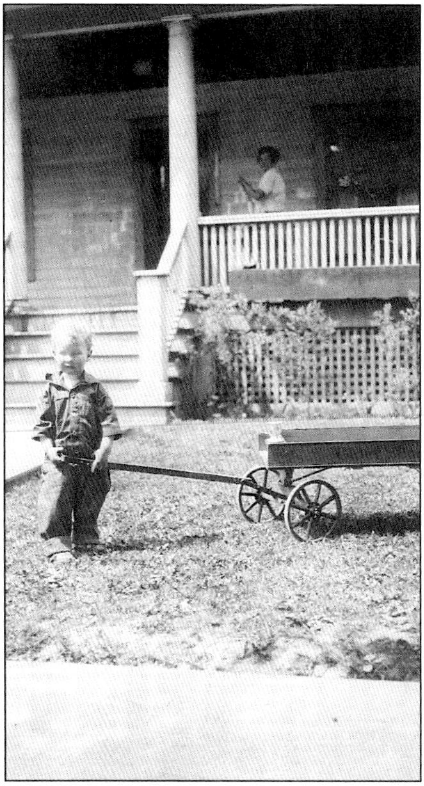

Little Jimmy Segbers holds his fortune—the great Chief Scout Wagon in 1923. Segbers used the wagon to peddle his newspaper route and later became one of Manchester's first high school kids to own a car. On his newspaper route, he would drive the car while his sisters Jess and Honey Mae and brother Bill Jr. would deliver the papers to Manchester residents.

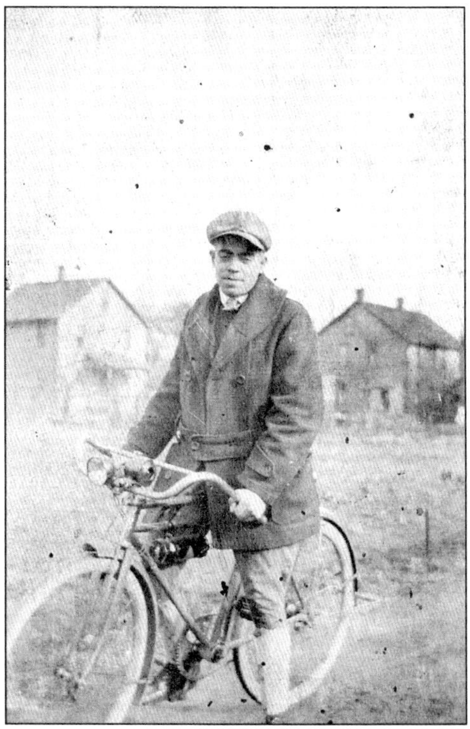

Born in 1903 as the only son of Italian Immigrants, Joseph Mottelo was raised on Merrick Circle near the LVRR house. Befriended by many railroad workers, Mottelo was offered a job on the LVRR and was eventually asked to run the railroad store. In 1918, he became the youngest member of the Railroaders at age 15. A year later, Ed Quigley left for Geneva, and Mottelo became Manchester's youngest champeen stretcher in team history.

Johnny Boardman is shown here collecting money for newspapers on his State Street route in Manchester in 1918. Jimmy Segbers eventually took over Boardman's route on State Street. Note the customary knickers of the era.

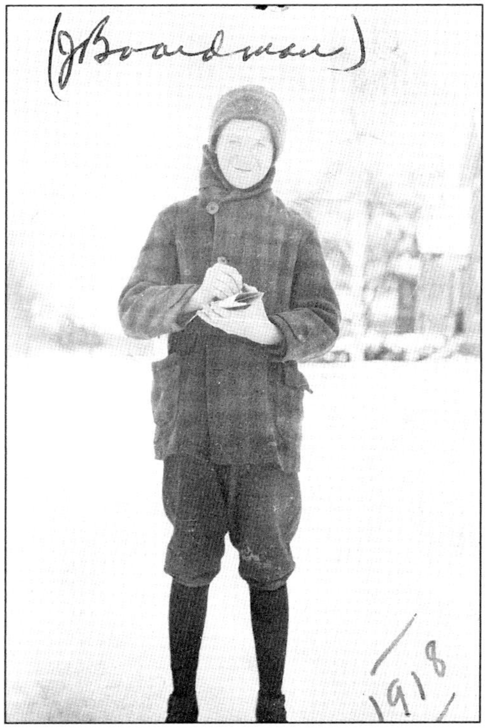

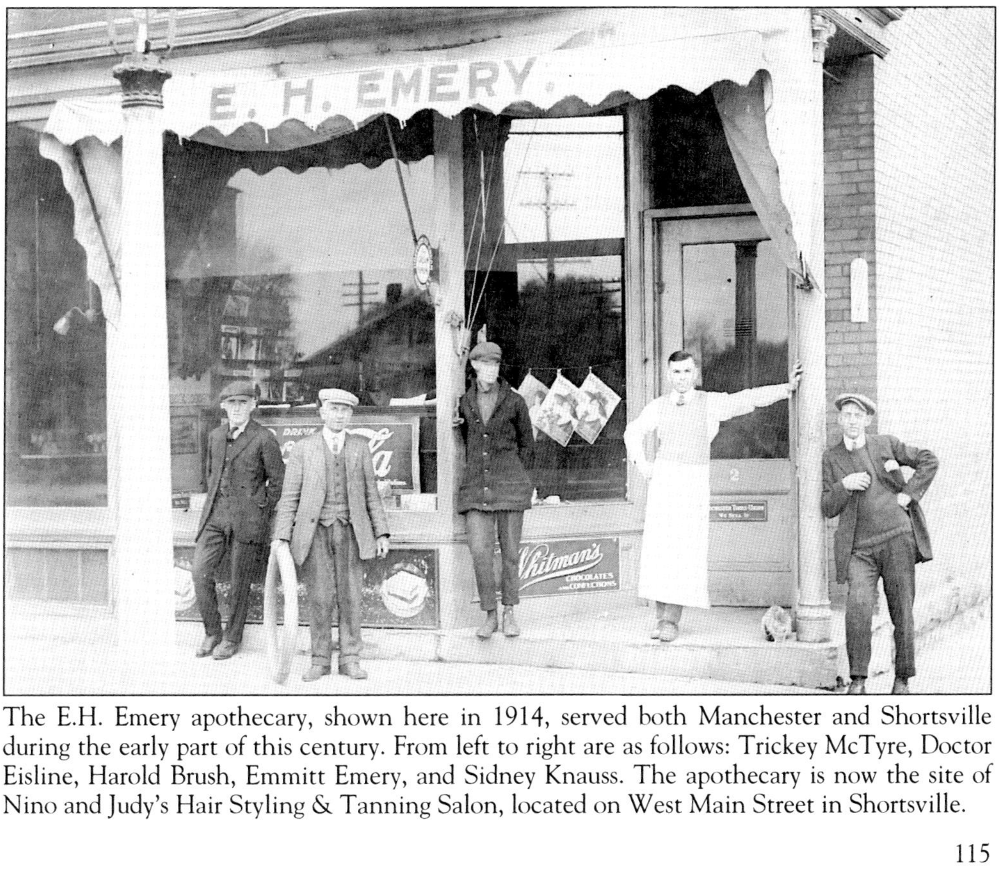

The E.H. Emery apothecary, shown here in 1914, served both Manchester and Shortsville during the early part of this century. From left to right are as follows: Trickey McTyre, Doctor Eisline, Harold Brush, Emmitt Emery, and Sidney Knauss. The apothecary is now the site of Nino and Judy's Hair Styling & Tanning Salon, located on West Main Street in Shortsville.

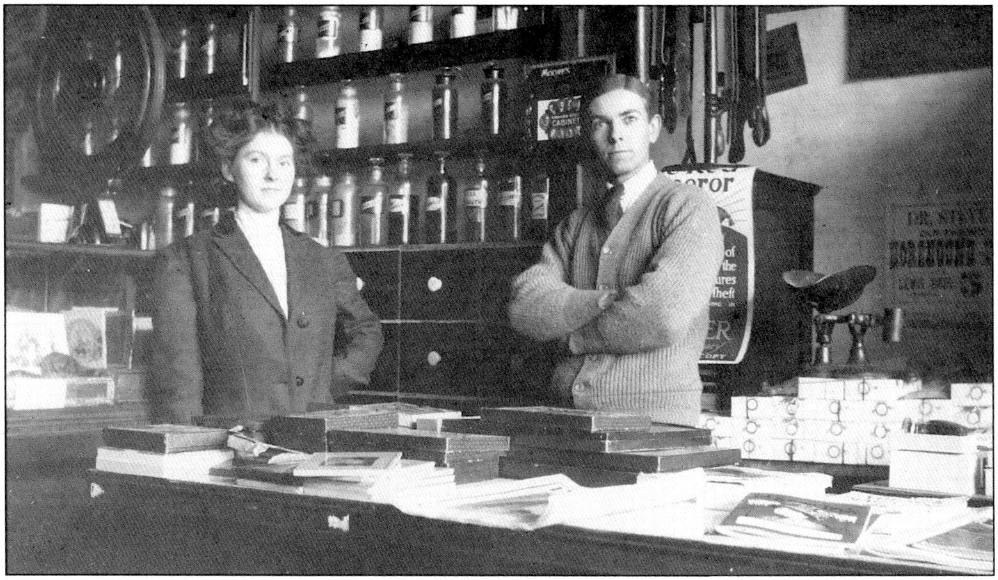

E.H. Emery and an unidentified co-worker pause inside the Emery store in 1909. The Emery store had a soda fountain along the back wall and a separate room with three tables. Emery, a quiet gentlemen who was known for wearing a white shirt and bow tie to work, produced the ever popular cherry soda, a favorite of many locals. He left the store in the early 1960s.

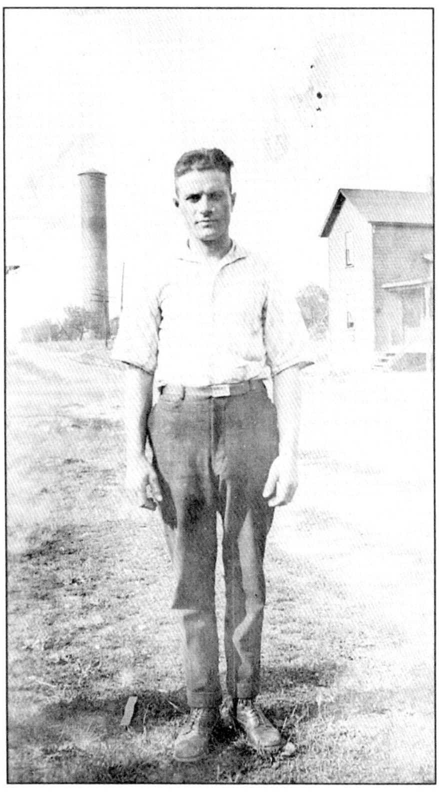

An immigrant from Ascoli, Italy, a mountain village in northern Italy on the coast of the Adriatic Sea, Frank Angeline came to Manchester seeking employment on the railroad. This picture of Angeline was taken in front of the old water tower on Merrick Avenue in Manchester.

Angeline and his wife, Caroline Mottelo Angeline, stand in front of the Mottelo's grocery store near the LVRR freight yard in 1943. Note the train in the distance. Frank Angeline became an American citizen after joining the army during World War I.

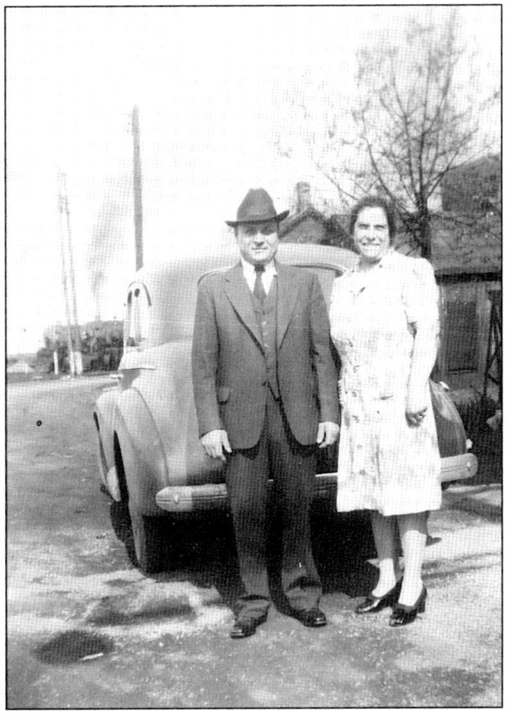

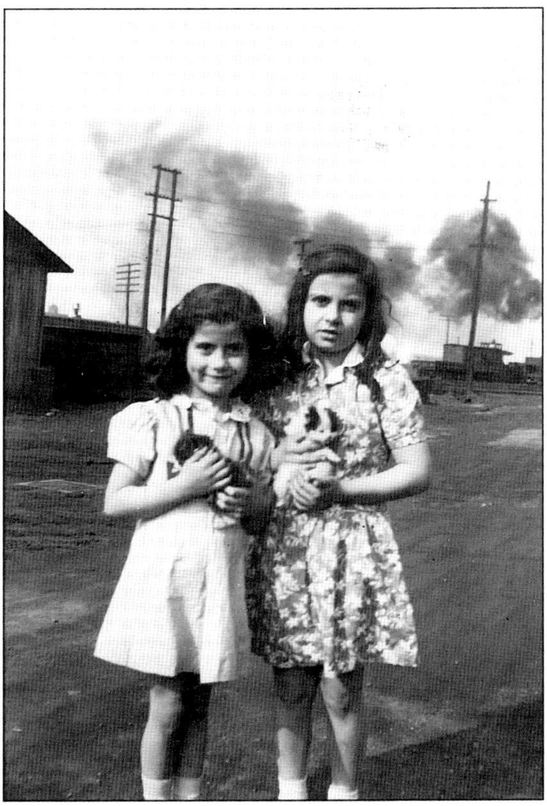

The Angeline sisters Lucy and Pauline hold their kittens near the rail yards in Manchester on April 12, 1942. It was a common sight to see stray cats roaming the yards of Manchester. Lucy went on to college at St. Mary's Hospital in Rochester, New York, and became an x-ray technician. Pauline went on to be a lifelong teacher in the Canandaigua school district.

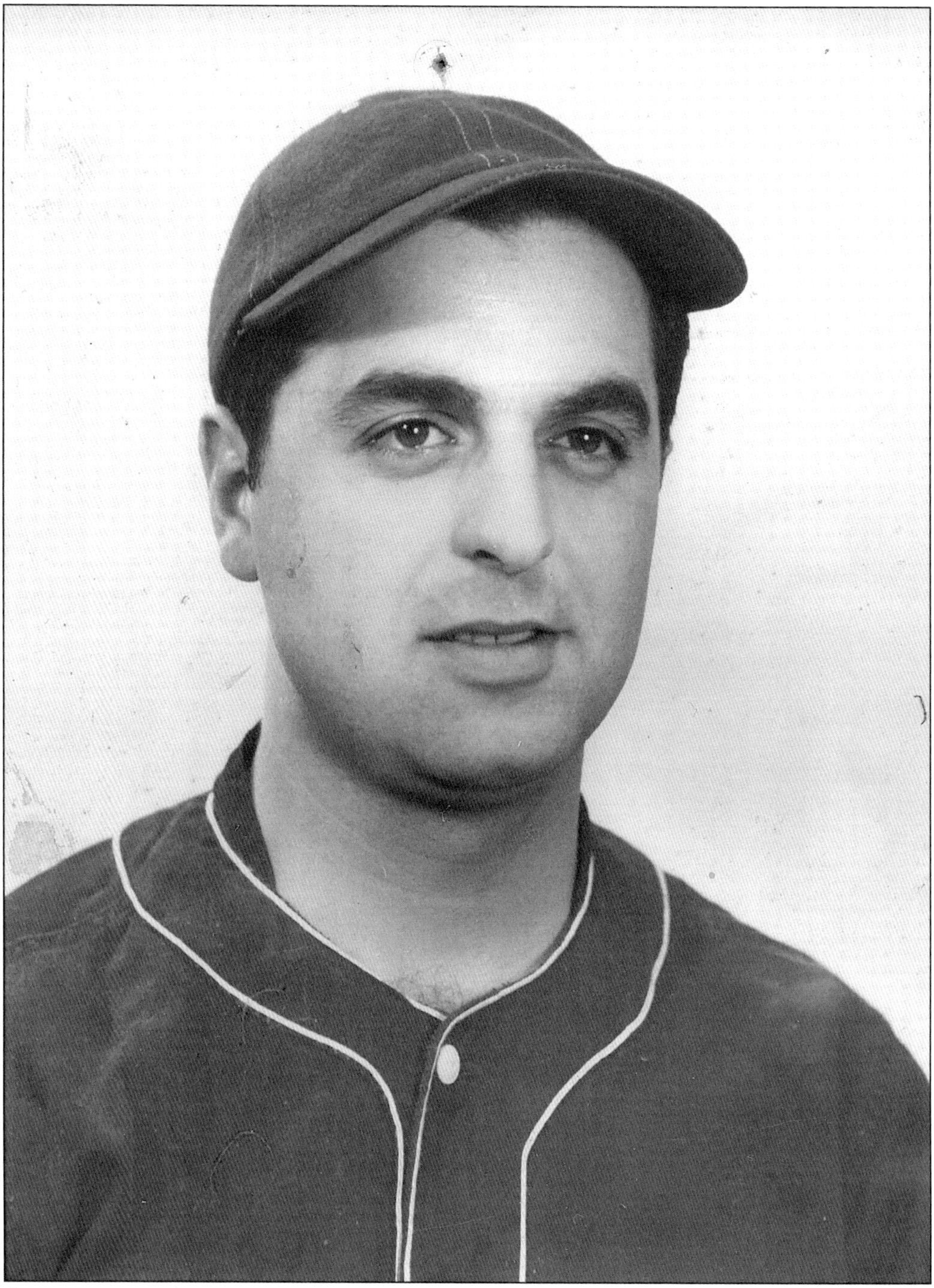

Ike Moses, son of a Syrian immigrant, poses in his 1949 softball uniform. Ike, a teammate of basketball hall of famer Bob Davies, was known for his swift speed around the bases. During a 1949 exhibition game against Eddie Feiner, Moses hit the winning home run against the King and his Court, which denied Feiner and the team a large sum of money. Heinz 57 had sponsored the team and proposed a $10,000 bonus if the team could win 57 consecutive games. Moses's homerun ended the streak at 56.

Ten

Then and Now

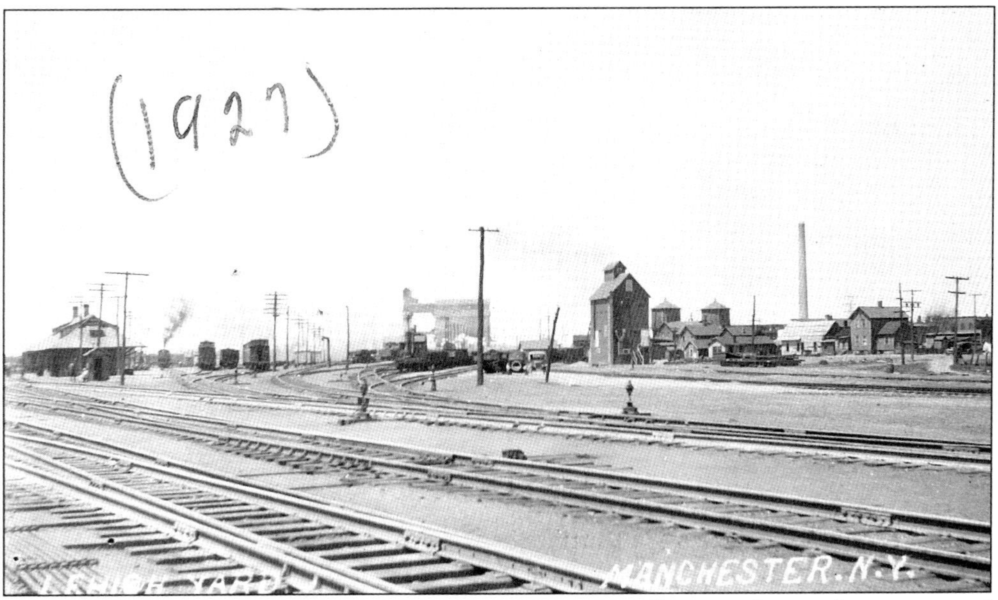

Manchester's transfer yards, shown here in 1927, remain partially intact despite their antiquated appearance. In 1938, the advent of the diesel engine eliminated many jobs on the railroad. Local men found employment in nearby factories and businesses. By June of 1970, all clerks and yard help of the LVVR were dismissed. In 1976, the Lehigh Valley line was bought out by Conrail, consequently closing the final chapter of the railroad in Manchester. The last Lehigh Valley train passed through Manchester on April 1, 1976.

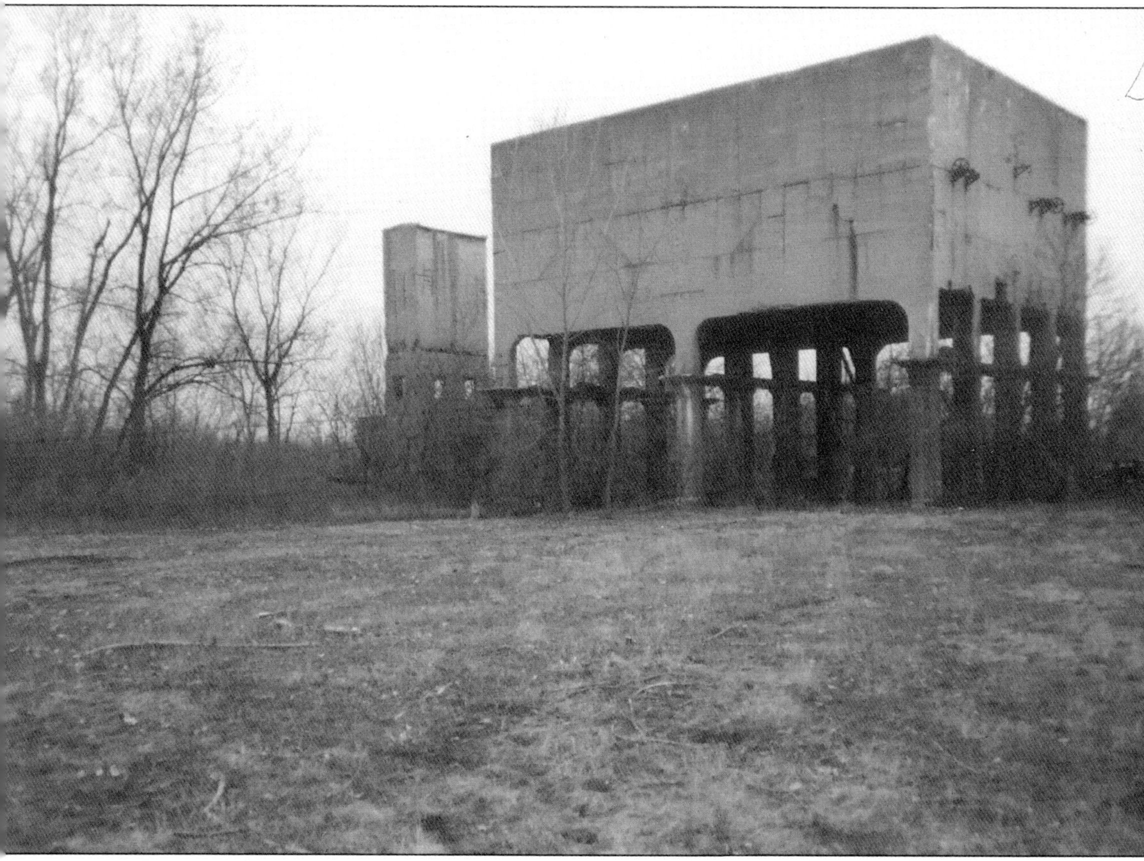

As this 1997 photograph illustrates, the quiescent coal pockets of the LVRR in Manchester still stand, though trivial and forgotten. Despite its ancient semblance, the structure, built in 1917, has withstood the elements for nearly a century.

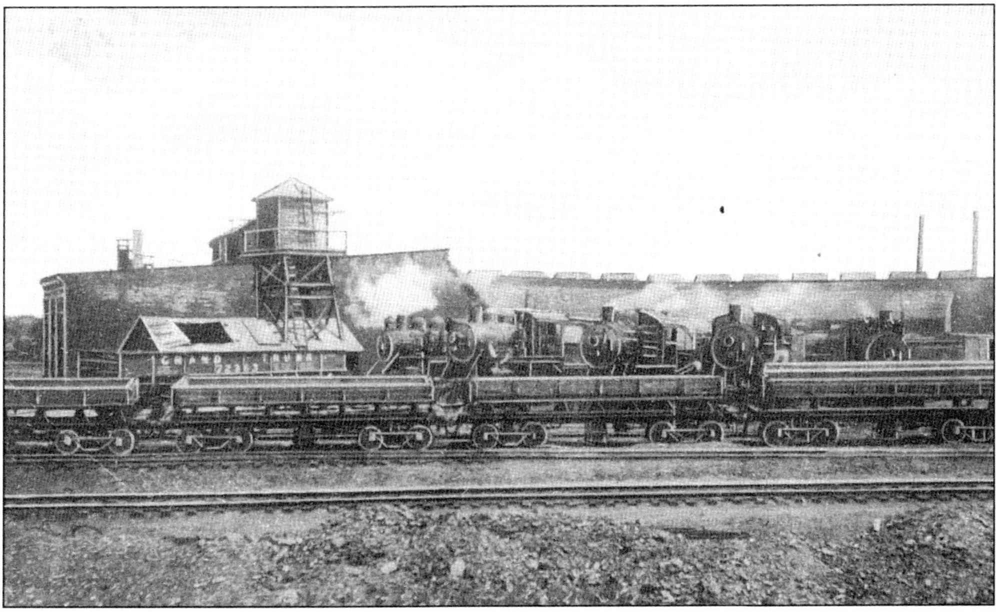

The Manchester roundhouse is shown here on August 12, 1917. During the peak of its operation, 35 steam locomotives were housed and repaired in the structure. The turntable became automated in 1903.

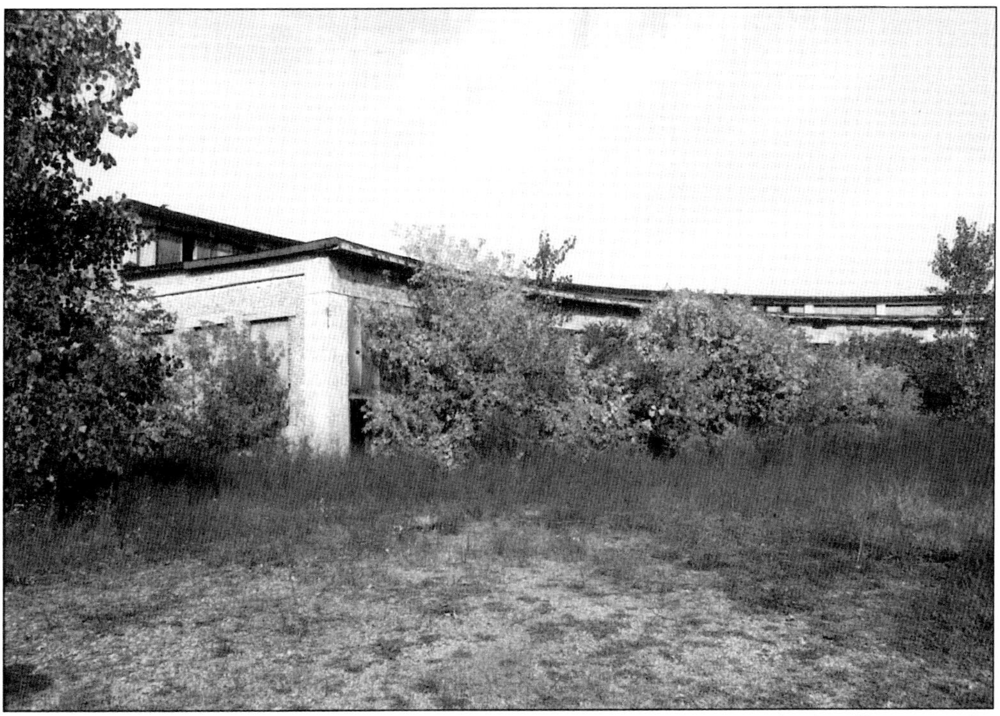

This 1998 photograph of the third roundhouse, overgrown by tree shrub, illustrates the appearance of abandonment as it descends unencumbered into the depths of time. The first roundhouse was built in 1892 and burned to the ground.

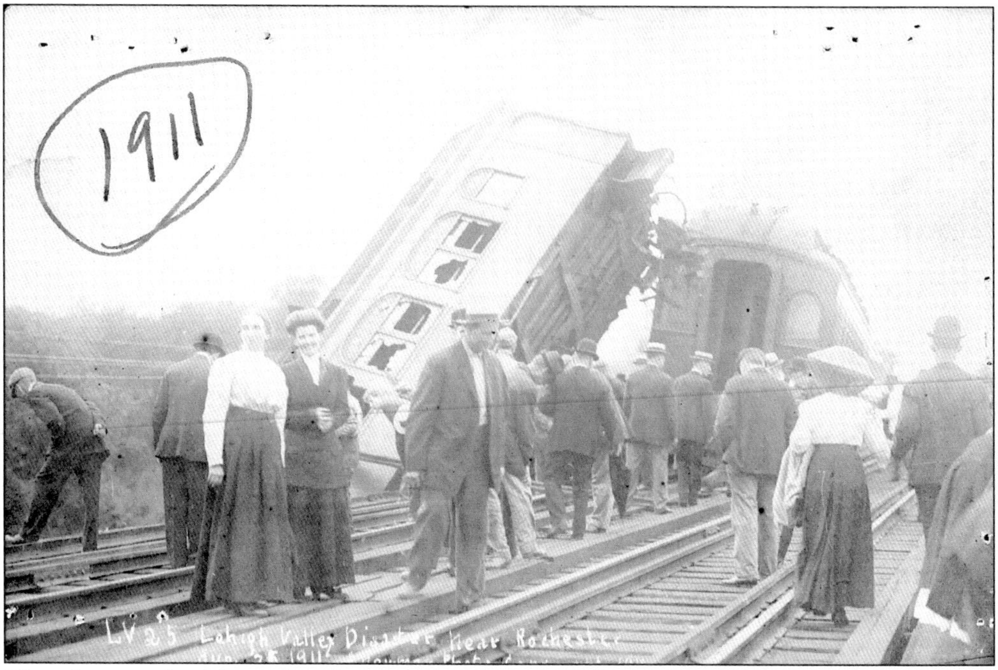

This photograph of the railroad tressel over the Canandaigua outlet in Manchester was taken during the 1911 derailment. The Washington Pullman, the eighth car of 14, can be seen in the background. Of the 29 victims, one died in the Washington Pullman.

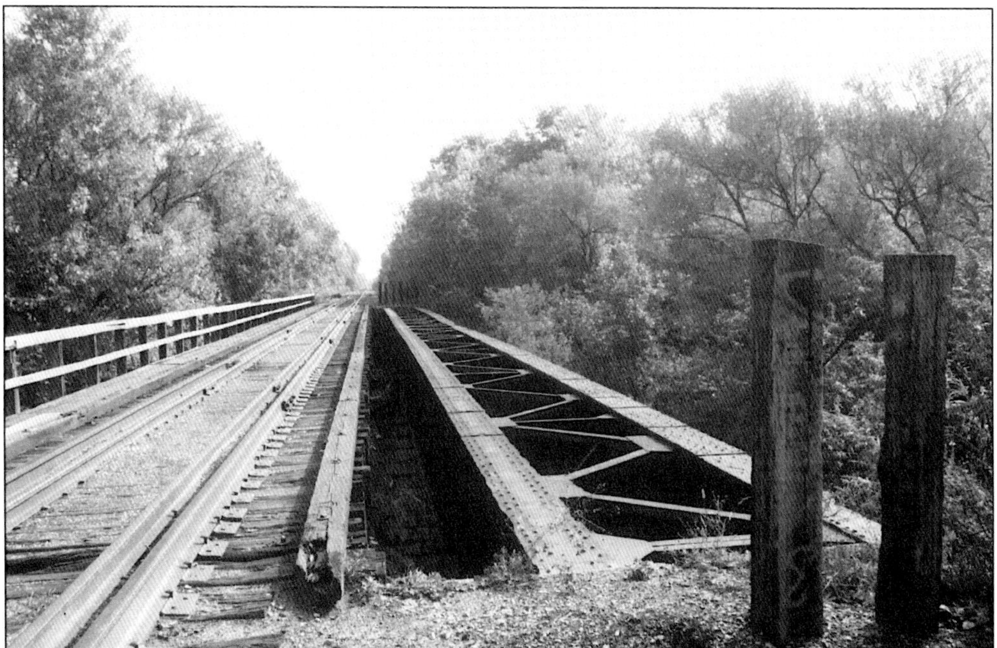

Today, the Ontario Central, a short track line, crosses the tressel twice a week when clay is shipped to Victor Insulator for various telephone line products. The tressel, a landmark in Manchester, is located near Smith Terrace. This is the former site of the LVRR restaurant and bunkhouse.

Florence Angeline, former LVRR store clerk, poses alongside Salsbury, an engineer from Sayre, Pennsylvania, at the Lehigh Valley oil house in 1943. The oil house served as the stock room and resource center for the LVRR. Western Union telegraphs were sent and received from the oil house.

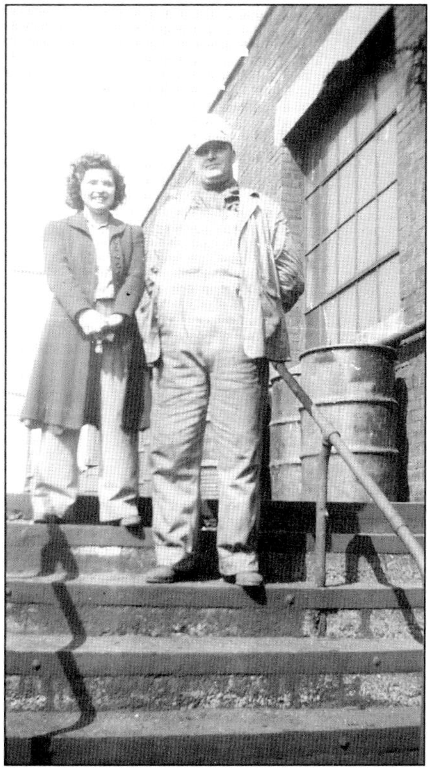

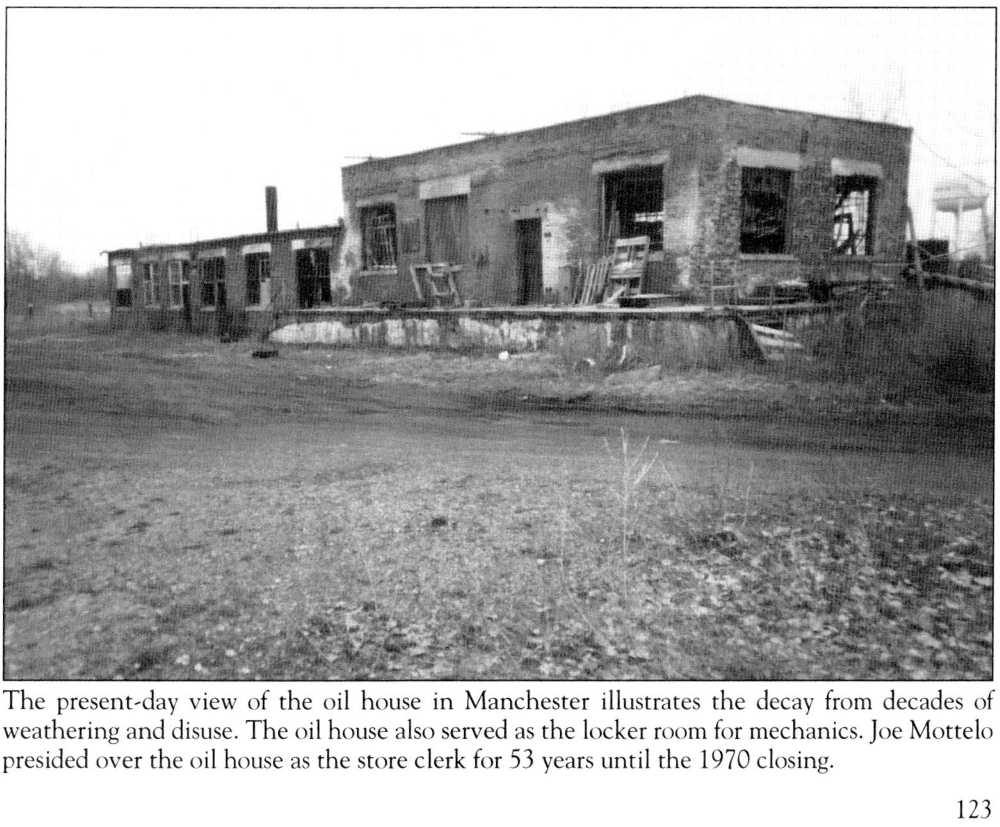

The present-day view of the oil house in Manchester illustrates the decay from decades of weathering and disuse. The oil house also served as the locker room for mechanics. Joe Mottelo presided over the oil house as the store clerk for 53 years until the 1970 closing.

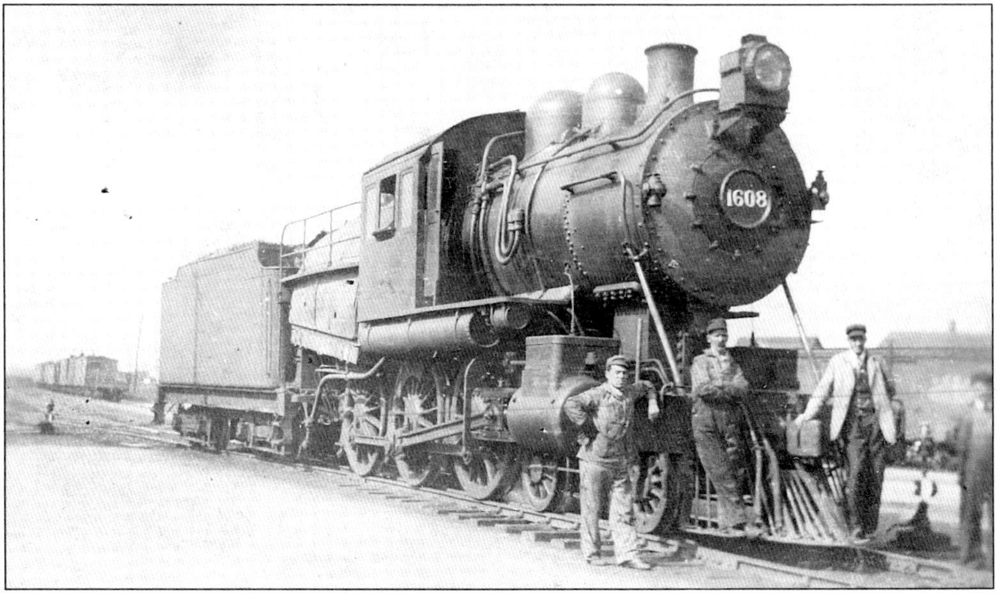

Steam locomotive 1608, once the workhorse of the LVRR freight yards, was decommissioned in the early part of the 20th century. Steamers like this Baldwin (pictured) were part of a series of trains nicknamed "Mother Hubbard."

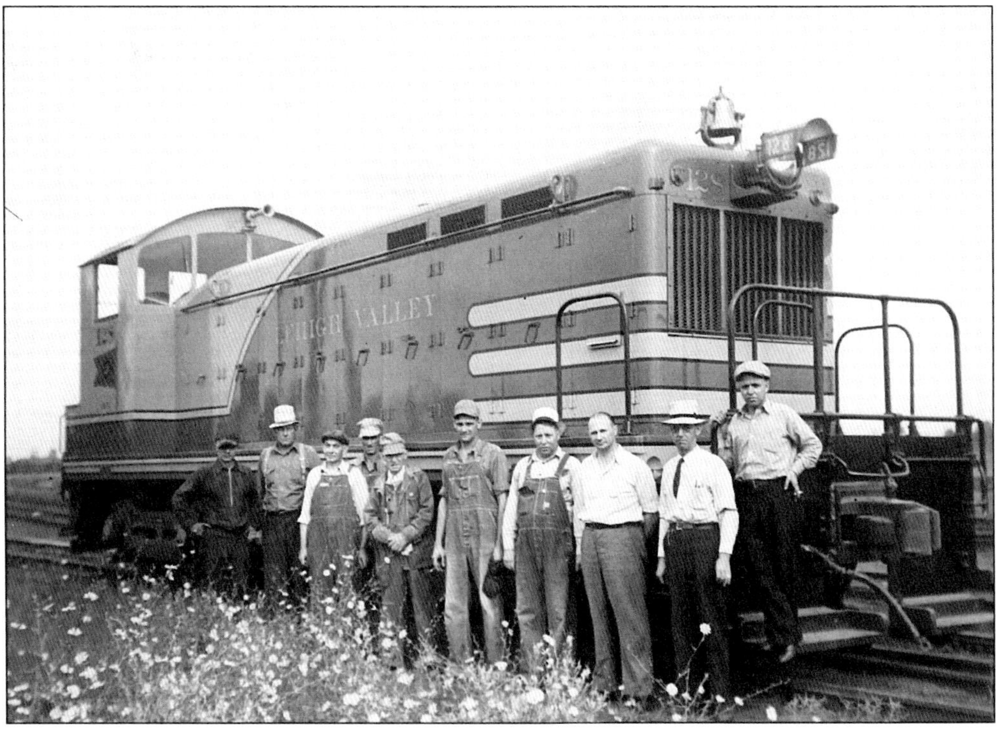

Diesel engines like this 128 gradually replaced steam locomotives in the 1930s and 1940s. "Gasoline" Gus Halderman (fourth from left) began his career as a fireman on the LVRR in 1912 and retired as an engineer in 1959. His son, Roger Halderman, has currently established a Lehigh Valley Railroad Historical Society in Manchester.

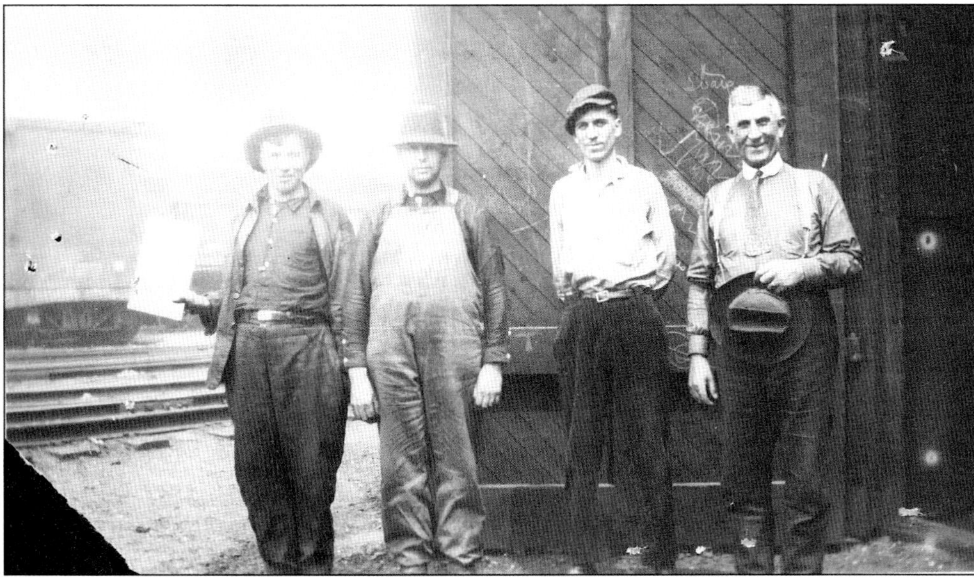

Four transfer yard workers stand before of a wooden boxcar in 1916. Presently, a small number of boxcars remain near the tracks in the old transfer yards of Manchester.

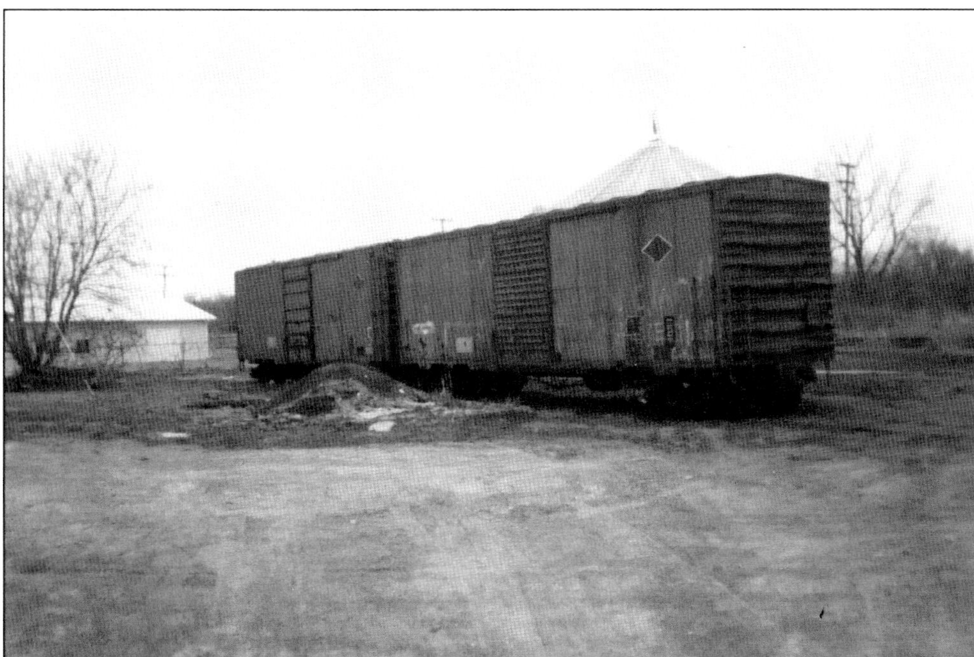

Pictured in 1997, a lone Lehigh Valley boxcar sits abandoned between the Wordingham Machine Shop and Crowell Feed Mill on Merrick Avenue in Manchester.

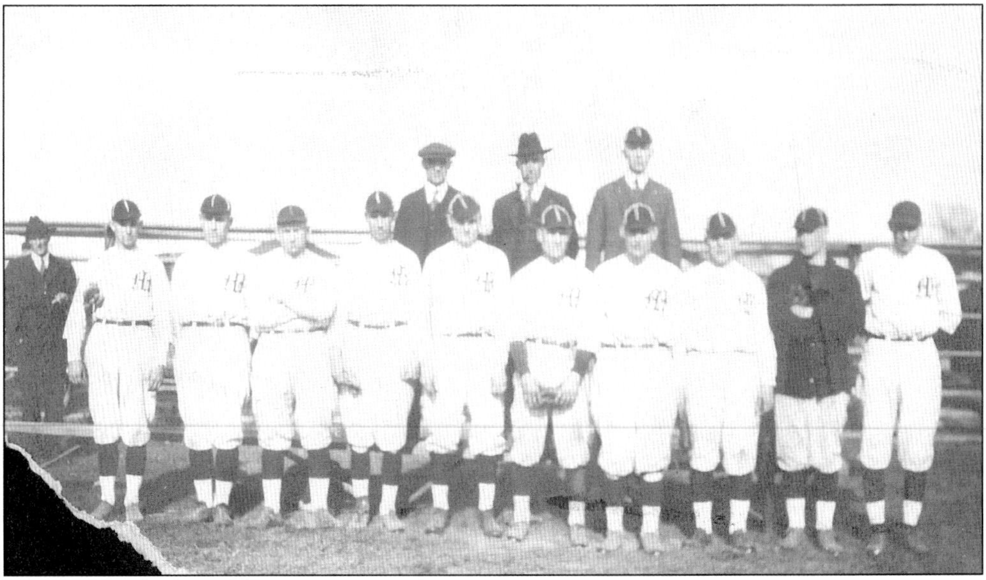

Standing before the bleachers at King's Diamond in 1919, the Railroaders introduced the first and seemingly the last semi-professional baseball team of Manchester.

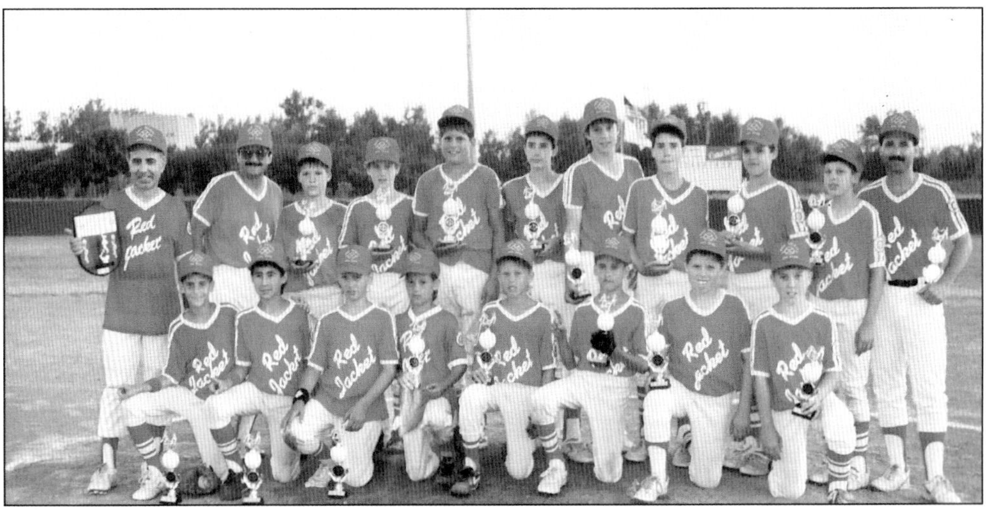

Ardency for small-town baseball remains steadfast. Recent local champions, such as this 1991 little league team of Manchester-Shortsville, are representative of the enduring allegiance fostered by the men known as champeen stretchers and gandy dancers. The Red Jacket Bambino All Stars (ages 11 and 12) were District 4 Tournament Champions and New York State Champions representing New York State at the Northeast U.S. Regional Tournament in North Bergin, New Jersey. This photograph was taken at the former site of King's Diamond, now called Westplex. Shown, from left to right, are as follows: (front row) Matt Vitticore, Bryan Rice, Josh Kesel, Eric Clarke, Jamie Lockwood, Marc Vitticore, Aaron Anderson, and Matt Shannon; (back row) Nino Macri (manager), Dom Vitticore, (coach), Dan Morphy, Don Batterson, Austin Reed, Josh Lopes, Beth Record, Jason Lopes, Matt Keyser, Bob Keyser, and Richard Rice (coach).

Acknowledgments

This book acknowledges the people and places in the small town of Manchester, from the dawn of its settlement to the twilight of its re-establishment. From the beginning, rural America has experienced a phenomenon of anonymity. Manchester, located in Ontario County, New York, represents the American small town, where the silence of anonymity was interrupted by the clearing of woods and the laying of track for the Lehigh Valley Railroad.

The arrival of the LVVR in 1892 marked a turning point for Manchester, as its composition and semblance were forever changed. During the golden years of the railroad, Manchester became the "Promised Land" for many immigrants, the site for the nation's largest freight transfer yard, and home of a celebrated semi-professional baseball team. From beginning to end, this period brought local dignity and national recognition to the small town of Manchester.

The largest source of village pride came by way of the Manchester Railroaders, the town's Industrial League baseball team. The Railroaders were known as "Davids" among International and Industrial League "Goliaths" like the Bronx Giants, the Brooklyn Bushwicks, the Buffalo Bisons, the Rochester Kay Pees (Kodak team), the Rochester Orioles, the Elmira Artics, the Auburn Lehighs, and the Toronto Leafs. Railroaders of Manchester played against the legendary Babe Ruth, swung successfully against Detroit's John Bogart (the pitcher who struck out Ruth), and defeated the 1919 World Series pitcher Roy Wilkinson of the Chicago White Sox.

With the help and contributions of many local families, this commemorative pictorial history will give readers, both locally and nationally, an intimate view of the past. For the purpose of brevity, we chose photographs we felt best represented the pertinent people and places of Manchester.

Though anonymity has once again silenced the small town of Manchester, it is our hope that this book, *The Golden Era of Railroads and Baseball,* will place Manchester in its rightful place among the great railroad and baseball towns of America.

Essentially, this book is a tribute long overdue.

— Tim Munn and Matthew Vitticore